# Python Geospatial Development

## *Third Edition*

Develop sophisticated mapping applications from
scratch using Python 3 tools for geospatial development

**Erik Westra**

BIRMINGHAM - MUMBAI

# Python Geospatial Development

*Third Edition*

First published: December 2010

Second edition: May 2013

Third edition: May 2016

Production reference: 1180516

Published by Packt Publishing Ltd.
Livery Place
35 Livery Street
Birmingham B3 2PB, UK.

ISBN 978-1-78528-893-7

www.packtpub.com

# Credits

**Author**
Erik Westra

**Reviewer**
Lou Mauget

**Commissioning Editor**
Kunal Parikh

**Acquisition Editors**
Shaon Basu
Aaron Lazar

**Content Development Editor**
Shaali Deeraj

**Technical Editor**
Nirant Carvalho

**Copy Editor**
Madhusudan Uchil

**Project Coordinator**
Sanchita Mandal

**Proofreader**
Safis Editing

**Indexer**
Hemangini Bari

**Graphics**
Kirk D'Penha

**Production Coordinator**
Shantanu N. Zagade

**Cover Work**
Shantanu N. Zagade

# About the Author

**Erik Westra** has been a professional software developer for over 25 years and has worked almost exclusively in Python for the past decade. Erik's early interest in graphical user interface design led to the development of one of the most advanced urgent courier dispatch systems used by messenger and courier companies worldwide. In recent years, Erik has been involved in the design and implementation of systems matching seekers and providers of goods and services across a range of geographical areas as well as real-time messaging and payments systems. This work has included the creation of real-time geocoders and map-based views of constantly changing data. Erik is based in New Zealand, and he works for companies worldwide.

He is also the author of the Packt titles *Python Geospatial Analysis* and *Building Mapping Applications* with QGIS as well as the forthcoming title *Modular Programming with Python*.

I would like to thank Ruth for being so awesome, and my children for their patience. Without you, none of this would have been possible.

# About the Reviewer

**Lou Mauget** learned to program long ago at Michigan State University while learning to use software to design a cyclotron. Afterward, he worked for 34 years at IBM. He went on to work for several consulting firms, including a long-term engagement with the railroad industry. He is currently consulting for Keyhole Software of Leawood, Kansas. Last spring, he wrote MockOla, a drag-drop wireframe prototyping tool for Keyhole. Lou has coded in C++, Java, and newer languages. His current interests include microservices, Docker, Node.js, NoSQL, geospatial systems, functional programming, mobile, single-page web applications — any new language or framework. Lou occasionally blogs about software technology. He is a coauthor of three computer books. He wrote two IBM DeveloperWorks XML tutorials and an LDAP tutorial for WebSphere Journal. Lou co-wrote several J2EE certification tests for IBM. He has been a reviewer for other publishers.

# www.PacktPub.com

## eBooks, discount offers, and more

Did you know that Packt offers eBook versions of every book published, with PDF and ePub files available? You can upgrade to the eBook version at www.PacktPub.com and as a print book customer, you are entitled to a discount on the eBook copy. Get in touch with us at customercare@packtpub.com for more details.

At www.PacktPub.com, you can also read a collection of free technical articles, sign up for a range of free newsletters and receive exclusive discounts and offers on Packt books and eBooks.

https://www2.packtpub.com/books/subscription/packtlib

Do you need instant solutions to your IT questions? PacktLib is Packt's online digital book library. Here, you can search, access, and read Packt's entire library of books.

## Why subscribe?

- Fully searchable across every book published by Packt
- Copy and paste, print, and bookmark content
- On demand and accessible via a web browser

# Table of Contents

# Preface

With the increasing use of map-based web sites and spatially aware devices and applications, geospatial development is a rapidly growing area. As a Python developer, you can't afford to be left behind. In today's location-aware world, every Python developer can benefit from understanding geospatial concepts and development techniques.

Working with geospatial data can get complicated because you are dealing with mathematical models of the earth's surface. Since Python is a powerful programming language with many high-level toolkits, it is ideally suited to geospatial development. This book will familiarize you with the Python tools required for geospatial development. It walks you through the key geospatial concepts of location, distance, units, projections, datums, and geospatial data formats. We will then examine a number of Python libraries and use these with freely available geospatial data to accomplish a variety of tasks. The book provides an in-depth look at storing spatial data in a database and how you can use spatial databases as tools to solve a range of geospatial problems.

It goes into the details of generating maps using the Mapnik map-rendering toolkit and helps you build a sophisticated web-based geospatial map-editing application using GeoDjango, Mapnik, and PostGIS. By the end of the book, you will be able to integrate spatial features into your applications and build complete mapping applications from scratch.

This book is a hands-on tutorial, teaching you how to access, manipulate, and display geospatial data efficiently using a range of Python tools for GIS development.

# What this book covers

*Chapter 1, Geospatial Development Using Python,* provides an overview of the Python programming language and the concepts behind geospatial development. Major use cases of geospatial development and recent and upcoming developments in the field are also covered.

*Chapter 2, GIS,* introduces the core concepts of location, distance, units, projections, shapes, datums, and geospatial data formats, before discussing the process of working with geospatial data by hand.

*Chapter 3, Python Libraries for Geospatial Development,* explores the major Python libraries available for geospatial development, including the available features, how to install them, the major concepts you need to understand about the libraries, and how they can be used.

*Chapter 4, Sources of Geospatial Data,* investigates the major sources of freely available geospatial data, what information is available, the data format used, and how to import the data once you have downloaded it.

*Chapter 5, Working with Geospatial Data in Python,* uses the libraries introduced earlier to perform various tasks using geospatial data, including changing projections, importing and exporting data, converting and standardizing units of geometry and distance, and performing geospatial calculations.

*Chapter 6, Spatial Databases,* introduces the concepts behind spatial databases before looking in detail at the PostGIS spatially enabled database and how to install and use it from a Python program.

*Chapter 7, Using Python and Mapnik to Produce Maps,* provides a detailed look at the Mapnik map-generation toolkit and how to use it to produce a variety of maps.

*Chapter 8, Working with Spatial Data,* works through the design and implementation of a complete geospatial application called DISTAL, using freely available geospatial data stored in a spatial database.

*Chapter 9, Improving the DISTAL Application,* improves the application written in the previous chapter to solve various usability and performance issues.

*Chapter 10, Tools for Web-based Geospatial Development,* examines the concepts of web application frameworks, web services, JavaScript UI libraries, and slippy maps. It introduces a number of standard web protocols used by geospatial applications and finishes with a survey of the tools and techniques that will be used to build the complete mapping application in the final three chapters of this book.

*Chapter 11, Putting it all Together – a Complete Mapping Application*, introduces ShapeEditor, a complete and sophisticated web application built using PostGIS, Mapnik, and GeoDjango. We start by designing the overall application, and we then build the ShapeEditor's database models.

*Chapter 12, ShapeEditor – Importing and Exporting Shapefiles*, continues with the implementation of the ShapeEditor system, concentrating on displaying a list of imported shapefiles, along with logic for importing and exporting shapefiles via a web browser.

*Chapter 13, ShapeEditor – Selecting and Editing Features*, concludes the implementation of the ShapeEditor, adding logic to let the user select and edit features within an imported shapefile. This involves the creation of a custom tile map server and the use of the OpenLayers JavaScript library to display and interact with geospatial data.

# What you need for this book

The third edition of this book has been extended to support Python 3, though you can continue to use Python 2 if you wish to. You will also need to download and install the following tools and libraries, though full instructions are given in the relevant sections of this book:

- GDAL/OGR
- GEOS
- Shapely
- Proj
- pyproj
- PostgreSQL
- PostGIS
- pyscopg2
- Mapnik
- Django

# Who this book is for

This book is aimed at experienced Python developers who want to get up to speed with open source geospatial tools and techniques in order to build their own geospatial applications or integrate geospatial technology into their existing Python programs.

# Conventions

In this book, you will find a number of styles of text that distinguish between different kinds of information. Here are some examples of these styles, and an explanation of their meaning.

Code words in text are shown as follows: "The dataset, an instance of gdal.Dataset, represents a file containing raster-format data."

A block of code is set as follows:

```
import pyproj

lat1,long1 = (37.8101274,-122.4104622)
lat2,long2 = (37.80237485,-122.405832766082)

geod = pyproj.Geod(ellps="WGS84")
angle1,angle2,distance = geod.inv(long1, lat1, long2, lat2)

print("Distance is {:0.2f} meters".format(distance))
```

When we wish to draw your attention to a particular part of a code block, the relevant lines or items are set in bold:

```
for value in values:
    if value != band.GetNoDataValue():
        try:
            histogram[value] += 1
        except KeyError:
            histogram[value] = 1
```

Any command-line input or output is written as follows:

```
% python calcBoundingBoxes.py
Afghanistan (AFG) lat=29.4061..38.4721, long=60.5042..74.9157
Albania (ALB) lat=39.6447..42.6619, long=19.2825..21.0542
Algeria (DZA) lat=18.9764..37.0914, long=-8.6672..11.9865
. . .
```

**New terms** and **important words** are shown in bold. Words that you see on the screen, in menus or dialog boxes for example, appear in the text like this: "Click on the **Download Domestic Names** hyperlink".

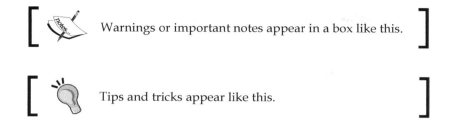

Warnings or important notes appear in a box like this.

Tips and tricks appear like this.

# Reader feedback

Feedback from our readers is always welcome. Let us know what you think about this book — what you liked or may have disliked. Reader feedback is important for us to develop titles that you really get the most out of.

To send us general feedback, simply send an e-mail to feedback@packtpub.com, and mention the book title through the subject of your message.

If there is a topic that you have expertise in and you are interested in either writing or contributing to a book, see our author guide on www.packtpub.com/authors.

# Customer support

Now that you are the proud owner of a Packt book, we have a number of things to help you to get the most from your purchase.

# Downloading the example code

You can download the example code files for this book from your account at http://www.packtpub.com. If you purchased this book elsewhere, you can visit http://www.packtpub.com/support and register to have the files e-mailed directly to you.

You can download the code files by following these steps:

1.  Log in or register to our website using your e-mail address and password.
2.  Hover the mouse pointer on the **SUPPORT** tab at the top.
3.  Click on **Code Downloads & Errata**.
4.  Enter the name of the book in the **Search** box.

5. Select the book for which you're looking to download the code files.

6. Choose from the drop-down menu where you purchased this book from.

7. Click on **Code Download**.

You can also download the code files by clicking on the **Code Files** button on the book's webpage at the Packt Publishing website. This page can be accessed by entering the book's name in the **Search** box. Please note that you need to be logged in to your Packt account.

Once the file is downloaded, please make sure that you unzip or extract the folder using the latest version of:

- WinRAR / 7-Zip for Windows
- Zipeg / iZip / UnRarX for Mac
- 7-Zip / PeaZip for Linux

The code bundle for the book is also hosted on GitHub at `https://github.com/PacktPublishing/Python-Geospatial-Development-Third-Edition`. We also have other code bundles from our rich catalog of books and videos available at `https://github.com/PacktPublishing/`. Check them out!

# Errata

Although we have taken every care to ensure the accuracy of our content, mistakes do happen. If you find a mistake in one of our books—maybe a mistake in the text or the code—we would be grateful if you would report this to us. By doing so, you can save other readers from frustration and help us improve subsequent versions of this book. If you find any errata, please report them by visiting `http://www.packtpub.com/support`, selecting your book, clicking on the **errata submission form** link, and entering the details of your errata. Once your errata are verified, your submission will be accepted and the errata will be uploaded to our website, or added to any list of existing errata, under the Errata section of that title.

# Piracy

Piracy of copyright material on the Internet is an ongoing problem across all media. At Packt, we take the protection of our copyright and licenses very seriously. If you come across any illegal copies of our works, in any form, on the Internet, please provide us with the location address or website name immediately so that we can pursue a remedy.

Please contact us at copyright@packtpub.com with a link to the suspected pirated material.

We appreciate your help in protecting our authors, and our ability to bring you valuable content.

# Questions

You can contact us at questions@packtpub.com if you are having a problem with any aspect of the book, and we will do our best to address it.

# 1
# Geospatial Development Using Python

This chapter provides an overview of the Python programming language and geospatial development. Please note that this is not a tutorial on how to use the Python language; Python is easy to learn, but the details are beyond the scope of this book.

In this chapter, we will see:

- What the Python programming language is and how it differs from other languages
- How the Python Standard Library and the Python Package Index make Python even more powerful
- What the terms **geospatial data** and **geospatial development** refer to
- An overview of the process of accessing, manipulating, and displaying geospatial data. How geospatial data can be accessed, manipulated, and displayed.
- Some of the major applications of geospatial development
- Some of the recent trends in the field of geospatial development

# Python

Python (`http://python.org`) is a modern, high-level language suitable for a wide variety of programming tasks. It is often used as a scripting language, automating and simplifying tasks at the operating system level, but it is equally suitable for building large and complex programs. Python has been used to write web-based systems, desktop applications, games, scientific programs, and even utilities and other higher-level parts of various operating systems.

Python supports a wide range of programming idioms, from straightforward procedural programming to object-oriented programming and functional programming.

Python is sometimes criticized for being an interpreted language, and can be slow compared to compiled languages such as C. However, the use of bytecode compilation and the fact that much of the heavy lifting is done by library code means that Python's performance is often surprisingly good—and there are many things you can do to improve the performance of your programs if you need to.

Open source versions of the Python interpreter are freely available for all major operating systems. Python is eminently suitable for all sorts of programming, from quick one-off scripts to building huge and complex systems. It can even be run in interactive (command-line) mode, allowing you to type in one-off commands and short programs and immediately see the results. This is ideal for doing quick calculations or figuring out how a particular library works.

One of the first things a developer notices about Python compared with other languages such as Java or C++ is how *expressive* the language is: what may take 20 or 30 lines of code in Java can often be written in half a dozen lines of code in Python. For example, imagine that you wanted to print a sorted list of the words that occur in a given piece of text. In Python, this is easy:

```
words = set(text.split())
for word in sorted(words):
    print(word)
```

Implementing this kind of task in other languages is often surprisingly difficult.

While the Python language itself makes programming quick and easy, allowing you to focus on the task at hand, the Python Standard Library makes programming even more efficient. This library makes it easy to do things such as converting date and time values, manipulating strings, downloading data from web sites, performing complex maths, working with e-mail messages, encoding and decoding data, XML parsing, data encryption, file manipulation, compressing and decompressing files, working with databases—the list goes on. What you can do with the Python Standard Library is truly amazing.

As well as the built-in modules in the Python Standard Library, it is easy to download and install custom modules, which could be written either in Python or C. The Python Package Index (`http://pypi.python.org`) provides thousands of additional modules that you can download and install. And if this isn't enough, many other systems provide Python bindings to allow you to access them directly from within your programs. We will be making heavy use of Python bindings in this book.

Python is in many ways an ideal programming language. Once you are familiar with the language and have used it a few times, you'll find it incredibly easy to write programs to solve various tasks. Rather than getting buried in a morass of type definitions and low-level string manipulation, you can simply concentrate on what you want to achieve. You almost end up thinking directly in Python code. Programming in Python is straightforward, efficient, and, dare I say it, *fun*.

# Python 3

There are two main flavors of Python in use today: the Python 2.x series has been around for many years and is still widely used today, while Python 3.x isn't backward compatible with Python 2 and is becoming more and more popular as it is seen as the main version of Python going forward.

One of the main things holding back the adoption of Python 3 is the lack of support for third-party libraries. This has been particularly acute for Python libraries used for geospatial development, which are often dependent on individual developers or have requirements that were not compatible with Python 3 for quite a long time. However, all the major libraries used in this book can now be run using Python 3, and so all the code examples in this book have been converted to use Python 3 syntax.

If your computer runs Linux or Mac OS X, then you can use Python 3 with all these libraries directly. If, however, your computer runs MS Windows, then Python 3 compatibility is more problematic. In this case, you have two options: you can attempt to compile the libraries yourself to work with Python 3 or you can revert to using Python 2 and make adjustments to the example code as required. Fortunately, the syntax differences between Python 2 and Python 3 are quite straightforward, so not many changes will be required if you do choose to use Python 2.x rather than Python 3.x.

# Geospatial development

The term **geospatial** refers to finding information that is located on the earth's surface. This can include, for example, the position of a cellphone tower, the shape of a road, or the outline of a country:

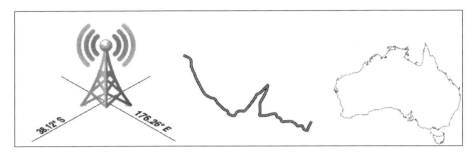

Geospatial data often associates some piece of information with a particular location. For example, the following map, taken from http://opendata.zeit.de/nuclear-reactors-usa, shows how many people live within 50 miles of a nuclear reactor within the eastern United States:

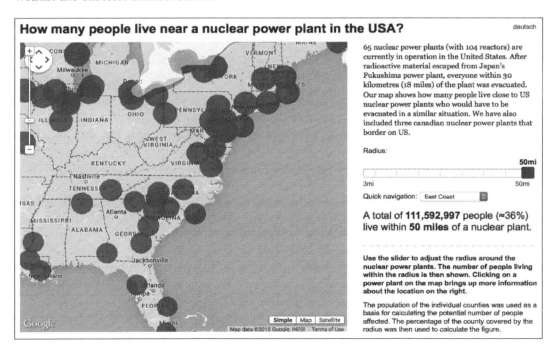

Geospatial development is the process of writing computer programs that can access, manipulate, and display this type of information.

Internally, geospatial data is represented as a series of **coordinates**, often in the form of latitude and longitude values. Additional **attributes**, such as temperature, soil type, height, or the name of a landmark, are also often present. There can be many thousands (or even millions) of data points for a single set of geospatial data. For example, the following outline of New Zealand consists of almost 12,000 individual data points:

Because so much data is involved, it is common to store geospatial information within a database. A large part of this book will be concerned with how to store your geospatial information in a database and access it efficiently.

Geospatial data comes in many different forms. Different **Geographical Information Systems** vendors have produced their own file formats over the years, and various organizations have also defined their own standards. It is often necessary to use a Python library to read files in the correct format when importing geospatial data into your database.

Unfortunately, not all geospatial data points are compatible. Just like a distance value of 2.8 can have very different meanings depending on whether you are using kilometers or miles, a given coordinate value can represent any number of different points on the curved surface of the earth, depending on which **projection** has been used.

A projection is a way of representing the earth's surface in two dimensions. We will look at projections in more detail in *Chapter 2, GIS*, but for now, just keep in mind that every piece of geospatial data has a projection associated with it. To compare or combine two sets of geospatial data, it is often necessary to convert the data from one projection to another.

> Latitude and longitude values are sometimes referred to as **unprojected coordinates**. We'll learn more about this in the next chapter.

In addition to the prosaic tasks of importing geospatial data from various external file formats and translating data from one projection to another, geospatial data can also be manipulated to solve various interesting problems. Obvious examples include the task of calculating the distance between two points, calculating the length of a road, or finding all data points within a given radius of a selected point. We will be using Python libraries to solve all of these problems and more.

Finally, geospatial data by itself is not very interesting. A long list of coordinates tells you almost nothing; it isn't until those numbers are used to draw a picture that you can make sense of it. Drawing maps, placing data points onto a map, and allowing users to interact with maps are all important aspects of geospatial development. We will be looking at all of these in later chapters.

# Applications of geospatial development

Let's take a brief look at some of the more common geospatial development tasks you might encounter.

# Analysing geospatial data

Imagine that you have a database containing a range of geospatial data for San Francisco. This database might include geographical features, roads, the location of prominent buildings, and other man-made features such as bridges, airports, and so on.

Such a database can be a valuable resource for answering various questions such as the following:

- What's the longest road in Sausalito?
- How many bridges are there in Oakland?
- What is the total area of Golden Gate Park?
- How far is it from Pier 39 to Coit Tower?

Many of these types of problems can be solved using tools such as the PostGIS spatially-enabled database toolkit. For example, to calculate the total area of Golden Gate Park, you might use the following SQL query:

```
select ST_Area(geometry) from features
  where name = "Golden Gate Park";
```

To calculate the distance between two locations, you first have to **geocode** the locations to obtain their latitude and longitude values. There are various ways to do this; one simple approach is to use a free geocoding web service such as the following:

```
http://nominatim.openstreetmap.org/search?format=json&q=Pier 39,San
Francisco, CA
```

This returns (among other things) a latitude value of `37.8101274` and a longitude value of `-122.4104622` for Pier 39 in San Francisco.

 These latitude and longitude values are in **decimal degrees**. If you don't know what these are, don't worry; we'll talk about decimal degrees in *Chapter 2, GIS*.

Similarly, we can find the location of Coit Tower in San Francisco using this query:

```
http://nominatim.openstreetmap.org/search?format=json&q=Coit Tower,
San Francisco, CA
```

This returns a latitude value of `37.80237485` and a longitude value of `-122.405832766082`.

Now that we have the coordinates for the two desired locations, we can calculate the distance between them using the `pyproj` Python library:

 If you want to run this example, you will need to install the `pyproj` library. We will look at how to do this in *Chapter 3, Python Libraries for Geospatial Development*.

```
import pyproj

lat1,long1 = (37.8101274,-122.4104622)
lat2,long2 = (37.80237485,-122.405832766082)

geod = pyproj.Geod(ellps="WGS84")
angle1,angle2,distance = geod.inv(long1, lat1, long2, lat2)

print("Distance is {:0.2f} meters".format(distance))
```

This prints the distance between the two points:

**Distance is 952.17 meters**

 Don't worry about the WGS84 reference at this stage; we'll look at what this means in *Chapter 2, GIS.*

Of course, you wouldn't normally do this sort of analysis on a one-off basis like this—it's much more common to create a Python program that will answer these sorts of questions for *any* desired set of data. You might, for example, create a web application that displays a menu of available calculations. One of the options in this menu might be to calculate the distance between two points; when this option is selected, the web application would prompt the user to enter the two locations, attempt to geocode them by calling an appropriate web service (and display an error message if a location couldn't be geocoded), then calculate the distance between the two points using pyproj, and finally display the results to the user.

Alternatively, if you have a database containing useful geospatial data, you could let the user select the two locations from the database rather than having them type in arbitrary location names or street addresses.

However you choose to structure it, performing calculations like this will often be a major part of your geospatial application.

# Visualizing geospatial data

Imagine you wanted to see which areas of a city are typically covered by a taxi during an average working day. You might place a GPS recorder in a taxi and leave it to record the taxi's position over several days. The result would be a series of timestamps and latitude and longitude values, like this:

```
2010-03-21 9:15:23   -38.16614499   176.2336626
2010-03-21 9:15:27   -38.16608632   176.2335635
2010-03-21 9:15:34   -38.16604198   176.2334771
2010-03-21 9:15:39   -38.16601507   176.2333958
...
```

By themselves, these raw numbers tell you almost nothing. But when you display this data visually, the numbers start to make sense:

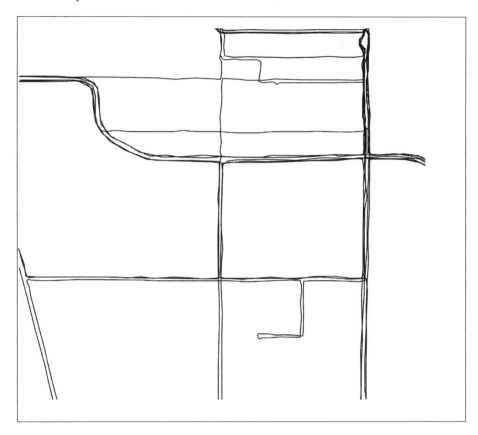

Detailed steps to download the code bundle are mentioned in the Preface of this book. Please have a look.

The code bundle for the book is also hosted on GitHub at `https://github.com/PacktPublishing/Python-Geospatial-Development-Third-Edition`. We also have other code bundles from our rich catalog of books and videos available at `https://github.com/PacktPublishing/`. Check them out!

You can immediately see that the taxi tends to go along the same streets again and again, and if you draw this data as an **overlay** on top of a street map, you can see exactly where the taxi has been:

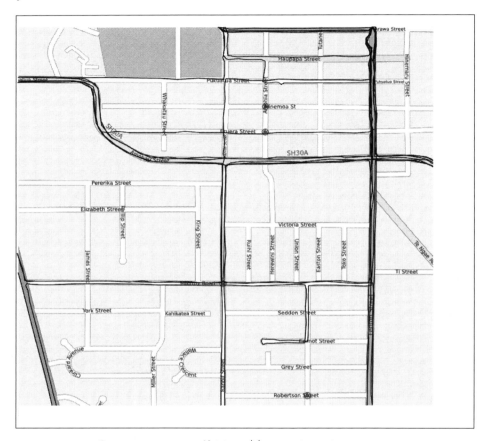

Street map courtesy of http://openstreetmap.org

While this is a simple example, visualization is a crucial aspect of working with geospatial data. How data is displayed visually, how different data sets are overlaid, and how the user can manipulate data directly in a visual format are all going to be major topics in this book.

# Creating a geospatial mash-up

The concept of a *mash-up* has become popular in recent years. Mash-ups are applications that combine data and functionality from more than one source. For example, a typical mash-up might collect details of houses for rent in a given city and plot the location of each rental on a map, like this:

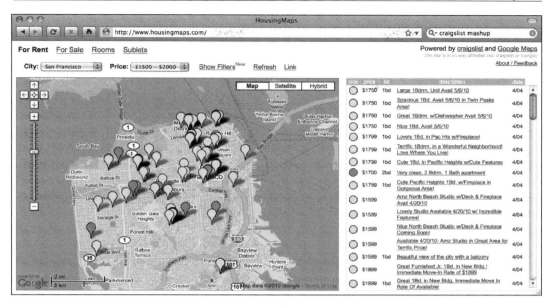

Image courtesy of `http://housingmaps.com`

The Google Maps API has been immensely popular in creating these types of mash-ups. However, Google Maps has some serious licensing and other limitations. It is not the only option, however tools such as Mapnik, OpenLayers, and MapServer, to name a few, also allow you to create mash-ups that overlay your own data onto a map.

Most of these mash-ups run as web applications across the Internet, running on a server that can be accessed by anyone who has a web browser. Sometimes, the mash-ups are private, requiring password access, but usually, they are publicly available and can be used by anyone. Indeed, many businesses (such as the housing maps site shown in the previous screen snapshot) are based on freely-available geospatial mash-ups.

# Recent developments

A decade ago, geospatial development was vastly more limited than it is today. Professional (and hugely expensive) geographical information systems were the norm for working with and visualizing geospatial data. Open-source tools, where they were available, were obscure and hard to use. What is more, everything ran on the desktop—the concept of working with geospatial data across the Internet was no more than a distant dream.

In 2005, Google released two products that completely changed the face of geospatial development: Google Maps and Google Earth made it possible for anyone with a web browser or desktop computer to view and work with geospatial data. Instead of requiring expert knowledge and years of practice, even a four-year-old could instantly view and manipulate interactive maps of the world.

Google's products are not perfect: the map projections are deliberately simplified, leading to errors and problems with displaying overlays. These products are only free for non-commercial use, and they include almost no ability to perform geospatial analysis. Despite these limitations, they have had a huge effect on the field of geospatial development. People became aware of what is possible, and the use of maps and their underlying geospatial data has become so prevalent that even cellphones now commonly include built-in mapping tools.

The **Global Positioning System (GPS)** has also had a major influence on geospatial development. Geospatial data for streets and other man-made and natural features used to be an expensive and tightly-controlled resource, often created by scanning aerial photographs and then manually drawing an outline of a street or coastline over the top to digitize the required features. With the advent of cheap and readily-available portable GPS units, as well as phones which have GPS built in, anyone who wishes to can now capture their own geospatial data. Indeed, many people have made a hobby of recording, editing, and improving the accuracy of street and topological data, which is then freely shared across the Internet. All this means that you're not limited to recording your own data or purchasing data from a commercial organization; volunteered information is now often as accurate and useful as commercially-available data, and may well be suitable for your geospatial application.

The open source software movement has also had a major influence on geospatial development. Instead of relying on commercial toolsets, it is now possible to build complex geospatial applications entirely out of freely-available tools and libraries. Because the source code for these tools is often available, developers can improve and extend these toolkits, fixing problems and adding new features for the benefit of everyone. Tools such as PROJ.4, PostGIS, OGR, and GDAL are all excellent geospatial toolkits that are benefactors of the open source movement. We will be making use of all these tools throughout this book.

As well as standalone tools and libraries, a number of geospatial **application programming interfaces** (**APIs**) have become available. Google has provided a number of APIs that can be used to include maps and perform limited geospatial analysis within a web site. Other sites, such as the OpenStreetMap geocoder we used earlier, allow you to perform various geospatial tasks that would be difficult to do if you were limited to using your own data and programming resources.

As more and more geospatial data becomes available from an increasing number of sources, and as the number of tools and systems that can work with this data also increases, it has become increasingly important to define **standards** for geospatial data. The Open Geospatial Consortium (http://www.opengeospatial.org) is an international standards organization that aims to do precisely this: provide a set of standard formats and protocols for sharing and storing geospatial data. These standards, including GML, KML, GeoRSS, WMS, WFS, and WCS, provide a shared language in which geospatial data can be expressed. Tools such as commercial and open source GIS systems, Google Earth, web-based APIs, and specialized geospatial toolkits such as OGR are all able to work with these standards. Indeed, an important aspect of a geospatial toolkit is the ability to understand and translate data between these various formats.

As devices with built-in GPS receivers have become more ubiquitous, it has become possible to record your location data while performing another task. **Geolocation**, the act of recording your location while you are doing something else, is becoming increasingly common. The Twitter social networking service, for example, now allows you to record and display your current location when you enter a status update. As you approach your office, sophisticated to-do list software can now automatically hide any tasks that can't be done at that location. Your phone can also tell you which of your friends are nearby, and search results can be filtered to only show nearby businesses.

All of this is simply the continuation of a trend that started when GIS systems were housed on mainframe computers and operated by specialists who spent years learning about them. Geospatial data and applications have been "democratized" over the years, making them available in more places, to more people. What was possible only in a large organization can now be done by anyone using a handheld device. As technology continues to improve and tools become more powerful, this trend is sure to continue.

# Summary

In this chapter, we briefly introduced the Python programming language and the main concepts behind geospatial development. We saw that Python is a very high-level language and that the availability of third-party libraries for working with geospatial data makes it eminently suited to the task of geospatial development. We learned that the term *geospatial data* refers to finding information that is located on the earth's surface using coordinates, and the term "geospatial development" refers to the process of writing computer programs that can access, manipulate, and display geospatial data.

We then looked at the types of questions that can be answered by analyzing geospatial data, saw how geospatial data can be used for visualization, and learned about geospatial mash-ups, which combine data (often geospatial data) in useful and interesting ways.

Next, we learned how Google Maps, Google Earth, and the development of cheap and portable GPS units have "democratized" geospatial development. We saw how the open source software movement has produced a number of high-quality, freely available tools for geospatial development and looked at how various standards organizations have defined formats and protocols for sharing and storing geospatial data.

Finally, we saw how geolocation is being used to capture and work with geospatial data in surprising and useful ways.

In the next chapter, we will look in more detail at traditional geographic information systems including a number of important concepts that you need to understand in order to work with geospatial data. Different geospatial formats will be examined, and we will finish by using Python to perform various calculations using geospatial data.

# 2

# GIS

The term **GIS** generally refers to **geographic information systems**, which are complex computer systems for storing, manipulating, and displaying geospatial data. GIS can also be used to refer to the more general **geographic information sciences**, which is the science surrounding the use of GIS systems.

In this chapter, we will look at:

- The central GIS concepts you will have to become familiar with: location, distance, units, projections, datums, coordinate systems, and shapes
- Some of the major data formats you are likely to encounter when working with geospatial data
- Some of the processes involved in working directly with geospatial data

## Core GIS concepts

Working with geospatial data is complicated because you are dealing with mathematical models of the Earth's surface. In many ways, it is easy to think of the Earth as a sphere on which you can place your data. That might be easy, but it isn't accurate—the Earth is more like an oblate spheroid than a perfect sphere. This difference, as well as other mathematical complexities that we won't get into here, means that representing points, lines, and areas on the surface of the Earth is a rather complicated process.

Let's take a look at some of the key GIS concepts you will have to become familiar with as you work with geospatial data.

# Location

Locations represent points on the surface of the Earth. One of the most common ways of measuring location is through the use of latitude and longitude coordinates. For example, my current location (as measured by a GPS receiver) is 38.167446 degrees south and 176.234436 degrees east. What do these numbers mean, and how are they useful?

Think of the Earth as a hollow sphere with $X$, $Y$, and $Z$ axis lines drawn through the center:

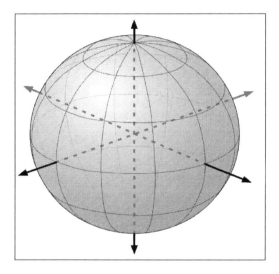

For any given point on the Earth's surface, you can draw a line that connects that point with the center of the Earth, like this:

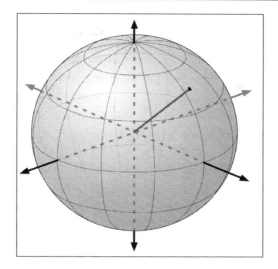

★ The point's **latitude** is the angle that this line makes in the north-south direction, relative to the equator:

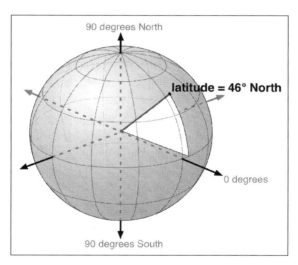

✦ In the same way, the point's **longitude** is the angle that this line makes in the east-west direction, relative to an arbitrary starting point (typically the location of the Royal Observatory in Greenwich, England):

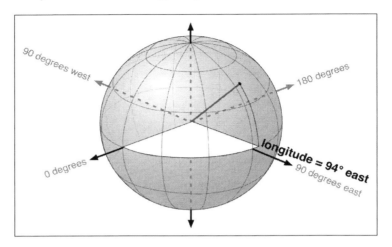

✦ By convention, positive latitude values are in the Northern Hemisphere, while negative latitude values are in the Southern Hemisphere. Similarly, positive longitude values are to the east of Greenwich, and negative longitude values are to the west. Thus, latitudes and longitudes cover the entire Earth, like this:

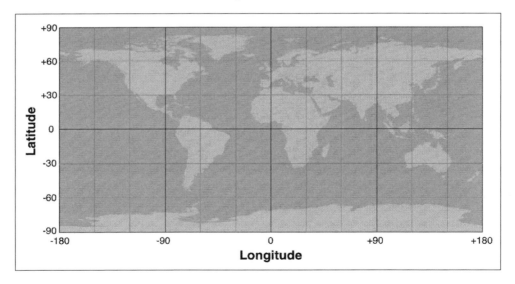

The horizontal lines, representing points of equal latitude, are called **parallels**, while the vertical lines, representing points of equal longitude, are called **meridians**. The meridian at zero longitude is often called the **prime meridian**. By definition, the parallel at zero latitude is the Earth's equator.

There are two things to remember when working with latitude and longitude values:

- Western longitudes are generally negative, but you may find situations (particularly when dealing with US-specific data) where western longitudes are given as positive values.

- The longitude values "wrap around" at the ±180° point. That is, as you travel east, your longitude will be 177, 178, 179, 180, -179, -178, -177, and so on. This can make basic distance calculations rather confusing if you do them yourself rather than relying on a library to do the work for you.

A latitude and longitude value refers to what is called a **geodetic location**.
A geodetic location identifies a precise point on the Earth's surface, regardless of what might be at that location. While much of the data we will be working with involves geodetic locations, there are other ways of describing a location you may encounter. For example, a **civic location** is simply a street address, which is another perfectly valid (though less scientifically precise) way of defining a location. Similarly, **jurisdictional locations** include information about which governmental boundary (such as an electoral ward, county, or city) the location is within, as this information is important in some contexts.

# Distance

The distance between two points on the Earth's surface can be thought of in different ways. Here are some examples:

**Angular distance**: this is the angle between two rays going out from the center of the Earth through two points.

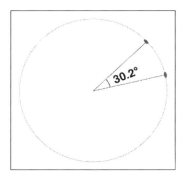

Angular distances are commonly used in seismology, and you may encounter them when working with geospatial data.

**Linear distance**: this is what people typically mean when they talk of distance—how far apart two points on the Earth's surface are.

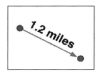

This is often described as an "as the crow flies" distance. We'll discuss this in more detail shortly, though be aware that linear distances aren't quite as simple as they might appear.

**Traveling distance:** linear ("as the crow flies") distances are all very well, but very few people can fly like crows. Another useful way of measuring distance is to measure how far you would actually have to travel to get from one point to another, typically following a road or other obvious route.

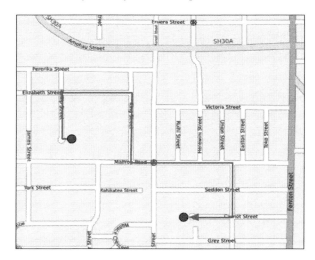

Most of the time, you will be dealing with linear distances. If the Earth were flat, linear distances would be simple to calculate—you would simply measure the length of a line drawn between the two points. Of course, the Earth is not flat, which means that actual distance calculations are rather more complicated:

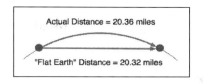

Because we are working with distances between points on the Earth's surface rather than points on a flat surface, we are actually using what is called the **great-circle distance**. The great-circle distance is the length of a semicircle going between two points on the surface of the Earth, where the semicircle is centered around the middle of the Earth:

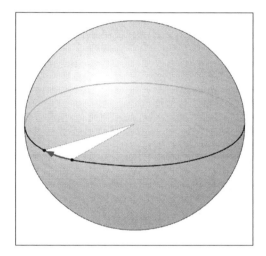

It is relatively straightforward to calculate the great-circle distance between any two points if you assume that the Earth is spherical; the **haversine formula** is often used for this. More complicated techniques that represent the shape of the Earth more accurately are available, though the haversine formula is sufficient in many cases.

[  We will learn how to use the haversine formula later in this chapter. ]

# Units

In September 1999, the Mars Climate Orbiter reached the outer edges of the Martian atmosphere, after having traveled through space for 286 days and cost a total of $327 million to create. As it approached its final orbit, a miscalculation caused it to fly too low, and the Orbiter was destroyed. An investigation revealed that the craft's thrusters were calculating force using imperial units, while the spacecraft's computer worked with metric units. The result was a disaster for NASA, and a pointed reminder of just how important it is to understand which units your data is in.

Geospatial values can be measured in a variety of units. Distances can be measured in metric and imperial, of course, but there are actually a lot of different ways in which a given distance can be measured, including:

- Millimeters
- Centimeters
- Inches
- International feet
- U.S. survey feet
- Meters
- Yards
- Kilometers
- International miles
- U.S. survey (statute) miles
- Nautical miles

Whenever you are working with distance data, it is important that you know which units those distances are in. You will also often find it necessary to convert data from one unit of measurement to another.

Angular measurements can also be in different units: degrees or radians. Once again, you will often have to convert from one to the other.

While these are not, strictly speaking, different units, you will often find yourself dealing with different ways of representing longitude and latitude values. Traditionally, longitude and latitude values have been written using "degrees, minutes, and seconds" notation, like this:

176° 14' 4"

★ Another possible way of writing these numbers is to use "degrees and decimal minutes" notation:

176° 14.066'

★ Finally, there is "decimal degrees" notation:

176.234436°

Decimal degrees are quite common now, mainly because they are simply floating-point numbers you can enter directly into your programs, but you may well need to convert longitude and latitude values from other formats before you can use them.

Another possible issue with longitude and latitude values is that the "quadrant" (east, west, north, or south) can sometimes be given as a different value rather than a positive or negative value. Here's an example:

176.234436° E

Fortunately, all these conversions are relatively straightforward. But it is important to know which units, and which format, your data is in—your software may not crash a spacecraft, but it will produce some very strange and incomprehensible results if you aren't careful.

# Projections

★
★ Creating a two-dimensional map from the three-dimensional shape of the Earth is a process known as **projection**. A projection is a mathematical transformation that "unwraps" the three-dimensional shape of the Earth and places it onto a two-dimensional plane.

Hundreds of different projections have been developed, but none of them are perfect. Indeed, it is mathematically impossible to represent the three-dimensional Earth's surface on a two-dimensional plane without introducing some sort of distortion; the trick is to choose a projection where the distortion doesn't matter for your particular use. For example, some projections represent certain areas of the Earth's surface accurately while adding major distortion to other parts of the Earth; these projections are useful for maps in the accurate portion of the Earth, but not elsewhere. Other projections distort the shape of a country while maintaining its area, while yet other projections do the opposite.

There are three main groups of projections: cylindrical, conical, and azimuthal. Let's look at each of these briefly.

# Cylindrical projections

An easy way to understand cylindrical projections is to imagine that the Earth is like a spherical Chinese lantern with a candle in the middle:

If you placed this lantern-Earth inside a paper cylinder, the candle would "project" the surface of the Earth onto the inside of the cylinder:

You could then "unwrap" this cylinder to obtain a two-dimensional image of the Earth:

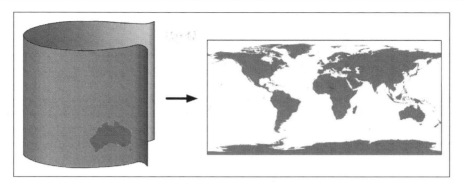

Of course, this is a simplification—in reality, map projections don't actually use light sources to project the Earth's surface onto a plane, but instead use sophisticated mathematical transformations to achieve the same effect.

Some of the main types of cylindrical projections include the **Mercator projection**, the **equal-area cylindrical projection**, and the **universal transverse Mercator projection**. The following map, taken from Wikipedia, is an example of a Mercator projection:

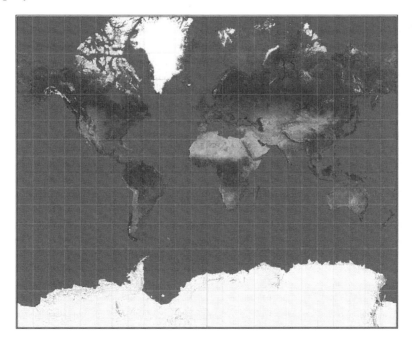

# Conic projections

A conic projection is obtained by projecting the Earth's surface onto a cone:

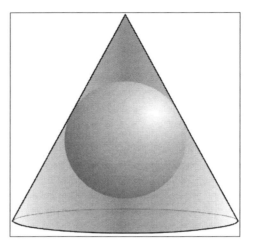

The cone is then "unwrapped" to produce the final map. Some of the more common types of conic projections include the **Albers equal-area projection**, the **Lambert conformal conic projection**, and the **equidistant projection**. The following is an example of a Lambert conformal conic projection, again taken from Wikipedia:

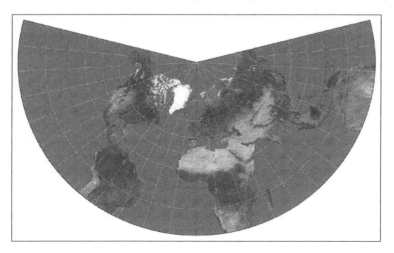

Polar-aligned conic projections are particularly useful when displaying areas that are wide but not very tall, such as a map of Russia.

# Azimuthal projections

An azimuthal projection involves projecting the Earth's surface directly onto a flat surface:

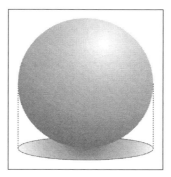

Azimuthal projections are centered around a single point and don't generally show the entire Earth's surface. They do, however, emphasize the spherical nature of the Earth. In many ways, azimuthal projections depict the Earth as it would be seen from space.

Some of the main types of azimuthal projections include the **gnomonic projection**, the **Lambert equal-area azimuthal projection**, and the **orthographic projection**. The following example, taken from Wikipedia, shows a gnomonic projection based around the North Pole:

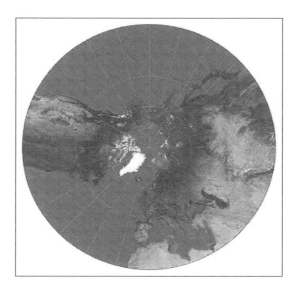

# The nature of map projections

As mentioned earlier, there is no such thing as a perfect projection—every projection distorts the Earth's surface in some way. Indeed, the mathematician Carl Gauss proved that it is mathematically impossible to project a three-dimensional shape such as a sphere onto a flat plane without introducing some sort of distortion. This is why there are so many different types of projection: some projections are more suited to a given purpose, but no projection can do everything.

Whenever you create or work with geospatial data, it is essential that you know which projection has been used to create that data. Without knowing the projection, you won't be able to plot data or perform accurate calculations.

# Coordinate systems

Closely related to map projections is the concept of a **coordinate system**. There are two types of coordinate systems you will need to be familiar with: **projected coordinate systems** and **unprojected coordinate systems**.

Latitude and longitude values are an example of an unprojected coordinate system. These are coordinates that refer directly to a point on the Earth's surface:

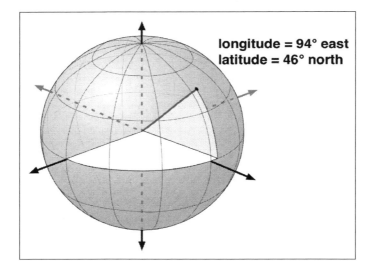

longitude = 94° east
latitude = 46° north

Unprojected coordinates are useful because they can accurately represent a desired point on the Earth's surface, but they also make it quite difficult to perform distance and other geospatial calculations.

Projected coordinates, on the other hand, are coordinates that refer to a point on a two-dimensional map that *represents* the surface of the Earth:

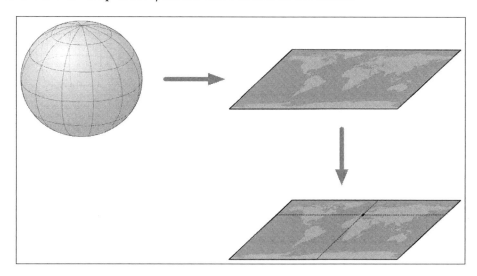

A projected coordinate system, as the name implies, makes use of a map projection to first convert the Earth into a two-dimensional Cartesian plane and then places points onto that plane. To work with a projected coordinate system, you need to know which projection was used to create the underlying map.

For both projected and unprojected coordinates, the coordinate system also implies a set of **reference points** that allow you to identify where a given point will be. For example, the unprojected lat/long coordinate system represents the longitude value of zero by a line running north-south through the Greenwich observatory in England. Similarly, a latitude value of zero represents a line running around the equator.

✖ For projected coordinate systems, you typically define an **origin** and the **map units**. Some coordinate systems also use **false northing** and **false easting** values to adjust the position of the origin, like this:

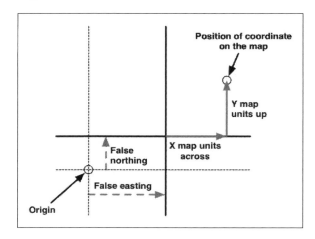

✖ To give a concrete example, the **Universal Transverse Mercator (UTM)** coordinate system divides the world into 60 different "zones", where each zone uses a different map projection to minimize projection errors. Within a given zone, the coordinates are measured as the number of meters from the zone's origin, which is the intersection of the equator and the central meridian for that zone. False northing and false easting values in meters are then added to the distance away from this reference point to avoid having to deal with negative numbers.

As you can imagine, working with projected coordinate systems like this can get quite complicated. The big advantage of projected coordinates, however, is that it is easy to perform geospatial calculations using these coordinates. For example, to calculate the distance between two points that both use the same UTM coordinate system, you simply calculate the length of the line between them. This length is the distance between the two points, measured in meters. This process is ridiculously easy compared with the work required to calculate distances using unprojected coordinates.

Of course, we are assuming that the two points are both in the same coordinate system. Since projected coordinate systems are generally only accurate over a relatively small area, you can get into trouble if the two points aren't both in the same coordinate system (for example, if they are in two different UTM zones). This is where unprojected coordinate systems have a big advantage: they cover the entire Earth.

# Datums

Roughly speaking, a **datum** is a mathematical model of the Earth used to describe locations on the Earth's surface. A datum consists of a set of reference points, often combined with a model of the shape of the Earth. The reference points are used to describe the location of other points on the Earth's surface, while the model of the Earth's shape is used when projecting the Earth's surface onto a two-dimensional plane. Thus, datums are used both by map projections and coordinate systems.

While there are hundreds of different datums in use throughout the world, most of these only apply to a localized area. There are three main **reference datums** that cover larger areas, and which you are likely to encounter when working with geospatial data:

- **NAD 27**: This is the North American Datum of 1927. It includes a definition of the Earth's shape (using a model called the Clarke Spheroid of 1866) and a set of reference points centered around Meades Ranch in Kansas. NAD 27 can be thought of as a local datum covering North America.

- **NAD 83**: This is the North American Datum of 1983. It makes use of a more complex model of the Earth's shape (the 1980 Geodetic Reference System, GRS 80). NAD 83 can be thought of as a local datum covering the United States, Canada, Mexico, and Central America.

- **WGS 84**: This is the World Geodetic System of 1984. This is a global datum covering the entire Earth. It makes use of yet another model of the Earth's shape (the Earth Gravitational Model of 1996, EGM 96) and uses reference points based on the IERS International Reference Meridian. WGS 84 is a very popular datum. When dealing with geospatial data covering the United States, WGS 84 is essentially identical to NAD 83. WGS 84 also has the distinction of being used by **Global Positioning System** (**GPS**) satellites, so all data captured by GPS units will use this datum.

While WGS 84 is the most common datum in use today, a lot of geospatial data makes use of other datums. Whenever you are dealing with a coordinate value, it is important to know which datum was used to calculate that coordinate. A given point in NAD 27, for example, may be several hundred feet away from that same coordinate expressed in WGS 84. Thus, it is vital that you know which datum is being used for a given set of geospatial data, and convert to a different datum where necessary.

# Shapes

Geospatial data often represents *shapes* in the form of points, paths, and outlines:

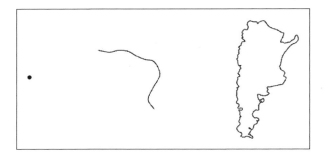

A **point**, of course, is simply a coordinate, described by two or more numbers within a projected or unprojected coordinate system.

A path is generally described using what is called a **LineString**:

A LineString represents a path as a connected series of line segments. A LineString is a deliberate simplification of a path—a way of approximating a curving path without having to deal with the complex mathematics required to draw and manipulate curves. LineStrings are often used in geospatial data to represent roads, rivers, contour lines, and so on.

 LineStrings are also sometimes referred to as *PolyLines*. Where a LineString is closed (that is, the last line segment finishes at the point where the first line segment starts), the LineString is often referred to as a *linear ring*.

✶| An outline is often represented in geospatial data using a **polygon**:

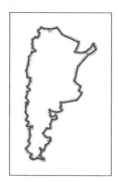

Polygons are commonly used in geospatial data to describe the outline of countries, lakes, cities, and so on. A polygon has an **exterior ring**, defined by a closed LineString, and may optionally have one or more **interior rings** within it, each also defined by a closed LineString. The exterior ring represents the polygon's outline, while the interior rings (if any) represent "holes" within the polygon:

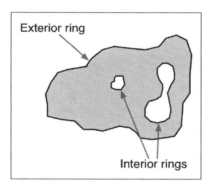

These holes are often used to depict interior features such as islands within a lake.

# GIS data formats

A GIS data format specifies how geospatial data is stored in a file (or multiple files) on disk. The format describes the logical structure used to store geospatial data within the file(s).

While we talk about storing information on disk, data formats can also be used to *transmit* geospatial information between computer systems. For example, a web service might provide map data on request, transmitting that data in a particular format.

A GIS data format will typically support:

- Geospatial data describing geographical **features**.

- Additional **meta-data** describing this data, including the datum and projection used, the coordinate system and units that the data is in, the date this file was last updated, and so on.

- **Attributes** providing additional information about the geographical features that are being described. For example, a city feature may have attributes such as *name*, *population*, *average temperature*, and so on.

- **Display information**, such as the color or line style to use when a feature is displayed.

There are two main types of GIS data: **raster format data** and **vector format data**. Raster formats are generally used to store bitmapped images, such as scanned paper maps or aerial photographs. Vector formats, on the other hand, represent spatial data using points, lines, and polygons. Vector formats are the most common type used by GIS applications as the data is smaller and easier to manipulate.

Some of the more common raster formats include:

- **Digital Raster Graphic (DRG)**: This format is used to store digital scans of paper maps

- **Digital Elevation Model (DEM)**: This is used to record elevation data

- **Band Interleaved by Line (BIL)**, **Band Interleaved by Pixel (BIP)**, **Band Sequential (BSQ)**: These data formats are typically used by remote sensing systems

Some of the more common vector formats include:

- **Shapefile**: This is an open specification developed by a company called the **Environmental Systems Research Institute (ESRI)** for storing and exchanging GIS data. A shapefile actually consists of a collection of files all with the same base name, for example, hawaii.shp, hawaii.shx, hawaii.dbf, and so on.

- **Simple Features**: This is an OpenGIS standard for storing geographical data (points, lines, and polygons) along with associated attributes.

- **TIGER/Line**: This is a text-based format previously used by the US Census Bureau to describe geographic features such as roads, buildings, rivers, and coastlines. More recent data comes in the Shapefile format, so the TIGER/Line format is only used for earlier Census Bureau datasets.

- **Coverage**: This is a proprietary data format used by ESRI's ARC/INFO system.

In addition to these "major" data formats, there are also so-called **micro-formats**, which are often used to represent individual pieces of geospatial data. These are often used to represent shapes within a running program or to transfer shapes from one program to another, but they aren't generally used to store data permanently. As you work with geospatial data, you are likely to encounter the following micro-formats:

- **Well-known Text (WKT)**: This is a simple text-based format for representing a single geographic feature such as a polygon or LineString

- **Well-known Binary (WKB)**: This alternative to WKT uses binary data rather than text to represent a single geographic feature

- **GeoJSON**: This is an open format for encoding geographic data structures and is based on the JSON data interchange format

- **Geography Markup Language (GML)**: This is an XML-based open standard for exchanging GIS data

Whenever you work with geospatial data, you need to know which format the data is in so that you can extract the information you need from the file(s) and, where necessary, transform the data from one format to another.

# Working with GIS data manually

Let's take a brief look at the process of working with GIS data manually. Before we can begin, there are two things you need to do:

- Obtain some GIS data

- Install the GDAL library and its Python bindings so that you can read the necessary data files

# Obtaining the data

Let's use the US Census Bureau's web site to download a set of vector maps for the various US states. The main site for obtaining GIS data from the US Census Bureau can be found at http://www.census.gov/geo/www/tiger.

To make things simpler, though, let's bypass the web site and directly download the file we need from http://www2.census.gov/geo/tiger/TIGER2014/STATE/ tl_2014_us_state.zip.

The file, tl_2014_us_state.zip, should be a ZIP-format archive. After uncompressing the archive, you should have a directory containing the following files:

- tl_2014_us_state.dbf
- tl_2014_us_state.prj
- tl_2014_us_state.shp
- tl_2014_us_state.shx

These files make up a shapefile containing the outlines of all the US states. Place these files together in convenient directory.

>  There will be a few extra files with a suffix of .xml. These contain additional information about the downloaded data but are not part of the shapefile itself.

# Installing GDAL

We next want to download and install the GDAL Python library. The main web site for GDAL can be found at http://gdal.org.

How you install GDAL depends on which operating system you are running.

## Installing GDAL on Linux

To install GDAL on a Linux machine, you would typically use your computer's package manager to install the GDAL package itself. For example, on Fedora Linux, you would use the following command:

```
yum install gdal gdal-devel
```

Note that you need to install the gdal-devel package as well as gdal itself. The gdal-devel package includes the files needed to compile the Python bindings for GDAL.

Once you have installed GDAL itself, you'll need to install and build the Python bindings. These Python bindings can be found at `https://pypi.python.org/pypi/GDAL`. Typically, you would use a command such as the following:

```
sudo easy_install GDAL
```

Obviously, you will need to have Python installed before you can install the Python bindings for GDAL.

# Installing GDAL on Mac OS X

To install GDAL on a Mac, you need to install the GDAL library itself, and then compile the Python bindings to use the version of GDAL you installed. Let's work through the various steps one at a time:

1. To download GDAL, go to `http://www.kyngchaos.com/software/frameworks`. You will need to install the *GDAL Complete* package. This package includes a precompiled version of GDAL, which you should install onto your computer.

2. Once you have installed GDAL, you next need to compile the Python bindings. To do this, you first need to install Xcode, which is Apple's development environment. Xcode can be downloaded for free from the Mac App store.

> Note that if your computer runs a version of Mac OS X lower than 10.9 (Yosemite), you will need to separately install the command-line tools for Xcode. To do this, start up Xcode and choose the **Preferences…** command from the **Xcode** menu. In the **Downloads** tab will be an option to install the command-line tools; enable this option and wait for the required tools to be installed.

3. Once you have Xcode installed, you can download and compile the Python bindings for GDAL. The easiest way to do this is to use **pip**, the Python package manager. If you don't already have pip, you can install it by following the instructions at `https://pip.pypa.io/en/latest/installing.html`.

4. Before you can compile the GDAL Python bindings, you will need to set a few environment variables so that Python can find the version of GDAL you installed. To do this, type the following in a Terminal window:

```
export CPLUS_INCLUDE_PATH=/Library/Frameworks/GDAL.framework/Headers
export C_INCLUDE_PATH=/Library/Frameworks/GDAL.framework/Headers
export LIBRARY_PATH=/Library/Frameworks/GDAL.framework/Versions/1.11/unix/lib
```

Make sure the version of GDAL in the `LIBRARY_PATH` variable definition matches the version you installed.

5. You can now install the Python bindings by typing the following:

```
pip install gdal==1.11
```

Once again, make sure that the version number matches the version of GDAL you installed.

All going well, the Python bindings for GDAL should compile successfully. You will see a few compiler warnings, but hopefully no errors.

## Installing GDAL on MS Windows

Unfortunately, there is currently no prebuilt installer for GDAL that uses Python 3. You can either attempt to build it yourself, or you will have to use Python 2. You can download a binary installer for GDAL that includes Python 2 support from `http://www.gisinternals.com`.

Because you won't be able to use Python 3, you will need to adjust the code you write to match the syntax for Python 2. For the code samples for this chapter, the only difference is that you don't use parentheses after the `print` keyword.

## Testing your GDAL installation

After installing GDAL, you can check whether it works by typing `import osgeo` into the Python command line; if the Python command prompt reappears with no error message, it means GDAL was successfully installed, and you are all set to go:

```
>>> import osgeo
>>>
```

## Examining the Downloaded Shapefile

Let's now use GDAL to look at the contents of the shapefile you downloaded earlier. You can either type the following directly into the command prompt, or else save it as a Python script so that you can run it whenever you wish to (let's call this script `analyze.py`):

```
import osgeo.ogr

shapefile = osgeo.ogr.Open("tl_2014_us_state.shp")
numLayers = shapefile.GetLayerCount()
```

```
print("Shapefile contains {} layers".format(numLayers))
print()

for layerNum in range(numLayers):
    layer = shapefile.GetLayer(layerNum)
    spatialRef = layer.GetSpatialRef().ExportToProj4()
    numFeatures = layer.GetFeatureCount()
    print("Layer {} has spatial reference {}".format(
            layerNum, spatialRef))
    print("Layer {} has {} features:".format(
            layerNum, numFeatures))
    print()

    for featureNum in range(numFeatures):
        feature = layer.GetFeature(featureNum)
        featureName = feature.GetField("NAME")

        print("Feature {} has name {}".
            format(featureNum, featureName))
```

This example assumes you've placed this script in the same directory as the `tl_2014_us_state.shp` file. If you've put it in a different directory, change the `osgeo.ogr.Open()` command to include the path to your shapefile. If you are running this on MS Windows, don't forget to use double backslash characters (\\) as directory separators.

Running this script will give us a quick summary of how the shapefile's data is structured:

```
Shapefile contains 1 layers

Layer 0 has spatial reference +proj=longlat +datum=NAD83 +no_defs
Layer 0 has 56 features:

Feature 0 has name West Virginia
Feature 1 has name Florida
Feature 2 has name Illinois
Feature 3 has name Minnesota
...
Feature 53 has name District of Columbia
Feature 54 has name Iowa
Feature 55 has name Arizona
```

This shows us that the data we downloaded consists of one layer, with 56 individual features corresponding to the various states and protectorates in the USA. It also tells us the "spatial reference" for this layer, which tells us that the coordinates are represented as latitude and longitude values using the NAD83 datum.

As you can see from the example, using GDAL to extract data from shapefiles is quite straightforward. Let's continue with another example. This time, we'll look at the details of feature number 12, New Mexico. Let's call this program `analyze2.py`:

```python
import osgeo.ogr

shapefile = osgeo.ogr.Open("tl_2014_us_state.shp")
layer = shapefile.GetLayer(0)
feature = layer.GetFeature(12)

print("Feature 12 has the following attributes:")
print()

attributes = feature.items()

for key,value in attributes.items():
  print("  {} = {}".format(key, value))

geometry = feature.GetGeometryRef()
geometryName = geometry.GetGeometryName()

print()
print("Feature's geometry data consists of a {}".format(
      geometryName))
```

Running this produces the following output:

```
Feature 12 has the following attributes:

  STUSPS = NM
  GEOID = 35
  REGION = 4
  ALAND = 314161410324.0
  MTFCC = G4000
  FUNCSTAT = A
  NAME = New Mexico
  STATEFP = 35
  LSAD = 00
```

```
STATENS = 00897535
AWATER = 755712514.0
DIVISION = 8
INTPTLON = -106.1316181
INTPTLAT = +34.4346843
```

`Feature's geometry data consists of a POLYGON`

The meaning of the various attributes is described on the US Census Bureau's web site, but what interests us right now is the feature's **geometry**. A geometry object is a complex structure that holds some geospatial data, often using nested geometry objects to reflect the way the geospatial data is organized. So far, we've discovered that New Mexico's geometry consists of a polygon. Let's now take a closer look at this polygon, using a program we'll call `analyze3.py`:

```
import osgeo.ogr

def analyzeGeometry(geometry, indent=0):
  s = []
  s.append("  " * indent)
  s.append(geometry.GetGeometryName())
  if geometry.GetPointCount() > 0:
    s.append(" with {} data points".format(geometry.GetPointCount()))
  if geometry.GetGeometryCount() > 0:
    s.append(" containing:")

  print("".join(s))

  for i in range(geometry.GetGeometryCount()):
    analyzeGeometry(geometry.GetGeometryRef(i), indent+1)

shapefile = osgeo.ogr.Open("tl_2014_us_state.shp")
layer = shapefile.GetLayer(0)
feature = layer.GetFeature(12)
geometry = feature.GetGeometryRef()

analyzeGeometry(geometry)
```

The recursive `analyzeGeometry()` function reveals the structure for this geometry:

```
POLYGON containing:
  LINEARRING with 7554 data points
```

As you can see, this geometry has a single linear ring, defining the outline of New Mexico. If we ran the same program over California (feature 13 in our shapefile), the output would be somewhat more complicated:

```
MULTIPOLYGON containing:
  POLYGON containing:
    LINEARRING with 121 data points
  POLYGON containing:
    LINEARRING with 191 data points
  POLYGON containing:
    LINEARRING with 77 data points
  POLYGON containing:
    LINEARRING with 152 data points
  POLYGON containing:
    LINEARRING with 392 data points
  POLYGON containing:
    LINEARRING with 93 data points
  POLYGON containing:
    LINEARRING with 10105 data points
```

As you can see, California is made up of seven distinct polygons, each defined by a single linear ring. This is because California is on the coast and includes six outlying islands as well as the main inland body of the state.

Let's finish this analysis of the US state shapefile by answering a simple question: what is the distance from the northernmost point to the southernmost point in California? There are various ways we could answer this question, but for now, we'll do it by hand. Let's start by identifying the northernmost and southernmost points in California:

```python
import osgeo.ogr

def findPoints(geometry, results):
    for i in range(geometry.GetPointCount()):
        x,y,z = geometry.GetPoint(i)
        if results['north'] == None or results['north'][1] < y:
            results['north'] = (x,y)
        if results['south'] == None or results['south'][1] > y:
            results['south'] = (x,y)
```

```
    for i in range(geometry.GetGeometryCount()):
      findPoints(geometry.GetGeometryRef(i), results)

  shapefile = osgeo.ogr.Open("tl_2014_us_state.shp")
  layer = shapefile.GetLayer(0)
  feature = layer.GetFeature(13)
  geometry = feature.GetGeometryRef()

  results = {'north' : None,
             'south' : None}

  findPoints(geometry, results)

  print("Northernmost point is ({:.4f}, {:.4f})".format(
        results['north'][0], results['north'][1]))
  print("Southernmost point is ({:.4f}, {:.4f})".format(
        results['south'][0], results['south'][1]))
```

The findPoints() function recursively scans through a geometry, extracting the individual points and identifying the points with the highest and lowest y (latitude) values, which are then stored in the results dictionary so that the main program can use these values.

As you can see, GDAL makes it easy to work with the complex geometry data structure. The code does require recursion, but it is still trivial compared with trying to read the data directly. If you run the above program, the following output will be displayed:

**Northernmost point is (-122.3782, 42.0095)**

**Southernmost point is (-117.2049, 32.5288)**

Now that we have these two points, we want to calculate the distance between them. As described earlier, we have to use a great-circle distance calculation here to allow for the curvature of the Earth's surface. We'll do this manually, using the haversine formula:

```
  import math

  lat1 = 42.0095
  long1 = -122.3782

  lat2 = 32.5288
  long2 = -117.2049
```

```
rLat1 = math.radians(lat1)
rLong1 = math.radians(long1)
rLat2 = math.radians(lat2)
rLong2 = math.radians(long2)

dLat = rLat2 - rLat1
dLong = rLong2 - rLong1
a = math.sin(dLat/2)**2 + math.cos(rLat1) * math.cos(rLat2) \
                          * math.sin(dLong/2)**2
c = 2 * math.atan2(math.sqrt(a), math.sqrt(1-a))
distance = 6371 * c

print("Great circle distance is {:0.0f} kilometers".format(
    distance))
```

Don't worry about the complex maths involved here; basically, we are converting the latitude and longitude values to radians, calculating the difference in latitude/longitude values between the two points, and then passing the results through some trigonometric functions to obtain the great-circle distance. The value of 6371 is the radius of the Earth, in kilometers.

More details about the haversine formula can be found at `http://mathforum.org/library/drmath/view/51879.html`.

If you run the program, your computer will tell you the distance from the northernmost to the southernmost point in California:

**Great circle distance is 1149 kilometers**

There are, of course, other ways of calculating this. You wouldn't normally type the haversine formula directly into your program, as there are libraries that will do this for you. But we deliberately did the calculation this way to show how it can be done.

If you would like to explore this further, you might like to try writing programs to calculate the following:

- The easternmost and westernmost points in California
- The midpoint of California

Hint: You can calculate the midpoint's longitude by taking the average of the easternmost and westernmost longitudes.

- The midpoint of Arizona
- The distance between the middle of California and the middle of Arizona

As you can see, working with GIS data manually isn't too onerous. While the data structures and maths involved can be rather complex, and you do have to be aware of the underlying GIS concepts, using tools such as GDAL makes your data accessible and easy to work with.

# Summary

In this chapter, we discussed many of the core concepts that underlie GIS development, examined some of the more common GIS data formats, and got our hands dirty exploring US state data downloaded from the US Census Bureau web site.

We saw that locations are often, but not always, represented using coordinates, learned that calculating the distance between two points requires you to take into account the curvature of the Earth's surface, and discovered why you must always be aware of the units used by geospatial data.

We then learned about map projections, which represent the three-dimensional shape of the Earth's surface as a two-dimensional plane, and saw that there are three main classes of map projection: cylindrical, conic, and azimuthal. We discovered that datums are mathematical models of the Earth's shape, and learned that the three most common datums in use are called NAD 27, NAD 83, and WGS 84.

We next examined the concept of coordinate systems and saw that these are used to describe how coordinates relate to a given point on the Earth's surface. We learned that unprojected coordinate systems directly represent points on the Earth's surface, while projected coordinate systems use a map projection to represent the Earth as a two-dimensional Cartesian plane onto which coordinates are then placed.

We examined the ways in which geospatial data can be used to represent shapes in the form of points, LineStrings, and polygons, and we looked at a number of standard GIS data formats you might encounter. We saw that some data formats work with raster data, while others use vector data.

Finally, we learned how to use Python to manually perform various geospatial calculations on data loaded from shapefiles.

In the next chapter, we will look in more detail at the various Python libraries that can be used for working with geospatial data.

# 3
# Python Libraries for Geospatial Development

This chapter examines a number of libraries and other tools that can be used for geospatial development in Python. In particular, we will cover:

- Python libraries for reading and writing geospatial data
- Python libraries for dealing with map projections
- Libraries for analyzing and manipulating geospatial data directly within your Python programs
- Tools for visualizing geospatial data

Note that two types of geospatial toolkits are not discussed in this chapter: geospatial databases and geospatial web toolkits. Both of these will be examined in detail later in this book.

## Reading and writing geospatial data

While you could, in theory, write your own parser to read a particular geospatial data format, it is much easier to use an existing Python library to do this. We will look at two popular libraries for reading and writing geospatial data: **GDAL** and **OGR**.

# GDAL/OGR

Unfortunately, the naming of these two libraries is rather confusing. **GDAL** (short for **Geospatial Data Abstraction Library**), was originally just a library for working with raster-format geospatial data, while the separate **OGR** library was intended to work with vector-format data. However, the two libraries are now partially merged and generally downloaded and installed together under the combined name of *GDAL*. To avoid confusion, we will call this combined library *GDAL/OGR* and use *GDAL* to refer to just the raster translation library.

A default installation of GDAL allows you to read data in 100 different raster file formats, and write data in 71 different formats. OGR, by default, supports reading data in 42 different vector file formats and writing data in 39 different formats. This makes GDAL/OGR one of the most powerful geospatial data translators available, and certainly the most useful freely-available library for reading and writing geospatial data.

## Installing GDAL/OGR

We saw how to install GDAL/OGR in the *Working with GIS data manually* section in the previous chapter. Refer to the instructions in that section for more information on installing GDAL and OGR onto your computer.

## Understanding GDAL

To read and write raster-format data, the GDAL library makes use of a **dataset** object. The dataset object, an instance of `gdal.Dataset`, represents a file containing raster-format data.

Each dataset is broken down into multiple **bands**, where each band contains a single piece of raster data. For example, a raster dataset representing a basemap image might consist of three bands, representing the red, green, and blue color components of the overall image:

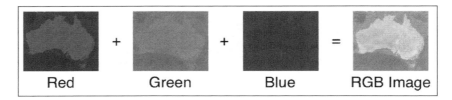

| Red | | Green | | Blue | | RGB Image |

Of course, bands aren't limited to storing RGB color values; they can hold any information you like. For example, one band might store elevation, a second band might store soil moisture levels, and a third band might hold a code indicating the type of vegetation found at that location. Each band within a raster dataset is represented by a `gdal.Band` object.

For each band, the raster data consists of a number of **cells** arranged into rows and columns:

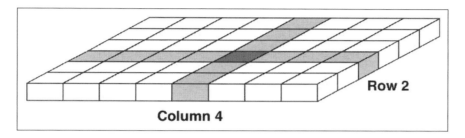

Each cell is then **georeferenced** onto a portion of the Earth's surface:

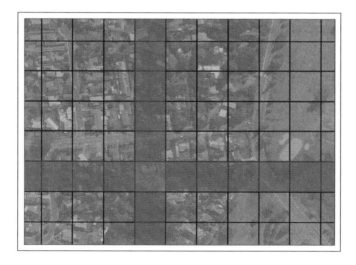

Within a band, each cell consists of a simple integer or floating-point value.

While raster datasets cover a rectangular area of the Earth's surface, there may not be a value for every cell. For example, a dataset that contains information for a particular country will not have values for the cells that lie beyond that country's borders, as shown in the following figure:

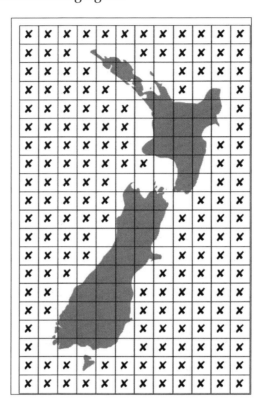

Each **X** in this figure represents a cell that doesn't have a value. To allow this, GDAL supports the concept of a **no data value**. This is a special value which is stored in the cell when the cell doesn't have an actual value associated with it.

Because each raster band typically has thousands (or even millions) of cells, you don't normally access the cells one at a time. Instead, you can use one of two possible techniques to access the band's data *en masse*:

- You can use the `band.ReadRaster()` method to read some or all of the band's data into a binary string and then use the built-in `struct` library to convert that string into an array of values

- You can use the `band.ReadArray()` method to read some of the band's data, storing the cell values directly into a `NumPy` array object

Both approaches have their advantages and disadvantages. Using `struct` allows you to access cell values as integers or floating-point values directly, but you can only easily extract one row of data at a time. Using the NumPy array approach makes it easier to read multiple rows of data at once but requires you to install the third-party NumPy library. NumPy also has the disadvantage that it stores each value as a custom NumPy object. For example, 16-bit integer values are stored as `numpy.uint16` objects; NumPy automatically converts these to integers as required, but doing so can slow your program down, so you may need to do this conversion yourself.

Note that the `gdal.Band` object has corresponding `WriterRaster()` and `WriteArray()` methods, allowing you to use either approach for writing raster data as well as reading it.

# GDAL example code

Let's take a look at how you can use GDAL to write raster-format data into a GeoTIFF formatted file. For our example, we'll divide the entire Earth's surface into 360 cells horizontally and 180 cells vertically, so that each cell covers one degree of latitude and longitude. For each cell, we'll store a single random number between 1 and 100.

We'll start by creating the file itself. To do this, we first ask GDAL to select a **driver** that can create the type of file we want, and then ask the driver to create the file:

```
from osgeo import gdal
driver = gdal.GetDriverByName("GTIFF")
dstFile = driver.Create("Example Raster.tiff", 360, 180, 1,
                gdal.GDT_INT16)
```
Int16

While this program is presented in sections so that that each step can be explained, the complete source code for the program is included in the example programs that can be downloaded for this chapter. Look for a file named `writeRaster.py`.

The `gdal.Driver.Create()` method takes the following parameters:

- The name of the raster file.
- The desired number of cells across.
- The desired number of cells down.
- The desired number of bands in the file.
- A constant defining the type of information to store in each cell. In our case, each cell will hold a 16-bit integer value.

Our next task is to set the **projection** that will be used to position our cells onto the surface of the earth. In our case, we will use WGS84, allowing us to refer to each cell's position using latitude and longitude values:

```
from gdal import osr
spatialReference = osr.SpatialReference()
spatialReference.SetWellKnownGeogCS("WGS84")
dstFile.SetProjection(spatialReference.ExportToWkt())
```

We next have to define the **georeferencing transform** to use for our data. This transform tells GDAL how to map each cell onto the surface of the Earth. The georeferencing transform is defined as a list of six numbers, known as an **affine transformation matrix**. Fortunately, we can ignore the mathematics of affine transformations and define our matrix using just four values:

- The *X* and *Y* position of the top-left corner of the top-left cell
- The width of each cell, measured in degrees of longitude
- The height of each cell, measured in degrees of latitude

Here is the Python code to set our file's georeferencing transform:

```
originX    = -180
originY    = 90
cellWidth  = 1.0
cellHeight = 1.0

dstFile.SetGeoTransform([originX, cellWidth, 0,
                         originY, 0, -cellHeight])
```

While we're at it, let's get a reference to the `gdal.Band` object we'll need to store data into our file's one and only raster band:

```
band = dstFile.GetRasterBand(1)
```

Now that we have set up our raster-format file, let's create some data to store into it. We'll use the built-in `random` module to create a list-of-lists holding one random number for each cell:

```
import random

values = []
for row in range(180):
    row_data = []
    for col in range(360):
        row_data.append(random.randint(1, 100))
    values.append(row_data)
```

To save these values to the file using the built-in `struct` module, we have to write them to disk one row at a time. Here's the code for doing this:

```
import struct

fmt = "<" + ("h" * band.XSize)

for row in range(180):
    scanline = struct.pack(fmt, *values[row])
    band.WriteRaster(0, row, 360, 1, scanline)
```

Alternatively, if you have NumPy installed, you can write the `values` array directly to the file as a NumPy array:

```
import numpy

array = numpy.array(values, dtype=numpy.int16)
band.WriteArray(array)
```

This completes our program. If you run it, you will create a file named `Example Raster.tiff`, which contains 360 x 180 random numbers. Let's now write a separate program that can read the contents of this file.

Fortunately, reading raster data is more straightforward than writing it. We'll start by opening the dataset and getting a reference to our (one and only) raster band:

```
from osgeo import gdal

srcFile = gdal.Open("Example Raster.tiff")
band = srcFile.GetRasterBand(1)
```

 This program is called `readRaster.py` and is included in the example programs that can be downloaded for this chapter.

We're now ready to read the contents of the file. Here is how we can do this using the built-in `struct` module:

```
import struct

fmt = "<" + ("h" * band.XSize)

for row in range(band.YSize):
    scanline = band.ReadRaster(0, row, band.XSize, 1,
                               band.XSize, 1,
                               band.DataType)
    row_data = struct.unpack(fmt, scanline)
    print(row_data)
```

> Don't worry about all the parameters to the `ReadRaster` method; because this method can scale the data as it is being read, we have to supply the number of cells across and down twice, as well as the starting cell position. You can look up the definition of this method in the GDAL documentation if you want to know the details.

As you can see, we're simply printing out the returned raster values so that you can see them. Let's do the same thing again, this time using NumPy:

```
values = band.ReadAsArray()
for row in range(band.XSize):
    print(values[row])
```

> Note that the `ReadAsArray()` method is only available if you have NumPy installed.

As you can see, reading raster data using GDAL is quite straightforward once you get past the complexity of converting the raw binary data back into Python using either `struct` or NumPy.

# Understanding OGR

As we have seen, OGR is used to read and write vector-format geospatial data. OGR uses the term **data source** to represent a file or other source of vector-format data. A data source consists of one or more **layers**, where each layer represents a set of related information. While many data sources consist of only one layer, other data sources may be more complex. For example, a single complex data source might store county outlines, roads, city boundaries, and the location of hospitals, each as a separate layer within the data source.

Each layer is made up of a list of **features**. A feature represents a single item that is being described. For example, for a "cities" layer, each feature would represent a single city.

For each feature, the layer has a **geometry**, which is the actual piece of geospatial data representing the feature's shape or position in space, along with a list of **attributes** that provide additional meta-information about the feature.

Finally, in addition to the features themselves, each layer has a **spatial reference** that identifies the projection and datum used by the layer's features.

The following illustration shows how all these elements relate to each other:

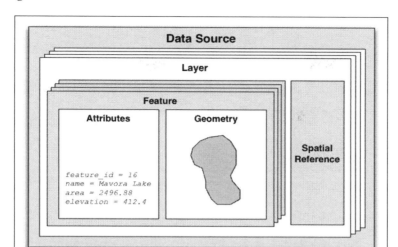

While this may seem like quite a complex design, the versatility of this approach allows OGR to work with all sorts of different vector data formats. For example, the shapefile format does not support multiple layers, but OGR uses a consistent model that represents a shapefile as a data source consisting of only one layer.

# OGR example code

Since you learned how to read from a shapefile using OGR in the previous chapter, let's now take a closer look at how you can write vector-format data using OGR. We'll write a simple Python program that generates a set of random Point geometries and stores them, along with some attribute values, in a shapefile.

Let's start by importing the required modules and creating a directory to hold the generated shapefile:

```
import os, os.path, shutil, random
from osgeo import ogr, osr

if os.path.exists("test-shapefile"):
    shutil.rmtree("test-shapefile")
os.mkdir("test-shapefile")
```

> The complete source code for this program is included in the
> example files for this chapter, in the file named `writeVector.py`.

Notice that we delete our shapefile's directory if it already exists. This allows us to
run the program multiple times without having to remember to delete the shapefile
each time.

We can now set up our shapefile as an OGR data source. As with GDAL, we first
select a **driver** for the type of data source we want to create and then ask the driver
to create the data source. Here is the relevant code:

```
driver = ogr.GetDriverByName("ESRI Shapefile")
path = os.path.join("test-shapefile", "shapefile.shp")
datasource = driver.CreateDataSource(path)
```

Next, we want to define our layer. To do this, we first have to define the spatial
reference we will use for our data:

```
spatialReference = osr.SpatialReference()
spatialReference.SetWellKnownGeogCS('WGS84')
```

We can then create the layer itself:

```
layer = datasource.CreateLayer("layer", spatialReference)
```

Since we want to store attribute information into our file, we next need to tell OGR
what those attributes will be and what type of data to store. This information is
added directly to the map layer using the `ogr.FieldDefn` class:

```
field = ogr.FieldDefn("ID", ogr.OFTInteger)
field.SetWidth(4)
layer.CreateField(field)

field = ogr.FieldDefn("NAME", ogr.OFTString)
field.SetWidth(20)
layer.CreateField(field)
```

Now that we've created our shapefile, let's store some information in it. We're going
to generate 100 Point geometries and calculate an ID and name to associate with each
feature. We'll use the built-in `random` module to do this:

```
for i in range(100):
    id   = 1000 + i
    lat  = random.uniform(-90, +90)
    long = random.uniform(-180, +180)
```

```
name = "point-{}".format(i)

wkt = "POINT({} {})".format(long, lat)
geometry = ogr.CreateGeometryFromWkt(wkt)
```

As you can see, we define the Point geometry as a WKT formatted string, which we then convert into an `ogr.Geometry` object. We next need to create an `ogr.Feature` object for each of our points and store the geometry and attribute values into the feature:

```
feature = ogr.Feature(layer.GetLayerDefn())
feature.SetGeometry(geometry)
feature.SetField("ID", id)
feature.SetField("NAME", name)
```

Finally, we have to tell the layer to create the feature and store it into the file:

```
layer.CreateFeature(feature)
```

This completes our program. If you run it, a directory named `test-shapefile` will be created, containing the various files that hold the shapefile's data.

To read through the contents of our generated shapefile, we use the same technique we covered in the previous chapter. Here is a simple program which will load the various Point geometries back into memory and display the coordinates as well as the attributes we stored earlier:

```
from osgeo import ogr

shapefile = ogr.Open("test-shapefile/shapefile.shp")
layer = shapefile.GetLayer(0)

for i in range(layer.GetFeatureCount()):
    feature  = layer.GetFeature(i)
    id       = feature.GetField("ID")
    name     = feature.GetField("NAME")
    geometry = feature.GetGeometryRef()
    print(i, name, geometry.GetX(), geometry.GetY())
```

 This program is available in the example code under the name `readVector.py`.

As you can see, using OGR to work with vector data sources is not difficult at all.

# GDAL/OGR documentation

GDAL and OGR are well documented, but there is a catch for Python programmers. The GDAL/OGR library and associated command-line tools are all written in C and C++. Bindings are available that allow access from a variety of other languages, including Python, but the documentation is all written for the C++ version of the libraries. This can make reading the documentation rather challenging—not only are all the method signatures written in C++, but the Python bindings have changed many of the method and class names to make them more "Pythonic".

Fortunately, the Python libraries are largely self-documenting, thanks to all the docstrings embedded in the Python bindings themselves. This means you can explore the documentation using tools such as Python's built-in `pydoc` utility, which can be run from the command line like this:

```
pydoc -g osgeo
```

This will open up a GUI window allowing you to read the documentation using a web browser. Alternatively, if you want to find out about a single method or class, you can use Python's built-in `help()` command from the Python command line, like this:

```
>>> from osgeo import ogr
>>> help(ogr.DataSource.CopyLayer)
```

Not all the methods are documented, so you may need to refer to the C++ docs on the GDAL web site for more information, and some of the docstrings that are there are copied directly from the C++ documentation—but the documentation for GDAL/OGR is excellent in general and should allow you to quickly come up to speed with using this library.

# Dealing with projections

One of the challenges of working with geospatial data is that geodetic locations (points on the Earth's surface) are often mapped onto a two-dimensional Cartesian plane using a cartographic projection. We looked at projections in the previous chapter: whenever you have some geospatial data, you need to know which projection that data uses. You also need to know the datum (model of the Earth's shape) assumed by the data.

A common challenge when dealing with geospatial data is that you have to convert data from one projection or datum to another. Fortunately, there is a Python library that makes this task easy: `pyproj`.

# pyproj

pyproj is a Python "wrapper" around another library called **PROJ.4**. PROJ.4 is an abbreviation for version 4 of the PROJ library. PROJ was originally written by the US Geological Survey for dealing with map projections and has been widely used in geospatial software for many years. The pyproj library makes it possible to access the functionality of PROJ.4 from within your Python programs.

# Installing pyproj

pyproj is available for MS Windows, Mac OS X, and any POSIX-based operating system. The main web page for pyproj can be found at https://github.com/jswhit/pyproj.

The way you install pyproj will vary depending on which operating system your computer is running:

- For MS Windows, you will first need to install the underlying PROJ.4 library. A binary installer for this can be found at https://github.com/OSGeo/proj.4/wiki. Once PROJ.4 itself has been installed, you need to install the pyproj library. A Python wheel (.whl) file for pyproj that works with your version of Python can be downloaded from http://www.lfd.uci.edu/~gohlke/pythonlibs/#pyproj. Once you have downloaded the appropriate .whl file, you can install it using pip, the Python package manager. Full instructions for installing a Python wheel using pip can be found at https://pip.pypa.io/en/latest/user_guide.html#installing-from-wheels.

- For Mac OS X, you can install pyproj along with the underlying PROJ.4 library by simply typing pip install pyproj from the command line.

> If this doesn't work, you can install a version of the PROJ.4 framework from http://www.kyngchaos.com/software/frameworks. Once this has been installed, pip should be able to successfully install the pyproj library.

- For Linux, you can install the PROJ.4 library using your favorite package manager and then install pyproj itself using pip. Alternatively, you can download the source code to pyproj and compile and install it yourself.

To ensure that the installation worked, start up the Python command line and try entering the following:

```
import pyproj
print(pyproj.__version__)
```

If this works without an error, then you have successfully installed `pyproj` onto your computer.

# Understanding pyproj

`pyproj` consists of just two classes: `Proj` and `Geod`. `Proj` converts between longitude and latitude values and native map *(x,y)* coordinates, while `Geod` performs various great-circle distance and angle calculations. Both are built on top of the PROJ.4 library. Let's take a closer look at these two classes.

# Proj

`Proj` is a cartographic transformation class, allowing you to convert geographic coordinates (that is, latitude and longitude values) into cartographic coordinates *((x, y)* values, by default in meters) and vice versa.

When you create a new `Proj` instance, you specify the projection, datum and other values used to describe how the coordinates are to be transformed. For example, to specify the transverse Mercator projection and the WGS84 ellipsoid, you would use the following Python code:

```
projection = pyproj.Proj(proj='tmerc', ellps='WGS84')
```

Once you have created a `Proj` instance, you can use it to convert a latitude and longitude to an *(x,y)* coordinate using the given projection. You can also use it to do an *inverse* projection, that is, converting from an *(x,y)* coordinate back into a latitude and longitude value.

The helpful `transform()` function can be used to directly convert coordinates from one projection value into another. You simply provide the starting coordinates, the `Proj` object that describes the starting coordinates' *projection*, and the desired ending projection. This can be very useful when converting coordinates, either singly or *en masse*.

# Geod

Geod is a geodetic computation class. This allows you to perform various great-circle calculations. We looked at great-circle calculations earlier, when considering how to accurately calculate the distance between two points on the Earth's surface. The Geod class, however, can do more than this:

- The fwd() method takes a starting point, an azimuth (angular direction), and a distance and returns the ending point and the back azimuth (the angle from the end point back to the start point):

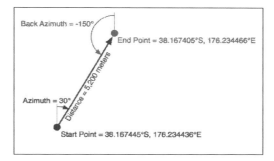

- The inv() method takes two coordinates and returns the forward and back azimuth as well as the distance between them:

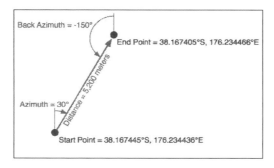

- The `npts()` method calculates the coordinates for a number of points spaced equidistantly along a geodesic line running from the start to the end point:

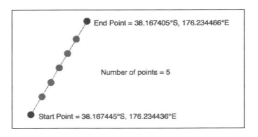

When you create a new `Geod` object, you specify the ellipsoid to use when performing the geodetic calculations. The ellipsoid can be selected from a number of predefined ellipsoids, or you can enter the parameters for the ellipsoid (equatorial radius, polar radius, and so on) directly.

# Example code

The following example starts with a location specified using UTM zone 17 coordinates. Using two `Proj` objects to define the UTM zone 17 and lat/long projections, it translates this location's coordinates into latitude and longitude values:

```
import pyproj

UTM_X = 565718.523517
UTM_Y = 3980998.9244

srcProj = pyproj.Proj(proj="utm", zone="11",
                ellps="clrk66", units="m")
dstProj = pyproj.Proj(proj='longlat', ellps='WGS84',
                datum='WGS84')

long,lat = pyproj.transform(srcProj, dstProj, UTM_X, UTM_Y)

print("UTM zone 17 coordinate " +
      "({:.4f}, {:.4f}) ".format(UTM_X, UTM_Y) +
      "= {:.4f}, {:.4f}".format(long, lat))
```

This second example takes the calculated lat/long values and, using a `Geod` object, calculates another point 10 km northeast of that location:

```
angle    = 315 # 315 degrees = northeast.
distance = 10000
```

```
geod = pyproj.Geod(ellps='clrk66')
long2,lat2,invAngle = geod.fwd(long, lat, angle, distance)

print("{:.4f}, {:.4f}".format(lat2, long2) +
      " is 10km northeast of " +
      "{:.4f}, {:.4f}".format(lat, long))
```

 Both of these examples can be found in the source code for this chapter, in the `pyproj_example.py` file.

# Documentation

The documentation available on the `pyproj` web site, and in the README file provided with the source code, is excellent as far as it goes. It describes how to use the various classes and methods, what they do, and what parameters are required. However, the documentation is rather sparse when it comes to the parameters used when creating a new `Proj` object. Here is what it says:

> "*A* `Proj` *class instance is initialized with* `proj` *map projection control parameter key/value pairs. The key/value pairs can either be passed in a dictionary, or as keyword arguments, or as a* `proj4` *string (compatible with the* `proj` *command).*"

The documentation does provide a link to a web site listing a number of standard map projections and their associated parameters, but understanding what these parameters mean generally requires you to delve into the PROJ documentation itself. The documentation for PROJ is dense and confusing, even more so because the main manual is written for PROJ version 3, with addendums for versions 4 and 4.3. Attempting to make sense of all this can be quite challenging.

Fortunately, in most cases, you won't need to refer to the PROJ documentation at all. When working with geospatial data using GDAL or OGR, you can easily extract the projection as a "proj4 string", which can be passed directly to the `Proj` initializer. If you want to hardwire the projection, you can generally choose a projection and ellipsoid using the `proj="..."` and `ellps="..."` parameters, respectively. If you want to do more than this, though, you will need to refer to the PROJ documentation for more details.

 To find out more about PROJ and read the original documentation, you can find everything you need at `https://github.com/OSGeo/proj.4/wiki`.

# Analyzing and manipulating Geospatial data

Because geospatial data works with geometrical features such as points, lines, and polygons, you often need to perform various calculations using these geometrical features. Fortunately, there are some very powerful tools for doing exactly this. For reasons we will describe shortly, the library of choice for performing this type of computational geometry in Python is **Shapely**.

# Shapely

Shapely is a Python package for the manipulation and analysis of two-dimensional geospatial geometries. It is based on the GEOS library, which implements a wide range of geospatial data manipulations in C++. GEOS is itself based on a library called the Java Topology Suite, which provides the same functionality for Java programmers. Shapely provides a Pythonic interface to GEOS, which makes it easy to use these manipulations directly from your Python programs.

# Installing Shapely

Shapely will run on all major operating systems, including MS Windows, Mac OS X, and Linux. Shapely's main web site can be found at `https://github.com/Toblerity/Shapely`. The Python Package Index page for Shapely also includes lots of useful information, and can be found at `https://pypi.python.org/pypi/Shapely`.

How you install Shapely depends on which operating system your computer is using:

- For Microsoft Windows, you can install a prebuilt Python Wheel file that includes Shapely as well as the underlying GEOS library. To do this, go to `http://www.lfd.uci.edu/~gohlke/pythonlibs/#shapely` and download the appropriate Python Wheel (`.whl`) file for the version of Python you are using. You can then follow the instructions at `https://pip.pypa.io/en/latest/user_guide.html#installing-from-wheels` to install the Wheel file onto your computer.

- For Mac OS X, you need to install the GEOS library before you can install Shapely. To do this, go to `http://www.kyngchaos.com/software/frameworks`, download the GEOS framework, and install it. Once this has been done, you can use pip, the Python package manager, to install Shapely itself. To ensure that Shapely will recognize the GEOS library, you should install Shapely by typing the following into a Terminal window:

```
export LDFLAGS=`/Library/Frameworks/GEOS.framework/Versions/3/
unix/bin/geos-config --libs`

export CFLAGS=`/Library/Frameworks/GEOS.framework/Versions/3/unix/
bin/geos-config --cflags`

pip install shapely
```

 You may get a warning about an incorrect file version, but you can ignore this as it won't stop Shapely from working.

- For a Linux-based computer, you should use your computer's package manager to first install the GEOS library and then install Shapely itself. If you need more information on installing GEOS, the web site for GEOS can be found at `http://trac.osgeo.org/geos`.

Once you have installed Shapely, start up your Python interpreter and try typing the following:

```
import shapely
import shapely.speedups
print(shapely.__version__)
print(shapely.speedups.available)
```

This will print the version of Shapely you have installed and whether or not the `shapely.speedups` module is available. If speedups are available, then Shapely will use the underlying GEOS library to do all the hard work; without speedups, Shapely will still mostly work but will be very slow.

# Understanding Shapely

The Shapely library is split up into a number of separate modules, which you import as required. The most commonly used Shapely modules include:

- `shapely.geometry`: This defines all the core geometric shape classes used by Shapely
- `shapely.wkt`: This provides functions to convert between Shapely geometry objects and well-known text (WKT)-formatted strings

- `shapely.wkb`: This provides functions for converting between Shapely geometry objects and well-known binary (WKB)-formatted binary data
- `shapely.ops`: This module provides functions for performing operations on a number of geometry objects at once

While you will almost always import the `shapely.geometry` module into your program, you would normally import the other modules only if you need them.

Let's take a closer look at the various geometry objects defined in the `shapely.geometry` module. There are eight fundamental geometry types supported by Shapely:

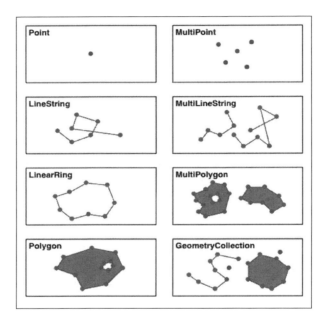

Each of these geometry types is implemented as a class within the `shapely.geometry` module:

- `shapely.geometry.Point` represents a single point in space. Points can be two-dimensional (*x,y*), or three-dimensional (*x,y,z*).
- `shapely.geometry.LineString` represents a sequence of points joined together to form a line. LineStrings can be *simple* (no crossing line segments) or *complex* (where two line segments within the LineString cross).
- `shapely.geometry.LinearRing` represents a LineString where the first and last coordinates are the same. The line segments within a LinearRing cannot cross or touch.

- `shapely.geometry.Polygon` represents a filled area, optionally with one or more "holes" inside it.

- `shapely.geometry.MultiPoint` represents a collection of Points.

- `shapely.geometry.MultiLineString` represents a collection of LineStrings.

- `shapely.geometry.MultiPolygon` represents a collection of Polygons.

- Finally, `shapely.geometry.GeometryCollection` represents a collection of any combination of Points, Lines, LinearRings, and Polygons.

As well as being able to represent these various types of geometries, Shapely provides a number of methods and attributes for manipulating and analyzing them. For example, the `LineString` class provides a `length` attribute that equals the length of all the line segments that make up the LineString, and a `crosses()` method that returns `True` if two LineStrings cross. Other methods allow you to calculate the intersection of two polygons, dilate or erode geometries, simplify a geometry, calculate the distance between two geometries, and build a polygon that encloses all the points within a given list of geometries (called a *convex hull*).

Note that Shapely is a *spatial* manipulation library rather than a geospatial manipulation library. It has no concept of geographical coordinates. Instead, it assumes that the geospatial data has been projected onto a two-dimensional Cartesian plane before it is manipulated, and the results can then be converted back into geographic coordinates if desired.

# Shapely example code

The following program creates two Shapely geometry objects, a circle and a square, and calculates their intersection. The intersection will be a polygon in the shape of a semicircle, as shown in the following diagram:

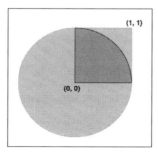

Here is the source code for our program:

```
import shapely.geometry
import shapely.wkt

pt = shapely.geometry.Point(0, 0)
circle = pt.buffer(1.0)

square = shapely.geometry.Polygon([(0, 0), (1, 0),
                                   (1, 1), (0, 1),
                                   (0, 0)])

intersect = circle.intersection(square)
for x,y in intersect.exterior.coords:
    print(x,y)
print(shapely.wkt.dumps(intersect))
```

 You can download the source code for this program. Look for a file named `shapely_example.py` in the book's code bundle.

Notice how the circle is constructed by taking a Point geometry and using the `buffer()` method to create a Polygon representing the outline of a circle.

# Shapely documentation

Complete and comprehensive documentation for the Shapely library can be found at `http://toblerity.org/shapely/manual.html`. It is well worth reading this manual, and if you are unsure about anything to do with Shapely, this web page should be your first port of call.

# Visualizing geospatial data

It's very hard, if not impossible, to understand geospatial data unless it is turned into a visual form—that is, until it is rendered as an image of some sort. Converting geospatial data into images requires a suitable toolkit. While there are several such toolkits available, we will look at one in particular: **Mapnik**.

# Mapnik

Mapnik is a freely-available library for building mapping applications. Mapnik takes geospatial data from a PostGIS database, shapefile, or any other format supported by GDAL/OGR, and turns it into clearly-rendered, good-looking images.

There are a lot of complex issues involved in rendering images well, and Mapnik does a good job of allowing the application developer to control the rendering process. Rules control which features should appear on the map, while "symbolizers" control the visual appearance of these features.

Mapnik allows developers to create XML stylesheets that control the map-creation process. Just as with CSS stylesheets, Mapnik's stylesheets allow you complete control over the way geospatial data is rendered. Alternatively, you can create the various styles by hand.

Mapnik itself is written in C++, though bindings are included that allow access to almost all of the Mapnik functionality via Python. Because these bindings are included in the main code base rather than being added by a third-party developer, support for Python is built right into Mapnik. This makes Python eminently suited to developing Mapnik-based applications.

Mapnik is heavily used by OpenStreetMap (`http://openstreetmap.org`) and EveryBlock (`http://everyblock.com`), among others. Since the output of Mapnik is simply an image, it is easy to include Mapnik as part of a web-based application, or you can display the output directly in a window as part of a desktop-based application. Mapnik works equally well on desktop and web platforms.

> Note that for this book, we will be using Mapnik version 2.2. At the time of writing this, Mapnik version 3.0 has just been released, but there are no prebuilt installers available. This makes installing the newer version of Mapnik difficult, so we have continued to use Mapnik 2. If you do use Mapnik 3, your code should still work as it is fully backward-compatible with Mapnik 2.

# Installing Mapnik

Mapnik runs on all major operating systems, including MS Windows, Mac OS X, and Linux. The main Mapnik web site can be found at `http://mapnik.org`.

> Unfortunately, at this time, there is no Mapnik installer for MS Windows that supports Python 3. For this reason, if you are using MS Windows, you will need to use Python 2.7 to use Mapnik. It is hoped that someone will build an installer for Mapnik that supports Python 3, but in the meantime, if you are using MS Windows, your only choice is to go back to using Python 2.

To install Mapnik onto your computer, follow these instructions:

- For MS Windows, you will need to use Python version 2.7. You can download the 32-bit Windows package for Mapnik from the Mapnik web site's download page. From there, follow the installation instructions provided.

> Note that you could try building Mapnik from source to be compatible with Python 3 on MS Windows. However, compiling Mapnik from source is very complicated and not something to be attempted unless you are very familiar with the required tools and willing to invest many hours to get it working.

- For Mac OS X, a binary installer that includes support for Python 3.3 is available from the Mapnik site. Simply download the `mapnik-osx-v2.2.0.dmg` file, double-click on it to open the disk image, and then run the installer. Once this has been done, follow the instructions in the `README.txt` file to update your system so that your Python 3.3 installation can find the Mapnik binaries.

- For Linux machines, you can try installing Mapnik using `pip`, the Python package manager:

```
pip install mapnik
```

> Mapnik has recently been updated to work with `pip`, as described in the blog entry at `http://mapnik.org/news/python-bindings`. If this does not work, you can use your favorite package manager to install Mapnik or even try compiling Mapnik from source.

Once you have installed Mapnik, you can check that your installation is working by opening up the Python shell and typing the following:

```
import mapnik
print(mapnik.mapnik_version())
```

The result should be an integer representing Mapnik's version number. For example, `200200` corresponds to Mapnik version 2.2.

If an error occurs, you may need to change your Python settings so that the Mapnik Python bindings can find the underlying Mapnik library. For example, you may need to edit your PYTHONPATH environment variable so that Mapnik can be found.

# Understanding Mapnik

When using Mapnik, the main object you are dealing with is called a **Map**. This diagram shows the parts of a Map object:

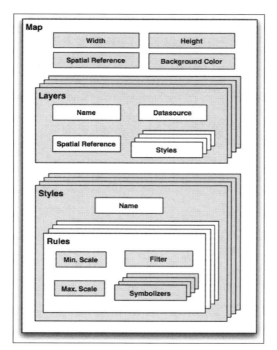

When creating a Map object, you tell it:

- The overall Width and Height of the map, in pixels
- The Spatial Reference to use for the map
- The Background Color to draw behind the contents of the map

You then define one or more **Layers**, which hold the map's contents. Each layer has:

- A Name.
- A Datasource object defining where to get the data for this layer. The data source can be a reference to a database, or it can be a shapefile or some other GDAL/OGR data source.
- A Spatial Reference to use for this layer. This can be different from the spatial reference used by the map as a whole, if appropriate.
- A list of Styles to apply to this layer. Each style is referred to by name, since the styles are actually defined elsewhere (possibly in an XML stylesheet).

Finally, you define one or more **Styles**, which tell Mapnik how to draw the various layers. Each Style has a **name** and of a list of **Rules** that make up the main part of the style's definition. Each Rule has:

- A **minimum scale** and **maximum scale** value (called the scale denominator). The Rule will only apply if the map's scale is within this range.
- A **filter** expression. The Rule will only apply to those features that match this filter expression.
- A list of **Symbolizers**. These define how the matching features will be drawn onto the map.

Mapnik implements a number of different types of Symbolizers, including:

- **LineSymbolizer**: This is used to draw a "stroke" along a line, a linear ring, or around the outside of a polygon.
- **LinePatternSymbolizer**: This uses the contents of an image file (specified by name) to draw the stroke along a line, a linear ring, or around the outside of a polygon.
- **PolygonSymbolizer**: This is used to draw the interior of a polygon.
- **PolygonPatternSymbolizer**: This uses the contents of an image file (again specified by name) to draw the interior of a polygon.
- **PointSymbolizer**: This uses the contents of an image file (specified by name) to draw a symbol at a point.

- **TextSymbolizer**: This draws a feature's text. The text to be drawn is taken from one of the feature's attributes, and there are numerous options to control how the text is to be drawn.

- **RasterSymbolizer**: This is used to draw raster data taken from any GDAL data source.

- **ShieldSymbolizer**: This draws a textual label and a point together. This is similar to the use of a PointSymbolizer to draw the image and a TextSymbolizer to draw the label, except that it ensures that both the text and the image are drawn together.

- **BuildingSymbolizer**: This uses a pseudo-3D effect to draw a polygon, to make it appear that the polygon is a three-dimensional building.

- **MarkersSymbolizer**: This draws blue directional arrows following the direction of polygon and line geometries. This is experimental and is intended to be used to draw one-way streets onto a street map.

When you instantiate a Symbolizer and add it to a style (either directly in code or via an XML stylesheet), you provide a number of parameters that define how the Symbolizer should work. For example, when using a `PolygonSymbolizer`, you can specify the fill color, the opacity, and a "gamma" value that helps draw adjacent polygons of the same color without the boundary being shown. For example:

```
p = mapnik.PolygonSymbolizer(mapnik.Color(127, 127, 0))
p.fill_opacity = 0.8
p.gamma = 0.65
```

If the Rule that uses this Symbolizer matches one or more polygons, those polygons will be drawn using the given color, opacity, and gamma value.

Different rules can, of course, have different Symbolizers as well as different filter values. For example, you might set up rules that draw countries in different colors depending on their population.

# Mapnik example code

The following example program displays a simple world map using Mapnik:

```
import mapnik

symbolizer = mapnik.PolygonSymbolizer(
                    mapnik.Color("darkgreen"))

rule = mapnik.Rule()
```

```
rule.symbols.append(symbolizer)

style = mapnik.Style()
style.rules.append(rule)

layer = mapnik.Layer("mapLayer")
layer.datasource = mapnik.Shapefile(
                        file="TM_WORLD_BORDERS-0.3.shp")
layer.styles.append("mapStyle")

map = mapnik.Map(800, 400)
map.background = mapnik.Color("steelblue")
map.append_style("mapStyle", style)
map.layers.append(layer)

map.zoom_all()
mapnik.render_to_file(map, "map.png", "png")
```

This example uses the World Borders Dataset, which you can download
from http://thematicmapping.org/downloads/world_
borders.php

Notice that this program creates a `PolygonSymbolizer` to display the country
polygons, and it then attaches the symbolizer to a Mapnik Rule object. The Rule
then becomes part of a Mapnik Style object. We then create a Mapnik Layer object,
reading the layer's map data from a shapefile data source. Finally, a Mapnik Map
object is created, the layer is attached, and the resulting map is rendered to a
PNG-format image file:

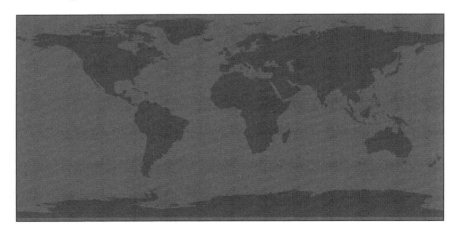

The source code for this program is available under the name
mapnik_example.py.

# Mapnik documentation

Unfortunately, Mapnik's web site makes it difficult to find the online documentation.
The Mapnik wiki can be found at https://github.com/mapnik/mapnik/wiki and
is an excellent source of useful information.

There is a set of Python-specific documentation for Mapnik available at http://
mapnik.org/docs, though unfortunately, this documentation is rather sparse and
confusing for Python programmers. Because the Python documentation is derived
from the C++ documentation and concentrates on describing how the Python
bindings are implemented rather than how an end user would work with Mapnik
using Python, there are a lot of technical details that aren't relevant to a Python
programmer, and it does not have enough Python-specific descriptions to be all
that useful.

The best way to get started with Mapnik is to follow the installation instructions and
then work your way through the two supplied tutorials. You can then check out the
*Learning Mapnik* page on the Mapnik wiki (https://github.com/mapnik/mapnik/
wiki/LearningMapnik)—the notes on these pages are rather brief and cryptic, but
there is useful information here if you're willing to dig.

It is worth looking at the Python API documentation, despite its limitations. The
main page lists the various classes available and a number of useful functions, many
of which are documented. The classes themselves list the methods and properties
(attributes) you can access, and even though many of these lack Python-specific
documentation, you can generally guess what they do.

 *Chapter 7, Using Python and Mapnik to Generate Maps,* includes
a detailed description of Mapnik; you may find this useful in
lieu of any other Python-based documentation.

# Summary

In this chapter, we looked at a number of important libraries for developing geospatial applications using Python. We investigated the GDAL and OGR libraries, which allow you to read and write geospatial data using a variety of formats. We also looked at how the `pyproj` library can be used to work with map projections and datums and how Shapely allows you to easily represent and work with geometry data. We then looked at how the Mapnik library can be used to generate good-looking maps.

While these tools are very powerful, you can't do anything with them unless you have some geospatial data to work with. Unless you are lucky enough to have access to your own source of data or are willing to pay large sums to purchase data commercially, your only choice is to make use of the geospatial data which is freely available on the Internet. These freely-available sources of geospatial data are the topic of the next chapter.

# 4
# Sources of Geospatial Data

When creating a geospatial application, the data you use will be just as important as the code you write. High-quality geospatial data, and in particular base maps and imagery, will be the cornerstone of your application. If your maps don't look good, then your application will be treated as the work of an amateur, no matter how well you write the rest of your program.

Traditionally, geospatial data has been treated as a valuable and scarce resource, being sold commercially for many thousands of dollars and with strict licensing constraints. Fortunately, with the trend towards "democratizing" geospatial tools, geospatial data is now increasingly becoming available for free and with little or no restriction on its use. There are still situations where you may have to pay for data, for example, to guarantee the quality of the data or if you need something that isn't available elsewhere. In general, however, you can simply download the data you need for free from a suitable server.

This chapter provides an overview of some of these major sources of freely available geospatial data. This is not intended to be an exhaustive list, but rather to provide information on the sources that are likely to be most useful to the Python geospatial developer.

In this chapter, we will cover the following:

- Some of the major freely available sources of vector-format geospatial data
- Some of the main freely available sources of raster geospatial data
- Sources of other types of freely available geospatial data, concentrating on databases of cities and other place names

# Sources of geospatial data in vector format

Vector-based geospatial data represents physical features as collections of points, lines, and polygons. Often, these features will have metadata associated with them. In this section, we will look at some of the major sources of free vector-format geospatial data.

## OpenStreetMap

OpenStreetMap (`http://openstreetmap.org`) is a site where people can collaborate to create and edit geospatial data. It is described as a "free, editable map of the whole world that is being built by volunteers largely from scratch and released with an open-content license."

The following screen snapshot shows a portion of a street map for Onchan, Isle of Man, based on data from OpenStreetMap:

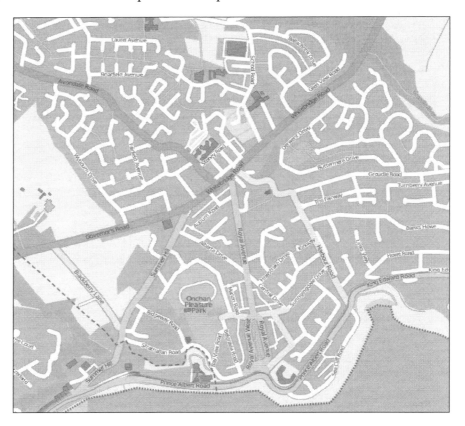

# The OpenStreetMap data format

OpenStreetMap does not use a standard format such as shapefiles to store its data. Instead, it has developed its own XML-based format for representing geospatial data in the form of **nodes** (single points), **ways** (sequences of points that define a line), **areas** (closed ways that represent polygons), and **relations** (collections of other elements). Any element (node, way, or relation) can have a number of **tags** associated with it that provide additional information about that element.

The following is an example of what the OpenStreetMap XML data looks like:

```
<osm>
  <node id="603279517" lat="-38.1456457"
   lon="176.2441646".../>
  <node id="603279518" lat="-38.1456583"
   lon="176.2406726".../>
  <node id="603279519" lat="-38.1456540"
   lon="176.2380553".../>
  ...
  <way id="47390936"...>
    <nd ref="603279517"/>
    <nd ref="603279518"/>
    <nd ref="603279519"/>
    <tag k="highway" v="residential"/>
    <tag k="name" v="York Street"/>
  </way>
  ...
  <relation id="126207"...>
    <member type="way" ref="22930719" role=""/>
    <member type="way" ref="23963573" role=""/>
    <member type="way" ref="28562757" role=""/>
    <member type="way" ref="23963609" role=""/>
    <member type="way" ref="47475844" role=""/>
    <tag k="name" v="State Highway 30A"/>
    <tag k="ref" v="30A"/>
    <tag k="route" v="road"/>
    <tag k="type" v="route"/>
  </relation>
</osm>
```

# Obtaining and using OpenStreetMap data

You can obtain geospatial data from OpenStreetMap in one of three ways:

- You can use the OpenStreetMap API to download a subset of the data you are interested in.

- You can download the entire OpenStreetMap database, called `Planet.osm`, and process it locally. Note that this is a multi-gigabyte download.

- You can make use of one of the mirror sites that provide OpenStreetMap data nicely packaged into smaller chunks and converted into other data formats. For example, you can download the data for North America on a state-by-state basis and in various formats, including shapefiles.

Let's take a closer look at each of these three options.

## The OpenStreetMap APIs

OpenStreetMap provides two APIs you can use:

- The **Editing API** (`http://wiki.openstreetmap.org/wiki/API`) can be used to retrieve and make changes to the OpenStreetMap dataset

- The **Overpass API** (`http://wiki.openstreetmap.org/wiki/Overpass_API`) provides a read-only interface to OpenStreetMap data

The Overpass API is most useful for retrieving data. It provides a sophisticated query language that you can use to obtain OpenStreetMap XML data based on the search criteria you specify. For example, you can retrieve a list of primary roads within a given bounding box using the following query:

```
way[highway=primary](-38.18, 176.13, -38.03, 176.38);out;
```

Using the `python-overpy` library (`https://github.com/DinoTools/python-overpy`), you can directly call the Overpass API from within your Python programs.

## Planet.osm

If you wish to download all of OpenStreetMap for processing on your computer, you will need to download the entire `Planet.osm` database. This database is available in two formats: a compressed XML-format file containing all the nodes, ways, and relations in the OpenStreetMap database, or a special binary format called PBF that contains the same information but is smaller and faster to read.

The `Planet.osm` database is currently 44 GB if you download it in compressed XML format or 29 GB if you download it in PBF format. Both formats can be downloaded from `http://planet.openstreetmap.org`.

The entire dump of the `Planet.osm` database is updated weekly, but **diff** files are created every week, day, hour, and minute. You can use these to update your existing copy of the `Planet.osm` database without having to download everything again.

## Mirror sites and extracts

Because of the size of the download, OpenStreetMap recommends that you use a mirror site rather than downloading `Planet.osm` directly from their servers. Extracts are also provided, which allow you to download the data for a given area rather than the entire world. These mirror sites and extracts are maintained by third parties; for a list of the URLs, refer to `http://wiki.openstreetmap.org/wiki/Planet.osm`.

Note that these mirrors and extracts are often available in alternative formats, including shapefiles and direct database dumps.

## Working with OpenStreetMap data

When you download `Planet.osm`, you will end up with an enormous file on your hard disk—currently, it is 576 GB if you download the data in XML format. You have two main options for processing this file using Python:

- You could use a Python library such as `imposm.parser` (`http://imposm.org/docs/imposm.parser/latest`) to read through the file and extract the information you want

- You could import the data into a database and then access that database from Python

In most cases, you will want to import the data into a database before you attempt to work with it. To do this, use the excellent `osm2pgsql` tool, which is available at `http://wiki.openstreetmap.org/wiki/Osm2pgsql`. `osm2pgsql` was created to import the entire `Planet.osm` data into a PostgreSQL database and is therefore highly optimized for this task.

Once you have imported the `Planet.osm` data into a database on your computer, you can use the `psycopg2` library, as described in *Chapter 6, Spatial Databases*, to access the OpenStreetMap data from your Python programs.

# TIGER

The United States Census Bureau have made available a large amount of geospatial data under the name **TIGER** (short for **Topologically Integrated Geographic Encoding and Referencing System**). The TIGER data includes information on streets, railways, rivers, lakes, geographic boundaries, legal and statistical areas such as school districts, and urban regions. Separate cartographic boundary and demographic files are also available for download.

The following diagram shows state and urban area outlines for California, based on data downloaded from the TIGER web site:

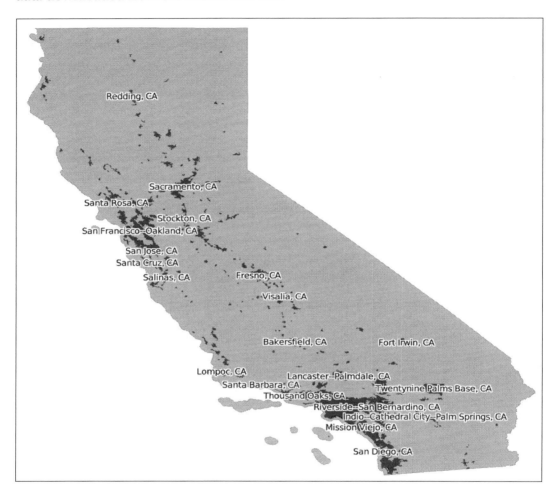

Because it is produced by the US government, TIGER only includes information for the United States and its protectorates (Puerto Rico, American Samoa, the Northern Mariana Islands, Guam, and the US Virgin Islands). For these areas, TIGER is an excellent source of geospatial data.

# The TIGER data format

Up until 2006, the US Census Bureau provided TIGER data in a custom text-based format called **TIGER/Line**. TIGER/Line files stored each type of record in a separate file and required custom tools to process. Fortunately, OGR supports TIGER/Line files, should you need to read them.

Since 2007, all TIGER data has been produced in the form of shapefiles, which are (somewhat confusingly) called TIGER/Line shapefiles.

You can download up-to-date shapefiles containing geospatial data such as street address ranges, landmarks, census blocks, metropolitan statistical areas, and school districts. For example, the *Core Based Statistical Area* shapefile contains the outline of each metropolitan and micropolitan area in the US:

This particular feature has the following metadata associated with it:

| Attribute name | Value |
| --- | --- |
| ALAND | 2606282680.0 |
| AWATER | 578761025.0 |
| CBSAFP | 18860 |
| CSAFP | None |
| GEOID | 18860 |
| INTPTLAT | +41.7499033 |
| INTPTLON | -123.9809983 |
| LSAD | M2 |
| MEMI | 2 |
| MTFCC | G3110 |
| NAME | Crescent City, CA |
| NAMELSAD | Crescent City, CA Micro Area |

Information on these various attributes can be found in the extensive documentation available on the TIGER web site.

You can also download shapefiles that include demographic data, such as population, number of houses, median age, and racial breakdown. For example, the following map tints each metropolitan area in California according to its total population as recorded in the latest (2010) census:

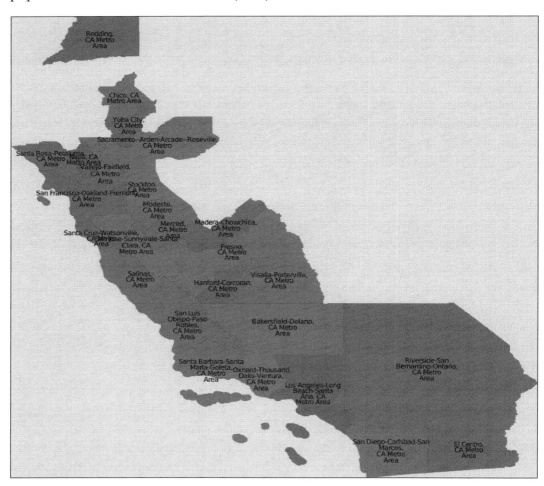

## Obtaining and using TIGER data

The TIGER data files can be downloaded from http://www.census.gov/geo/maps-data/data/tiger.html.

Make sure that you download the technical documentation, as it describes the various files you can download and all the attributes associated with each feature. For example, if you want to download the current set of urban areas for the US, the shapefile you are looking for is in a ZIP archive named `tl_2015_us_uac10.zip` and includes information such as the city or town name and the size of the urban area in square meters.

# Natural Earth

Natural Earth (`http://www.naturalearthdata.com`) is a web site that provides public-domain vector and raster map data at high, medium, and low resolutions. Two types of vector map data are provided:

- **Cultural map data**: This includes polygons for country, state or province, urban areas, and park outlines as well as point and line data for populated places, roads, and railways:

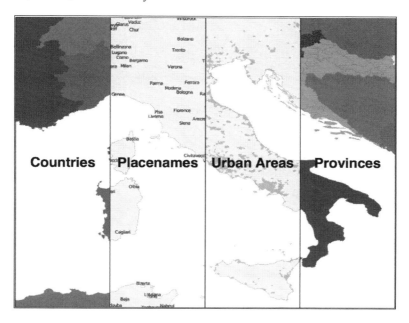

- **Physical map data**: This includes polygons and linestrings for land masses, coastlines, oceans, minor islands, reefs, rivers, lakes, and so on

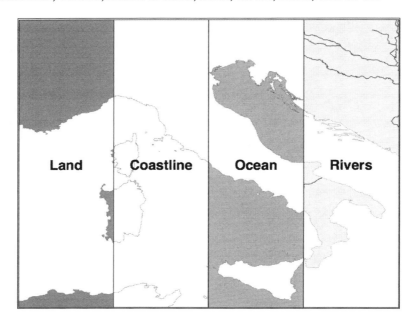

All of this can be downloaded and used freely in your geospatial programs, making the Natural Earth site an excellent source of data for your application.

# The Natural Earth data format

All the vector-format data on the Natural Earth web site is provided in the form of shapefiles. All the data is in geographic (latitude and longitude) coordinates, using the standard WGS84 datum, making it very easy to use these files in your own application.

# Obtaining and using Natural Earth vector data

The Natural Earth site is uniformly excellent, and downloading the files you want is easy: simply click on the **Get the Data** link on the main page. You can then choose the resolution and type of data you are looking for. You can also choose to download either a single shapefile or a number of shapefiles all bundled together. Once they have been downloaded, you can use the Python libraries discussed in the previous chapter to work with the contents of those shapefiles.

The Natural Earth web site is very comprehensive; it includes detailed information about the geospatial data you can download and a forum where you can ask questions and discuss any problems you may have.

# The Global Self-consistent, Hierarchical, High-resolution Geography Database (GSHHG)

The US National Geophysical Data Center (part of the NOAA) provides high-quality vector shoreline data for the entire world in the form of a database called the **Global Self-consistent, Hierarchical, High-resolution Geography Database (GSHHG)**. This database includes detailed vector data for shorelines, lakes, and rivers in five different resolutions. The data has been broken out into four different levels: ocean boundaries, lake boundaries, island-in-lake boundaries, and pond-on-island-in-lake boundaries.

The following image shows European shorelines, lakes, and islands, taken from the GSHHG database:

The GSHHG database has been constructed out of two public-domain geospatial databases: the **World Data Bank II** database includes data on coastlines, lakes, and rivers, while the **World Vector Shorelines** database only provides coastline data. Because the World Vector Shorelines database has more accurate data but lacks information on rivers and lakes, the two databases were combined to provide the most accurate information possible. After merging the databases, the author manually edited the data to make it consistent and remove a number of errors. The result is a high-quality database of land and water boundaries worldwide.

 More information about the process used to create the GSHHG database can be found at `http://www.soest.hawaii.edu/pwessel/papers/1996/JGR_96/jgr_96.html`

## The GSHHG data format

The GSHHG database can be downloaded in Shapefile format, among others. If you download the data in Shapefile format, you will end up with a total of twenty separate shapefiles, one for every combination of resolution and level:

- The **resolution** represents the amount of detail in the map:

| Value | Resolution | Includes |
| --- | --- | --- |
| c | Crude | Features greater than 500 sq. km. |
| l | Low | Features greater than 100 sq. km. |
| i | Intermediate | Features greater than 20 sq. km. |
| h | High | Features greater than 1 sq. km. |
| f | Full | Every feature |

- The **level** indicates the type of boundaries that are included in the shapefile:

| Value | Includes |
| --- | --- |
| 1 | Ocean boundaries |
| 2 | Lake boundaries |
| 3 | Island-in-lake boundaries |
| 4 | Pond-on-island-in-lake boundaries |

The name of the shapefile tells you the resolution and level of the included data. For example, the shapefile for ocean boundaries at full resolution would be named `GSHHS_f_L1.shp`.

 The GSSHG database was previously called the Global Self-consistent, Hierarchical, High-Resolution **Shoreline** Database, which is the why the abbreviation GSHHS persists in a few places, like these filenames.

Each shapefile consists of a single layer containing the various polygon features making up the given type of boundary.

## Obtaining the GSHHG database

The main GSHHG web site can be found at `http://www.ngdc.noaa.gov/mgg/shorelines/gshhs.html`.

Follow the download link on this page to see the list of files you can download. To download the data in shapefile format, you will want a file with a name like `gshhg-shp-2.3.4.zip`, where `2.3.4` is the version number of the database you are downloading.

Once you have downloaded and decompressed the file, you can extract the data from the individual shapefiles using OGR, as described in the previous chapter.

# The World Borders Dataset

Many of the data sources we have examined so far are rather complex. If all you are looking for is some simple vector data covering the entire world, the World Borders Dataset may be all you need. While some of the country borders are apparently disputed, the simplicity of the World Borders Dataset makes it an attractive choice for many basic geospatial applications.

The following map was generated using the World Borders Dataset:

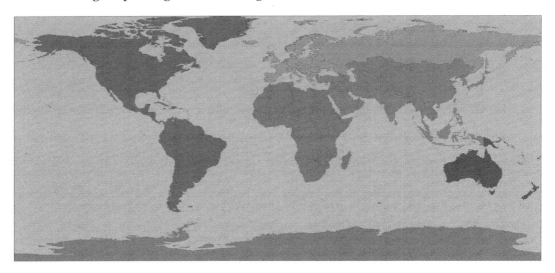

The World Borders Dataset will be used extensively throughout this book. Indeed, you have already seen an example program in *Chapter 3, Python Libraries for Geospatial Development*, where we used Mapnik to generate a world map using the World Borders Dataset shapefile.

# The World Borders Dataset data format

The World Borders Dataset is available in the form of a shapefile with a single layer, with one feature for each country. For each country, the corresponding feature has one or more polygons that define the country's boundary along with useful attributes, including the name of the country or area; various ISO, FIPS, and UN codes identifying the country; a region and subregion classification; and the country's population, land area, and latitude/longitude.

The various codes make it easy to match the features against your own country-specific data, and you can also use information such as the population and area to highlight different countries on the map. For example, the preceding map used the `region` field to draw each geographic region in a different color.

## Obtaining the World Borders Dataset

The World Borders Dataset can be downloaded from `http://thematicmapping.` `org/downloads/world_borders.php`.

This web site also provides more details about the contents of the dataset, including links to the United Nations' site where the region and subregion codes are listed.

# Sources of geospatial data in raster format

One of the most enthralling aspects of programs such as Google Earth is the ability to "see" the Earth as you appear to fly above it. This is achieved by displaying satellite and aerial photographs carefully stitched together to provide the illusion that you are viewing the Earth's surface from above.

While writing your own version of Google Earth would be an almost impossible task, it is possible to obtain free satellite imagery in the form of raster-format geospatial data, which you can then use in your own geospatial applications.

Raster data is not just limited to images of the Earth's surface, however; other useful information can be found in raster format—for example, **digital elevation maps (DEMs)** contain the height of each point on the Earth's surface, which can then be used to calculate the elevation of any desired point. DEM data can also be used to generate two-dimensional images that represent different heights using different shades or colors or to simulate the shading effect of hills using a technique called **shaded relief imagery**.

In this section, we will look at the world's most comprehensive source of satellite imagery, Landsat, as well as the raster-format data available on the Natural Earth site and some freely-available sources of digital elevation data.

# Landsat

**Landsat** is an ongoing effort to collect images of the Earth's surface. The name is derived from *land and satellite*. A group of dedicated satellites have been continuously gathering images since 1972. Landsat imagery includes black and white and traditional red/green/blue (RGB) color images as well as infrared and thermal imaging. The color images are typically at a resolution of 30 meters per pixel, while the black and white images from Landsat 7 are at a resolution of 15 meters per pixel.

The following image shows color-corrected Landsat satellite imagery for the city of Rotorua, New Zealand. The city itself is on the southern (bottom) edge of a lake:

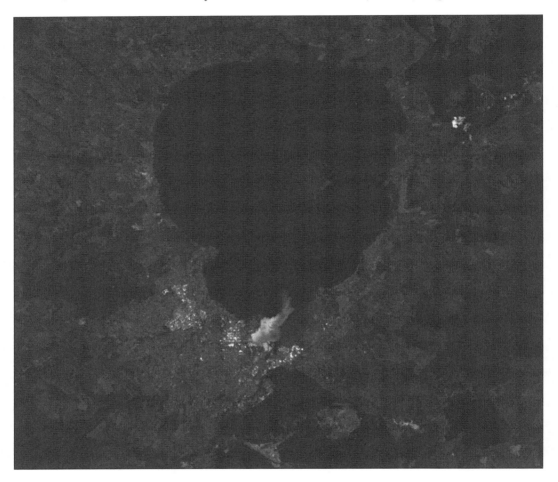

# The Landsat data format

Landsat images are typically available in the form of **GeoTIFF** files. GeoTIFF is a geospatially tagged TIFF image file format, allowing images to be georeferenced onto the Earth's surface. Most GIS software and tools, including GDAL, are able to read GeoTIFF-formatted files.

Because the images come directly from a satellite, the files you can download typically store separate bands of data in separate files. Depending on the satellite the data came from, there can be up to eight different bands of data—for example, Landsat 7 generates separate red, green, and blue bands as well as three different infrared bands, a thermal band, and a high-resolution "panchromatic" (black-and-white) band.

To understand how this works, let's take a closer look at the process required to create the preceding image. The raw satellite data consists of eight separate GeoTIFF files, one for each band. band 1 contains the blue color data, band 2 contains the green color data, and band 3 contains the red color data. These separate files can then be combined using GDAL to produce a single color image, as follows:

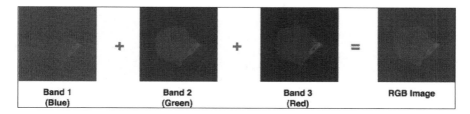

Another complication with the Landsat data is that the images produced by the satellites are distorted by various factors, including the ellipsoid shape of the Earth, the elevation of the terrain being photographed, and the orientation of the satellite as the image is taken. The raw data is therefore not a completely accurate representation of the features being photographed. Fortunately, a process known as **orthorectification** can be used to correct these distortions. In most cases, orthorectified versions of the satellite images can be downloaded directly.

# Obtaining Landsat imagery

The easiest way to access Landsat imagery is to make use of the University of
Maryland's *Global Land Cover Facility* web site (`http://glcf.umd.edu/data/`
`landsat`). Click on the **Download via Search and Preview Tool (ESDI)** link, and
then click on **Map Search**. Select **ETM+** from the **Landsat Imagery** list, and if you
zoom in on the desired part of the Earth, you will see the areas covered by various
Landsat images:

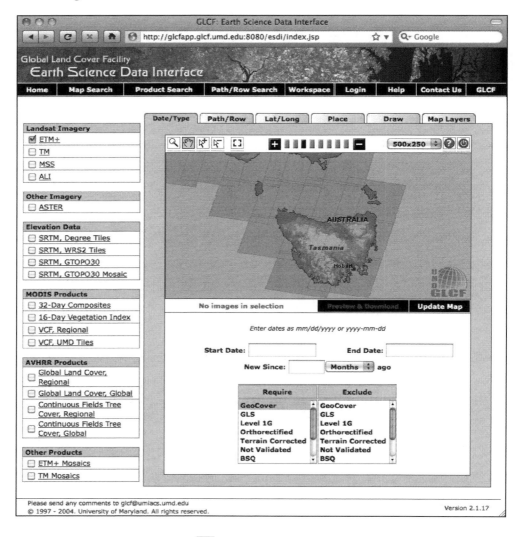

If you choose the selection tool ($\boxed{\text{ⱪ}^{+}}$), you will be able to click on a desired area and
then select **Preview & Download** to choose the image to download.

Alternatively, if you know the path and row number of the desired area of the Earth, you can directly access the files via FTP. The path and row number (as well as the **world reference system (WRS)** number used by the data) can be found on the **Preview & Download** page:

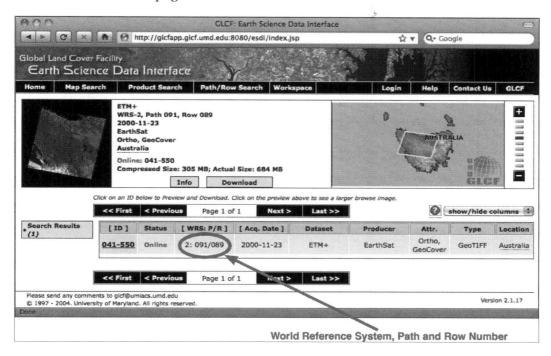

World Reference System, Path and Row Number

If you want to download the image files via FTP, the main FTP site is at `ftp://ftp.glcf.umd.edu/glcf/Landsat`.

The directories and files have complex names that include the WRS, the path and row number, the satellite number, the date at which the image was taken, and the band number. For example, a file named `p091r089_7t20001123_z55_nn10.tif.gz` refers to path `091` and row `089`, which happens to be the portion of Tasmania highlighted in the preceding screen snapshot. The `7` refers to the number of the Landsat satellite that took the image, and `20001123` is a datestamp indicating when the image was taken. The final part of the filename, `nn10`, tells us that the file is for band 1.

By interpreting the filename in this way, you can download the correct files and match the files against the desired bands. For more information on what all these different satellites and bands mean, refer to the documentation links in the **Landsat Imagery** section in the upper right-hand corner of the **Global Land Cover Facility** web site (`http://glcf.umd.edu/data/landsat`).

# Natural Earth

In addition to providing vector map data, the Natural Earth web site (`http://www.naturalearthdata.com`) makes available five different types of raster maps at both a 1:10-million and 1:50-million scale:

- The rather esoterically-named **Cross-Blended Hypsometric Tints** provide visualizations where the color is selected based on both elevation and climate. These images are then often combined with shaded-relief images to produce a realistic-looking view of the Earth's surface.

- **Natural Earth 1** and **Natural Earth 2** are more idealized views of the Earth's surface; they use a light palette and softly blended colors, providing an excellent backdrop for drawing your own geospatial data.

- The **Ocean Bottom** dataset uses a combination of shaded relief imagery and depth-based coloring to provide a visualization of the ocean floor.

- The **Shaded Relief** imagery uses greyscale to "shade" the surface of the Earth based on high-resolution elevation data.

The following diagram shows what these raster maps look like:

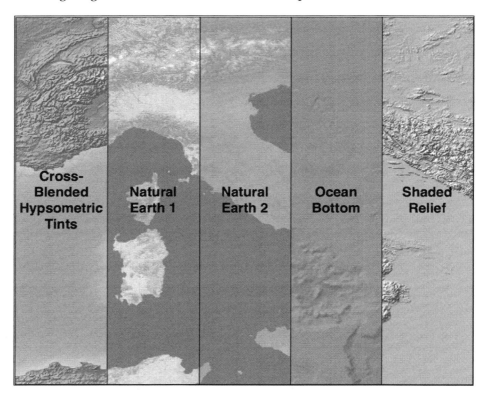

An additional raster dataset is available that provides bathymetry (underwater depth) visualizations at a 1:50-million scale. The following diagram is an example of the bathymetry data for the oceans surrounding New Zealand:

# The Natural Earth data format

Most of the raster-format data on the Natural Earth site is in the standard TIFF image format. The one exception is the bathymetry data, which is provided in the form of a layered Adobe Photoshop file with differing shades of blue associated with each depth band.

In all cases, the raster data is in geographic (latitude/longitude) projection and uses the standard WGS84 datum, making it easy to translate between latitude and longitude coordinates and pixel coordinates within the raster image.

## Obtaining and using Natural Earth raster data

As with the vector data, the raster-format data on the Natural Earth site is easy to download: simply go to the web site (http://www.naturalearthdata.com) and follow the **Get the Data** link to download the raster-format data. You can choose to download the data at either a 1:10-million scale or a 1:50-million scale, and you can also choose to download the large- or small-size version of each file.

Once you have downloaded the TIFF format data, you can open the file in an image editor or use a command-line utility such as gdal_translate to manipulate the image. For the bathymetry data, you can open the file directly in Adobe Photoshop or use a cheaper alternative such as GIMP or Flying Meat's Acorn. Each depth band is a separate layer in the file and is associated with a specific shade of blue by default. You can choose different colors if you prefer and select which layers to show or hide. When you are finished, you can flatten the image and save it as a TIFF file for use in your programs.

# Global Land One-kilometer Base Elevation (GLOBE)

GLOBE is an international effort to produce high-quality, medium-resolution **digital elevation model (DEM)** data for the entire world. The result is a set of freely-available DEM files, which can be used for many types of geospatial analysis and development.

The following diagram shows GLOBE DEM data for northern Chile, converted to a grayscale image:

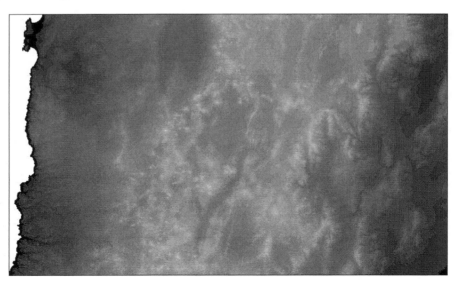

# The GLOBE data format

Like all DEM data, GLOBE uses raster values to represent the elevation at a given point on the Earth's surface. In the case of GLOBE, this data consists of 32-bit signed integers representing the height above (or below) sea level, in meters. Each cell or "pixel" within the raster data represents the elevation of a square on the Earth's surface that is 30 arc-seconds of longitude wide and 30 arc-seconds of latitude high:

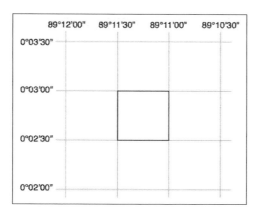

Note that 30 arc-seconds equal approximately 0.00833 degrees of latitude or longitude, which equates to a square roughly one kilometer wide and high. This means that the GLOBE data has a resolution of approximately 1 kilometer per cell or "pixel".

The raw GLOBE data is simply a long list of 32-bit integers in big-endian format, where the cells are read left to right and then top to bottom, like this:

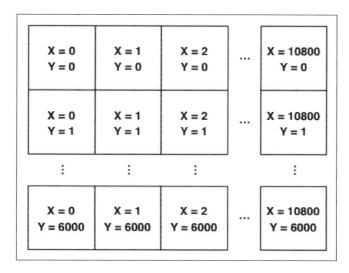

A separate header (.hdr) file provides more detailed information about the DEM data, including the width and height and its georeferenced location. Tools such as GDAL are able to read the raw data as long as the header file is provided.

## Obtaining and using GLOBE data

The main web site for the GLOBE project can be found at http://www.ngdc. noaa.gov/mgg/topo/globe.html, and you can download a detailed manual describing the GLOBE dataset at http://www.ngdc.noaa.gov/mgg/topo/report/ globedocumentationmanual.pdf.

The GLOBE elevation data is made available as a series of 16 "tiles" covering the entire Earth's surface. You can download any of the tiles that you wish by clicking on the **Get Data Online** link from the main page.

Unfortunately, the tile data you download only includes the raw elevation data itself. There is no information provided for georeferencing the elevation data onto the surface of the Earth or to tell GDAL what format the data is in. If you don't want to calculate this information yourself, you will need to download a .hdr file corresponding to each tile. These .hdr files can be found at http://www.ngdc.noaa. gov/mgg/topo/elev/esri/hdr.

Once you have downloaded the data, simply place the raw DEM file into the same directory as the .hdr file. You can then open the file directly using GDAL, like this:

```
import osgeo.gdal
dataset = osgeo.gdal.Open("j10g.bil")
```

The dataset will consist of a single band of raster data, which you can then read using GDAL.

 To see an example of using GDAL to process DEM data, please refer to the GDAL section in *Chapter 3, Python Libraries for Geospatial Development*.

## The National Elevation Dataset (NED)

The **National Elevation Dataset** (NED) is a high-resolution digital elevation model provided by the US Geological Survey. It covers the continental United States, Alaska, Hawaii, and other US territories. Most of the United States is covered by elevation data at a resolution of either 30 or 10 meters per cell, with selected areas available at 3 meters per cell. Alaska is generally only available at a resolution of 60 meters per cell.

The following shaded relief image was generated using NED elevation data for the Marin Headlands in San Francisco:

# The NED data format

NED data can be downloaded in various formats, including IMG, GeoTIFF, and ArcGRID, all of which can be processed using GDAL.

As with other DEM data, each cell in the raster image represents the height of a given area on the Earth's surface. For NED data, the height is in meters above or below a reference height known as the *North American Vertical Datum of 1988*. This roughly equates to the height above sea level, allowing for tidal and other variations.

# Obtaining and using NED data

The main web site for the National Elevation Dataset can be found at: `http://ned.usgs.gov`.

This site describes the NED dataset; to download the data, you'll have to use the **National Map Viewer**, which is available at `http://viewer.nationalmap.gov/viewer/`.

To use the viewer, zoom in to the area you are interested in, and then click on the **Download Data** link at the top of the page:

Click on the option to download by the current map extent, and then select the **Elevation DEM Products** option from the provided list. When you click on the **Next** button, you will be presented with a list of the available DEM datasets that cover the visible portion of the map:

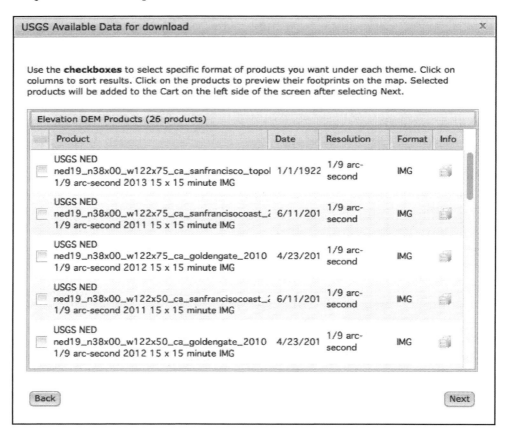

Choose the dataset you are interested in and click on the **Info** icon beside the dataset.

 Note that at a resolution of one-ninth of an arc-second, each cell in the dataset will be approximately 3 meters square.

When you click on the **Info** icon, a new tab will be opened in your browser, giving you lots of information about the selected dataset. In particular, you will see a map showing the area covered by this dataset:

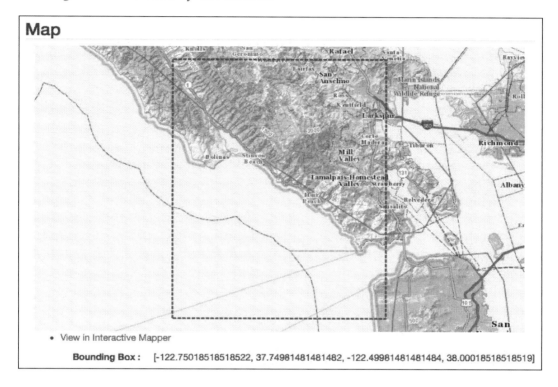

**Map**

- View in Interactive Mapper

**Bounding Box :**    [-122.75018518518522, 37.74981481481482, -122.49981481481484, 38.00018518518519]

If you scroll down to the **Links (External Sources)** section of the page, you will see a direct download link for the dataset. Clicking on this will immediately download the file.

 The National Map Viewer includes a shopping cart option for downloading multiple datasets at once. You can ignore this, though, and simply download the dataset directly.

You will end up with a compressed `.zip` format file containing the data you want, along with a large number of metadata files and documentation about the dataset. Once you have decompressed the `.zip` archive, you can open the dataset in GDAL just like you would open any other raster dataset:

```
import osgeo.gdal
dataset = osgeo.gdal.Open("dem.tif")
```

Finally, if you are working with DEM data, you might like to check out the `gdaldem` utility, which is included as a part of the GDAL download. This program makes it easy to view and manipulate DEM raster data. The preceding shaded relief image was created using this utility, like this:

```
gdaldem hillshade dem.tif image.tiff
```

# Sources of other types of geospatial data

The vector and raster geospatial data we have looked at so far is generally used to provide images or information about the Earth itself. However, geospatial applications often have to place data onto the surface of the Earth, that is, georeference something such as a place or event. In this section, we will look at two additional databases that provide information about the location of cities, towns, natural features, and points of interest on the surface of the Earth.

This data can be used in two important ways. First, it can be used to *label* features, for example, to place the label "London" onto a georeferenced image of southern England. Secondly, this data can be used to *locate* something by name, for example, by allowing the user to choose a city from a drop-down list and then draw a map centered around that city.

## The GEOnet Names Server

The **GEOnet Names Server** provides a large database of place names. It is an official repository of non-American place names, as decided by the US Board on Geographic Names.

The following is an extract from the GEOnet Names Server database:

| LAT | LONG | FC | DSG | ELEV | NT | FULL_NAME |
|---|---|---|---|---|---|---|
| -46.333333 | 168.716667 | S | RSTN | | N | Kamahi |
| -46.816667 | 168.25 | T | ISL | | N | North Island |
| -40.959722 | 175.6575 | P | PPL | | N | Masterton |
| -52.556111 | 169.136667 | H | COVE | | N | Camp Cove |
| -39.455556 | 173.858333 | P | PPL | | N | Opunake |
| -52.501389 | 169.120556 | T | ISL | 76 | N | Gomez Island |
| -39.591667 | 174.283333 | P | PPL | | N | Hawera |
| -36.641944 | 175.360833 | T | RKS | | N | Motupotaka Rocks |
| -41.255833 | 173.263333 | S | TOWR | | N | Boulder Bank Lighthouse |
| -36.605278 | 174.9175 | T | RK | | N | Shearer Rock |
| -36.610556 | 174.705556 | P | PPL | | N | Red Beach |
| -46.5625 | 169.619444 | T | ISL | | N | Cosgrove Island |
| -42.133333 | 171.616667 | T | MT | | N | Mount McHardy |
| -39.266667 | 174.616667 | T | MT | | N | Turakirai |
| -37.433333 | 174.7 | T | HLL | | N | Nihonui |
| -44.033333 | 169.25 | H | STM | | N | Cowan Creek |
| -44.65 | 170.35 | H | STM | | N | Deep Creek |
| -40.966667 | 173.916667 | H | BAY | | V | Waitara Bay |
| -42.183333 | 173.466667 | H | STM | | N | Spray Stream |
| -39.45 | 173.833333 | H | STM | | N | Heimama Stream |
| -46.1 | 166.466667 | H | CHNM | | V | Eastern Entrance |
| -36.766667 | 174.4 | T | BCH | | N | Muriwai Beach |
| -38.983333 | 177.45 | T | HLL | | N | Ohinemaemae |
| -41.25 | 174.116667 | H | BAY | | N | Kahikatea Bay |
| -36.583333 | 174.6 | P | PPL | | N | Parakakau |
| -41.152222 | 173.438333 | H | COVE | | N | Pier Cove |
| -39.183333 | 177.85 | H | STM | | N | Mangatea Stream |
| -41.383333 | 172.583333 | T | MT | | N | Mount Gomorrah |
| -42.55 | 171.966667 | H | STM | | N | Waiheke River |

As you can see from this example, this database includes longitude and latitude values as well as codes indicating the type of place (populated place, administrative district, natural feature, and so on), the elevation (where relevant), and a code indicating the type of name (official, conventional, historical, and so on).

The GEOnet Names Server database contains approximately 6 million features and 10 million names. It includes every country other than the US and Antarctica.

# The GEOnet Names Server data format

The GEOnet Names Server's data is provided as a simple tab-delimited text file, where the first row in the file contains the field names, and subsequent rows contain the various features, one per row. Importing this name data into a spreadsheet or database is trivial.

For more information on the supplied fields and what the various codes mean, refer to `http://geonames.nga.mil/gns/html/gis_countryfiles.html`.

# Obtaining and using GEOnet Names Server data

The main site for the GEOnet Names Server is `http://geonames.nga.mil/gns/html`.

The main interface to the GEOnet Names Server is through various search tools that provide filtered views of the data. To download the data directly rather than searching, go to `http://geonames.nga.mil/gns/html/namefiles.html`.

Each country is listed; simply click on the hyperlink for the country you want data for, and your browser will download a `.zip` file containing a number of tab-delimited text files containing all the features within that country. The data for each country is provided both as a single combined file as well as a separate file for each feature type.

As well as downloading each country's data individually, there is also an option to download all the countries in one file, which is a 460MB download.

Once you have downloaded the files and decompressed them, you can load the files directly into a spreadsheet or database for further processing. By filtering on the **Feature Classification (FC)**, **Feature Designation Code (DSG)**, and other fields, you can select the particular set of place names you want and then use that data directly in your application.

# The Geographic Names Information System (GNIS)

The **Geographic Names Information System (GNIS)** is the US equivalent of the GEOnet Names Server—it contains name information for the United States.

The following is an extract from the GNIS database:

| FEATURE_NAME | FEATURE_CLASS | STATE_ALPHA | PRIM_LAT_DEC | PRIM_LONG_DEC | ELEVATION |
|---|---|---|---|---|---|
| Abbott Ranch | Locale | CA | 36.2305176 | -121.4657686 | 250 |
| Abbott Reservoir | Reservoir | CA | 40.9060035 | -120.8613504 | 1760 |
| Abbott Spring | Spring | CA | 40.9093369 | -120.8535725 | 1794 |
| Abbotts Lagoon | Lake | CA | 38.1174233 | -122.9533306 | 0 |
| Abbotts Peak | Summit | CA | 37.9763136 | -120.6224262 | 471 |
| Abbotts Upper Cabin | Building | CA | 41.4295777 | -123.1875457 | 1477 |
| ABC Camp Rustic Campsite | Locale | CA | 36.0232958 | -121.4299341 | 756 |
| ABC-TV Heliport | Airport | CA | 34.1033427 | -118.2834088 | 129 |
| Abel Canyon | Valley | CA | 34.8233155 | -119.8643049 | 524 |
| Abel Canyon Campground | Locale | CA | 34.82276 | -119.8626382 | 524 |
| Abel Canyon Spring | Spring | CA | 34.8710918 | -119.816803 | 1190 |
| Abel Square Shopping Center | Locale | CA | 37.427717 | -121.9080126 | 5 |
| Abelardo Cabin | Locale | CA | 36.3102401 | -120.7585092 | 1146 |
| Abelian Group Math School | School | CA | 37.8685219 | -122.2876776 | 23 |
| Abels Apple Acres | Locale | CA | 38.7465695 | -120.748544 | 797 |
| Aberdeen | Populated Place | CA | 36.9779897 | -118.2534321 | 1193 |
| Aberdeen Bypass Ditch | Canal | CA | 36.9616004 | -118.2362091 | 1173 |
| Aberdeen Canyon | Valley | CA | 34.1155644 | -118.2889647 | 196 |
| Aberdeen Ditch | Canal | CA | 36.9646558 | -118.225931 | 1174 |
| Aberdeen-Inverness Residence Hall | Building | CA | 33.978349 | -117.3253209 | 331 |
| Abernathy Meadow | Flat | CA | 37.8752015 | -119.8993467 | 1292 |
| Abestos Number 1 Prospect | Mine | CA | 36.8940982 | -118.069813 | 2033 |
| Abilene | Populated Place | CA | 36.145507 | -119.053714 | 124 |
| Able Spring | Spring | CA | 39.1473909 | -122.6310973 | 924 |
| Ables Drain | Canal | CA | 37.4274355 | -120.9690959 | 19 |
| Abney Butte | Summit | CA | 41.9759586 | -123.1603266 | 1269 |
| Abolitos Park | Park | CA | 32.9833782 | -117.0600321 | 175 |
| Abraham Lincoln Continuation High School | School | CA | 33.9711265 | -117.3661556 | 275 |
| Abraham Lincoln Elementary School | School | CA | 33.6100221 | -117.8606119 | 89 |

GNIS includes natural, physical, and cultural features, though it does not include road or highway names.

As with the GEOnet Names Server, the GNIS database contains the official names used by the US government, as decided by the US Board on Geographic Names. GNIS is run by the US Geological Survey and currently contains over 2.2 million features.

# The GNIS data format

GNIS names are available for download as pipe-delimited compressed text files. This format uses the pipe character ( | ) to separate the various fields:

```
FEATURE_ID|FEATURE_NAME|FEATURE_CLASS|...
1397658|Ester|Populated Place|...
1397926|Afognak|Populated Place|...
```

The first line contains the field names, and subsequent lines contain the various features. The available information includes the name of the feature, its type, elevation, the county and state the feature is in, the latitude/longitude coordinate of the feature itself, and the latitude/longitude coordinate of the origin of the feature (for streams, valleys, and so on).

## Obtaining and using GNIS data

The main GNIS web site can be found at `http://geonames.usgs.gov/domestic`.

Click on the **Download Domestic Names** hyperlink, and you will be given options to download all the GNIS data on a state-by-state basis or download all the features in a single large download. You can also download "topical gazetteers" that include selected subsets of the data—all populated places, all historical places, and so on.

If you click on one of the **File Format** hyperlinks, a pop-up window will appear describing the structure of the files in more detail.

Once you have downloaded the data you want, you can simply import the file into a database or spreadsheet. To import into a spreadsheet, use the **Delimited** format and enter | as the custom delimiter character. You can then sort or filter the data in whatever way you want so that you can use it in your application.

# Choosing your geospatial data source

If you need to obtain map data, images, elevations, or place names for use in your geospatial applications, the sources we have covered should give you everything you need. Of course, this is not an exhaustive list—other sources of data are available, and can be found online using a search engine or sites such as `http://freegis.org`.

The following table lists the various requirements you may have for geospatial data in your application development and which data source(s) may be most appropriate in each case:

| Requirement | Suitable data sources |
| --- | --- |
| Simple base map | World Borders Dataset |
| Shaded relief (pseudo-3D) maps | GLOBE or NED data processed using `gdaldem`; Natural Earth raster images |
| Street map | OpenStreetMap |
| City outlines | TIGER (US); Natural Earth urban areas |
| Detailed country outlines | GSHHG Level 1 |
| Photorealistic images of the Earth | Landsat |
| List of names of cities and places | GNIS (US) or Geonet Names Server (elsewhere) |

# Summary

In this chapter, we surveyed a number of sources of freely-available geospatial data. For vector-format data, we looked at OpenStreetMap, a collaborative site where people can create and edit vector maps worldwide; TIGER, which is a service of the US Census Bureau; the Natural Earth Data web site; the GSHHG high-resolution shoreline database; and the simple but effective World Borders Dataset.

For geospatial data in raster format, we looked at Landsat imagery, the GLOBE digital elevation model, and the high-resolution National Elevation Dataset for the US and its protectorates.

We then looked at two sources of place name data: the GEOnet Names Server, which provides information about official place names for every country other than the US and Antarctica, and GNIS, which provides official place names for the United States.

This completes our survey of geospatial data sources. In the next chapter, we will use the Python toolkits described in *Chapter 3, Python Libraries for Geospatial Development*, to work with some of this geospatial data in interesting and useful ways.

# 5
# Working with Geospatial Data in Python

In this chapter, we will combine the Python libraries and geospatial data covered earlier and use them to accomplish a variety of tasks. These tasks have been chosen to demonstrate various techniques for working with geospatial data in your Python programs; while in some cases there are quicker and easier ways to achieve these results (for example, using command-line utilities) we will create these solutions in Python so that you can learn how to work with geospatial data in your own Python programs.

This chapter will cover the following topics:

- Working with geospatial data in both vector and raster format
- Changing the datums and projections used by geospatial data
- Performing geospatial calculations on points, lines, and polygons
- Converting and standardizing units of geometry and distance

This chapter is formatted like a cookbook, detailing various real-world tasks you might want to perform and providing "recipes" for accomplishing them.

# Pre-requisites

If you want to follow through the examples in this chapter, make sure you have the following Python libraries installed on your computer:

- GDAL/OGR version 1.11 or later (`http://gdal.org`)
- `pyproj` version 1.9.4 or later (`http://code.google.com/p/pyproj`)
- Shapely version 1.5.9 or later (`https://pypi.python.org/pypi/Shapely`)

For more information about these libraries and how to use them, please refer to *Chapter 3, Python Libraries for Geospatial Development*.

# Working with geospatial data

In this section, we will look at some examples of tasks you might want to perform that involve using geospatial data in both vector and raster format.

# Task – calculate the bounding box for each country in the world

In this slightly contrived example, we will make use of a shapefile to calculate the minimum and maximum latitude/longitude values for each country in the world. This "bounding box" can be used, among other things, to generate a map centered on a particular country. For example, the bounding box for Turkey would look like this:

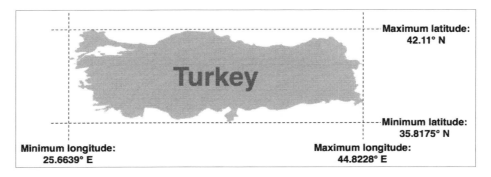

Start by downloading the World Borders Dataset from `http://thematicmapping.org/downloads/world_borders.php`. Make sure you download the file named `TM_WORLD_BORDERS-0.3.zip` rather than the simplified `TM_WORLD_BORDERS_SIMPL-0.3.zip` file. Decompress the `.zip` archive and place the various files that make up the shapefile (the `.dbf`, `.prj`, `.shp`, and `.shx` files) together in a suitable directory.

Next, we need to create a Python program that can read the borders for each country. Fortunately, using OGR to read through the contents of a shapefile is simple:

```
from osgeo import ogr

shapefile = ogr.Open("TM_WORLD_BORDERS-0.3.shp")
layer = shapefile.GetLayer(0)

for i in range(layer.GetFeatureCount()):
    feature = layer.GetFeature(i)
```

This complete program, along with all the other examples in this chapter, can be downloaded as part of the sample code for this chapter.

The feature will consist of a geometry defining the outline of the country, along with a set of attributes providing information about that country. According to the Readme.txt file, the attributes in this shapefile include the ISO-3166 three-letter code for the country (in a field called ISO3) as well as the name for the country (in a field called NAME). This allows us to obtain the country code and name for the feature:

```
countryCode = feature.GetField("ISO3")
countryName = feature.GetField("NAME")
```

We can also obtain the country's border polygon using the GetGeometryRef() method:

```
geometry = feature.GetGeometryRef()
```

To solve this task, we will need to calculate the bounding box for this geometry. OGR uses the term **envelope** to refer to the geometry's bounding box, so we can get the bounding box in the following way:

```
minLong,maxLong,minLat,maxLat = geometry.GetEnvelope()
```

Let's put all this together into a complete working program:

```
# calcBoundingBoxes.py

from osgeo import ogr

shapefile = ogr.Open("TM_WORLD_BORDERS-0.3.shp")
layer = shapefile.GetLayer(0)

countries = [] # List of (code, name, minLat, maxLat,
```

```
                             # minLong, maxLong) tuples.

    for i in range(layer.GetFeatureCount()):
        feature = layer.GetFeature(i)
        countryCode = feature.GetField("ISO3")
        countryName = feature.GetField("NAME")
        geometry = feature.GetGeometryRef()
        minLong,maxLong,minLat,maxLat = geometry.GetEnvelope()

        countries.append((countryName, countryCode,
                            minLat, maxLat, minLong, maxLong))

    countries.sort()

    for name,code,minLat,maxLat,minLong,maxLong in countries:
        print("{} ({}) lat={:.4f}..{:.4f},long={:.4f}..{:.4f}"
            .format(name,code,minLat,maxLat,minLong,maxLong))
```

 If you aren't storing the TM_WORLD_BORDERS-0.3.shp shapefile in the same directory as the script itself, you will need to add the directory where the shapefile is stored to your ogr.Open() call.

Running this program produces the following output:

```
% python calcBoundingBoxes.py
Afghanistan (AFG) lat=29.4061..38.4721, long=60.5042..74.9157
Albania (ALB) lat=39.6447..42.6619, long=19.2825..21.0542
Algeria (DZA) lat=18.9764..37.0914, long=-8.6672..11.9865
...
```

# Task – calculate the border between Thailand and Myanmar

In this recipe, we will make use of the World Borders Dataset to obtain polygons defining the borders of Thailand and Myanmar. We will then transfer these polygons into Shapely and use Shapely's capabilities to calculate the common border between these two countries, saving the result into another shapefile.

If you haven't already done so, download the World Borders Dataset from the Thematic Mapping web site, http://thematicmapping.org/downloads/world_borders.php.

The World Borders Dataset conveniently includes the ISO-3166 two-character country code for each feature, so we can identify the features corresponding to Thailand and Myanmar as we read through the shapefile. We can then extract the outline of each country, converting the outlines into Shapely geometry objects. Here is the relevant code, which forms the start of our calcCommonBorders.py program:

```
# calcCommonBorders.py

import os, os.path, shutil
from osgeo import ogr, osr
import shapely.wkt

shapefile = ogr.Open("TM_WORLD_BORDERS-0.3.shp")
layer = shapefile.GetLayer(0)

thailand = None
myanmar = None

for i in range(layer.GetFeatureCount()):
    feature = layer.GetFeature(i)
    if feature.GetField("ISO2") == "TH":
        geometry = feature.GetGeometryRef()
        thailand = shapely.wkt.loads(geometry.ExportToWkt())
    elif feature.GetField("ISO2") == "MM":
        geometry = feature.GetGeometryRef()
        myanmar = shapely.wkt.loads(geometry.ExportToWkt())
```

 Once again, this code assumes that you have placed the TM_ WORLD_BORDERS-0.3.shp shapefile in the same directory as the Python script. If you've placed it into a different directory, you'll need to adjust the ogr.Open() statement to match it.

Now that we have the country outlines in Shapely, we can use Shapely's computational geometry capabilities to calculate the common border between these two countries:

```
commonBorder = thailand.intersection(myanmar)
```

The result will be a LineString (or a MultiLineString if the border is broken up into more than one part). Let's now save this common border into a new shapefile:

```
if os.path.exists("common-border"):
    shutil.rmtree("common-border")
os.mkdir("common-border")
```

```
spatialReference = osr.SpatialReference()
spatialReference.SetWellKnownGeogCS('WGS84')

driver = ogr.GetDriverByName("ESRI Shapefile")
dstPath = os.path.join("common-border", "border.shp")
dstFile = driver.CreateDataSource(dstPath)
dstLayer = dstFile.CreateLayer("layer", spatialReference)

wkt = shapely.wkt.dumps(commonBorder)

feature = ogr.Feature(dstLayer.GetLayerDefn())
feature.SetGeometry(ogr.CreateGeometryFromWkt(wkt))
dstLayer.CreateFeature(feature)
```

If we were to display the results on a map, we could clearly see the common border between these two countries:

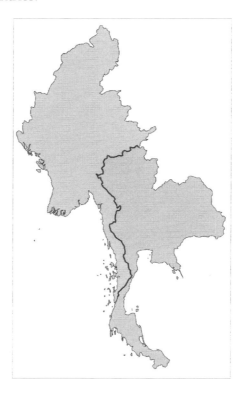

 We will learn how to draw maps like this in *Chapter 7, Using Python and Mapnik to Generate Maps.*

The contents of the `common-border/border.shp` shapefile is represented by the heavy line along the countries' common border.

Note that we will use this shapefile later in this chapter to calculate the length of the Thailand-Myanmar border, so make sure you generate and keep a copy of this shapefile.

# Task – analyze elevations using a digital elevation map

A **digital elevation map** (**DEM**) is a raster geospatial data format where each pixel value (or cell) represents the height of a point on the earth's surface. We encountered DEM files in the previous chapter, where we saw two examples of data sources that supply this type of information: the National Elevation Dataset covering the United States, and GLOBE which provides DEM files covering the entire Earth.

Because a DEM file contains elevation data, it can be interesting to analyze the elevation values for a given area. For example, we could draw a histogram showing how much of a country's area is at a certain elevation. Let's take some DEM data from the GLOBE dataset and calculate an elevation histogram using that data.

To keep things simple, we will choose a small country surrounded by ocean: New Zealand.

> We're using a small country so that we don't have too much data to work with. We're also using a country surrounded by ocean so that we can check all the points within a bounding box rather than having to use a polygon to exclude points outside of the country's boundaries. This makes our task much easier.

To download the DEM data, go to the GLOBE web site (http://www.ngdc.noaa.gov/mgg/topo/globe.html) and click on the **Get Data Online** hyperlink. We're going to use the data already calculated for this area of the world, so click on the **Any or all 16 "tiles"** hyperlink. New Zealand is in tile **L**, so click on the hyperlink for this tile to download it.

The file you download will be called `l10g.zip` (or `l10g.gz` if you chose to download the tile in GZIP format). If you decompress it, you will end up with a single file called `l10g`, containing the raw elevation data.

By itself, this file isn't very useful—it needs to be georeferenced onto the earth's surface so that you can match up each elevation value with its position on the earth. To do this, you need to download the associated header file. Suitable header files for the premade tiles can be found at `http://www.ngdc.noaa.gov/mgg/topo/elev/esri/hdr`. Download the file named `l10g.hdr` and place it into the same directory as the `l10g` file you downloaded earlier. You can then read the DEM file using GDAL, just like we did earlier:

```
from osgeo import gdal
dataset = gdal.Open("l10g")
```

You probably noticed when you downloaded the `l10g` tile that it covers much more than just New Zealand—all of Australia is included, as well as Malaysia, Papua New Guinea, and several other east-Asian countries. To work with the elevation data for just New Zealand, we will need to identify the relevant portion of the raster DEM, that is, the range of $x$ and $y$ coordinates that cover New Zealand. We will start by looking at a map and identifying the minimum and maximum latitude/longitude values that enclose all of New Zealand, but no other country:

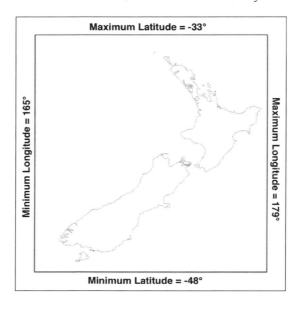

Rounded to the nearest degree, we get a longitude/latitude bounding box of (165, -48)...(179, -33). This is the area we want to scan to cover all of New Zealand.

There is, however, a problem: the raster data consists of pixels or "cells" identified by $x$ and $y$ coordinates, not longitude and latitude values. We have to convert from longitudes and latitudes to $x$ and $y$ coordinates. To do this, we need to make use of GDAL's coordinate transformation features.

We'll start by obtaining our dataset's coordinate transformation:

```
t = dataset.GetGeoTransform()
```

Using this transformation, we can convert an $(x, y)$ coordinate to its corresponding latitude and longitude value. In this case, however, we want to do the opposite — we want to take a latitude and longitude and calculate the associated $x$ and $y$ coordinates. To do this, we have to *invert* the transformation. Once again, GDAL will do this for us:

```
success,tInverse = gdal.InvGeoTransform(t)
if not success:
    print("Failed!")
    sys.exit(1)
```

There are some cases where a transformation can't be inverted. This is why gdal.InvGeoTransform() returns a success flag as well as the inverted transformation. With this particular set of DEM data, however, the transformation should always be invertible, so this is unlikely to happen.

Now that we have the inverse transformation, it is possible to convert from a latitude and longitude to an $x$ and $y$ coordinate, like this:

```
x,y = gdal.ApplyGeoTransform(tInverse, longitude, latitude)
```

Using this, we can finally identify the minimum and maximum $(x, y)$ coordinates that cover the area we are interested in:

```
x1,y1 = gdal.ApplyGeoTransform(tInverse, minLong, minLat)
x2,y2 = gdal.ApplyGeoTransform(tInverse, maxLong, maxLat)

minX = int(min(x1, x2))
maxX = int(max(x1, x2))
minY = int(min(y1, y2))
maxY = int(max(y1, y2))
```

Now that we know the $x$ and $y$ coordinates for the portion of the DEM that we're interested in, we can use GDAL to read in the individual height values. We start by obtaining the raster band that contains the DEM data:

```
band = dataset.GetRasterBand(1)
```

GDAL band numbers start from 1. There is only one raster band in the DEM data we're using.

We next want to read the elevation values from our raster band. If you remember, there are two ways you can use GDAL to read raster data: as raw binary data, which you then extract using the `struct` module, or using the NumPy library to automatically read data into an array.

Let's assume that you don't have NumPy installed; we'll use the `struct` method instead. Using the technique we covered in *Chapter 3, Python Libraries for Geospatial Development*, we can use the `ReadRaster()` method to read the raw binary data and then the `struct.unpack()` function to convert the binary data to a list of elevation values. Here is the relevant code:

```
fmt = "<" + ("h" * width)
scanline = band.ReadRaster(X, y, width, height,
                           width, height, gdalconst.GDT_Int16)
values = struct.unpack(fmt, scanline)
```

Putting all this together, we can use GDAL to open the raster data file and read all the elevation values within the bounding box surrounding New Zealand. We'll then count how often each elevation value occurs and print out a simple histogram using the elevation values. Here is the resulting code:

```
# histogram.py

import sys, struct
from osgeo import gdal
from osgeo import gdalconst

minLat   = -48
maxLat   = -33
minLong = 165
maxLong = 179

dataset = gdal.Open("l10g")
band = dataset.GetRasterBand(1)

t = dataset.GetGeoTransform()
success,tInverse = gdal.InvGeoTransform(t)
if not success:
    print("Failed!")
    sys.exit(1)
```

```
x1,y1 = gdal.ApplyGeoTransform(tInverse, minLong, minLat)
x2,y2 = gdal.ApplyGeoTransform(tInverse, maxLong, maxLat)

minX = int(min(x1, x2))
maxX = int(max(x1, x2))
minY = int(min(y1, y2))
maxY = int(max(y1, y2))

width = (maxX - minX) + 1
fmt = "<" + ("h" * width)

histogram = {} # Maps elevation to number of occurrences.

for y in range(minY, maxY+1):
    scanline = band.ReadRaster(minX, y, width, 1,
                               width, 1,
                               gdalconst.GDT_Int16)
    values = struct.unpack(fmt, scanline)

    for value in values:
        try:
            histogram[value] += 1
        except KeyError:
            histogram[value] = 1

for height in sorted(histogram.keys()):
    print(height, histogram[height])
```

 Don't forget to add a directory path to the gdal.Open()
statement if you placed the 110g file in a different directory.

If you run this, you will see a list of heights (in meters) and how many cells have that height value:

```
-500 2607581
1 6641
2 909
3 1628
...
3097 1
3119 2
3173 1
```

This reveals one final problem: there is a large number of cells with an elevation value of -500. What is going on here? Clearly, -500 is not a valid height value. The GLOBE documentation provides the answer:

> *"Every tile contains values of -500 for oceans, with no values between -500 and the minimum value for land noted here."*

So all those points with a value of -500 represent cells that are over the ocean. If you remember from our description of the GDAL library in *Chapter 3, Python Libraries for Geospatial Development*, GDAL includes a **no data value** for exactly this purpose. Indeed, the gdal.RasterBand object has a GetNoDataValue() method that will tell us what this value is. This allows us to add the following highlighted line to our program to exclude the cells without any data:

```
for value in values:
    if value != band.GetNoDataValue():
        try:
            histogram[value] += 1
        except KeyError:
            histogram[value] = 1
```

This finally gives us a histogram of the heights across New Zealand. You could create a graph using this data if you wished. For example, the following chart shows the total number of pixels at or below a given height:

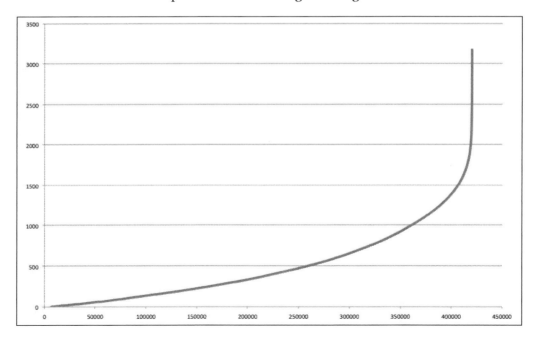

# Changing datums and projections

In *Chapter 2, GIS,* we saw that a **datum** is a mathematical model of the earth's shape, while a **projection** is a way of translating points on the earth's surface into points on a two-dimensional map. There are a large number of available datums and projections—whenever you are working with geospatial data, you must know which datum and which projection (if any) your data uses. If you are combining data from multiple sources, you will often have to change your geospatial data from one datum to another or from one projection to another.

# Task – changing projections to combine shapefiles using geographic and UTM coordinates

In this recipe, we will work with two shapefiles that have different projections. We haven't yet encountered any geospatial data that uses a projection—all the data we've seen so far used geographic (unprojected) latitude and longitude values. So, let's start by downloading some geospatial data in the **Universal Transverse Mercator (UTM)** projection.

The WebGIS web site (`http://www.webgis.com`) provides shapefiles describing land use and land cover, called LULC data files. For this example, we will download a shapefile for southern Florida (Dade County, to be exact), which uses the UTM projection.

You can download this shapefile from `http://www.webgis.com/MAPS/fl/lulcutm/miami.zip`.

The decompressed directory contains the shapefile, `miami.shp`, along with a `datum_reference.txt` file describing the shapefile's coordinate system. This file tells us the following:

```
The LULC shape file was generated from the original USGS GIRAS LULC
file by Lakes Environmental Software.
Datum: NAD83
Projection: UTM
Zone: 17
Data collection date by U.S.G.S.: 1972
Reference: http://edcwww.cr.usgs.gov/products/landcover/lulc.html
```

So, this particular shapefile uses UTM zone 17 projection and a datum of NAD83.

Let's take a second shapefile, this time in geographic coordinates. We'll use the GSHHS shoreline database, which uses the WGS84 datum and geographic (latitude/longitude) coordinates.

> You don't need to download the GSHHS database for this example; while we will display a map overlaying the LULC data over the top of the GSHHS data, you only need the LULC shapefile to complete this recipe. Drawing maps such as the one shown in this recipe will be covered in *Chapter 7, Using Python and Mapnik to Generate Maps*.

We can't directly compare the coordinates in these two shapefiles; the LULC shapefile has coordinates measured in UTM (that is, in meters from a given reference line), while the GSHHS shapefile has coordinates in latitude and longitude values (in decimal degrees):

```
LULC:   x=485719.47, y=2783420.62
        x=485779.49, y=2783380.63
        x=486129.65, y=2783010.66
        . . .

GSHHS: x=180.0000, y=68.9938
       x=180.0000, y=65.0338
       x=179.9984, y=65.0337
```

Before we can combine these two shapefiles, we first have to convert them to use the same projection. We'll do this by converting the LULC shapefile from UTM-17 to geographic (latitude/longitude) coordinates. Doing this requires us to define an OGR **coordinate transformation** and then apply that transformation to each of the features in the shapefile.

Here is how you can define a coordinate transformation using OGR:

```python
from osgeo import osr

srcProjection = osr.SpatialReference()
srcProjection.SetUTM(17)

dstProjection = osr.SpatialReference()
dstProjection.SetWellKnownGeogCS('WGS84') # Lat/long.

transform = osr.CoordinateTransformation(srcProjection,
                                         dstProjection)
```

Using this transformation, we can transform each of the features in the shapefile from UTM projections back into geographic coordinates:

```
for i in range(layer.GetFeatureCount()):
    feature = layer.GetFeature(i)
    geometry = feature.GetGeometryRef()
    geometry.Transform(transform)
```

Putting all this together with the techniques we explored earlier for copying the features from one shapefile to another, we end up with the following complete program:

```
# changeProjection.py

import os, os.path, shutil
from osgeo import ogr
from osgeo import osr
from osgeo import gdal

# Define the source and destination projections, and a
# transformation object to convert from one to the other.

srcProjection = osr.SpatialReference()
srcProjection.SetUTM(17)

dstProjection = osr.SpatialReference()
dstProjection.SetWellKnownGeogCS('WGS84') # Lat/long.

transform = osr.CoordinateTransformation(srcProjection,
                                         dstProjection)

# Open the source shapefile.

srcFile = ogr.Open("miami/miami.shp")
srcLayer = srcFile.GetLayer(0)

# Create the dest shapefile, and give it the new projection.

if os.path.exists("miami-reprojected"):
    shutil.rmtree("miami-reprojected")
os.mkdir("miami-reprojected")

driver = ogr.GetDriverByName("ESRI Shapefile")
dstPath = os.path.join("miami-reprojected", "miami.shp")
dstFile = driver.CreateDataSource(dstPath)
```

```
dstLayer = dstFile.CreateLayer("layer", dstProjection)

# Reproject each feature in turn.

for i in range(srcLayer.GetFeatureCount()):
    feature = srcLayer.GetFeature(i)
    geometry = feature.GetGeometryRef()

    newGeometry = geometry.Clone()
    newGeometry.Transform(transform)

    feature = ogr.Feature(dstLayer.GetLayerDefn())
    feature.SetGeometry(newGeometry)
    dstLayer.CreateFeature(feature)
```

 Note that this example doesn't copy field values into the new shapefile; if your shapefile has metadata, you will want to copy the fields across as you create each new feature. Also, the preceding code assumes that the miami.shp shapefile has been placed into a miami subdirectory; you'll need to change the ogr.Open() statement to use the appropriate path name if you've stored this shapefile in a different place.

After running this program over the miami.shp shapefile, the coordinates for all the features in the shapefile will have been converted from UTM-17 to geographic coordinates:

```
Before reprojection:  x=485719.47, y=2783420.62
                      x=485779.49, y=2783380.63
                      x=486129.65, y=2783010.66
                      ...


 After reprojection: x=-81.1417, y=25.1668
                     x=-81.1411, y=25.1664
                     x=-81.1376, y=25.1631
```

To see whether this worked, let's draw a map showing the reprojected LULC data overlaid on top of the GSHHS shoreline data:

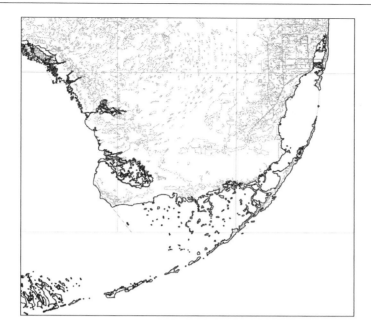

The light gray outlines show the various polygons within the LULC shapefile, while the black outline shows the shoreline as defined by the GLOBE shapefile. Both of these shapefiles now use geographic coordinates and, as you can see, the coastlines match exactly.

If you have been watching closely, you may have noticed that the LULC data uses the NAD83 datum, while the GSHHS data and our reprojected version of the LULC data both use the WGS84 datum. We can do this without error because the two datums are identical for points within North America.

# Task – changing the datums to allow older and newer TIGER data to be combined

For this example, we will need to obtain some geospatial data that uses the NAD27 datum. This datum dates back to 1927 and was commonly used for North American geospatial analysis up until the 1980s, when it was replaced by NAD83.

The US Geological Survey makes available a set of road data that uses the older NAD27 datum. To obtain this data, go to `http://pubs.usgs.gov/dds/dds-81/TopographicData/Roads` and download the files named `roads.dbf`, `roads.prj`, `roads.shp`, and `roads.shx`. These four files together make up the "roads" shapefile. Place them into a directory named `roads`.

This sample shapefile covers an area of the Sierra Nevada mountains in the United States, including a portion of both California and Nevada. The town of Bridgeport, CA, is covered by this shapefile.

Using the `ogrinfo` command-line tool, we can see that this shapefile does indeed use the older NAD27 datum:

```
% ogrinfo -so roads.shp roads
INFO: Open of `roads.shp'
      using driver `ESRI Shapefile' successful.


Layer name: roads
Geometry: Line String
Feature Count: 10050
Extent: (-119.637220, 37.462695) - (-117.834877, 38.705226)
Layer SRS WKT:
GEOGCS["GCS_North_American_1927",
    DATUM["North_American_Datum_1927",
        SPHEROID["Clarke_1866",6378206.4,294.9786982]],
    PRIMEM["Greenwich",0],
    UNIT["Degree",0.0174532925199433]]
...
```

If we were to assume that this shapefile uses the more common WGS84 datum, all the features would appear in the wrong places:

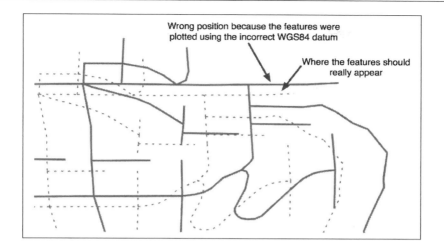

To make the features appear in the correct places and to be able to combine these features with other data that uses the WGS84 datum, we need to convert the shapefile to use WGS84. Changing a shapefile from one datum to another requires the same basic process we used earlier to change a shapefile from one projection to another.

First, you choose the source and destination datums and define a coordinate transformation to convert from one to the other:

```
srcDatum = osr.SpatialReference()
srcDatum.SetWellKnownGeogCS('NAD27')

dstDatum = osr.SpatialReference()
dstDatum.SetWellKnownGeogCS('WGS84')

transform = osr.CoordinateTransformation(srcDatum, dstDatum)
```

You then process each feature in the shapefile, transforming the feature's geometry using the coordinate transformation:

```
for i in range(srcLayer.GetFeatureCount()):
    feature = srcLayer.GetFeature(i)
    geometry = feature.GetGeometryRef()
    geometry.Transform(transform)
```

Here is the complete Python program to convert the `roads` shapefile from the
NAD27 datum to WGS84:

```python
# changeDatum.py

import os, os.path, shutil
from osgeo import ogr
from osgeo import osr
from osgeo import gdal

# Define the source and destination datums, and a
# transformation object to convert from one to the other.

srcDatum = osr.SpatialReference()
srcDatum.SetWellKnownGeogCS('NAD27')

dstDatum = osr.SpatialReference()
dstDatum.SetWellKnownGeogCS('WGS84')

transform = osr.CoordinateTransformation(srcDatum, dstDatum)

# Open the source shapefile.

srcFile = ogr.Open("roads/roads.shp")
srcLayer = srcFile.GetLayer(0)

# Create the dest shapefile, and give it the new projection.

if os.path.exists("roads-reprojected"):
    shutil.rmtree("roads-reprojected")
os.mkdir("roads-reprojected")

driver = ogr.GetDriverByName("ESRI Shapefile")
dstPath = os.path.join("roads-reprojected", "roads.shp")
dstFile = driver.CreateDataSource(dstPath)
dstLayer = dstFile.CreateLayer("layer", dstDatum)

# Reproject each feature in turn.
```

```
for i in range(srcLayer.GetFeatureCount()):
    feature = srcLayer.GetFeature(i)
    geometry = feature.GetGeometryRef()

    newGeometry = geometry.Clone()
    newGeometry.Transform(transform)

    feature = ogr.Feature(dstLayer.GetLayerDefn())
    feature.SetGeometry(newGeometry)
    dstLayer.CreateFeature(feature)
```

The preceding code assumes that the `roads` folder is in the same directory as the Python script itself; if you placed this folder somewhere else, you'll need to change the `ogr.Open()` statement to use the appropriate directory path.

If we now plot the reprojected features using the WGS84 datum, the features will appear in the correct places:

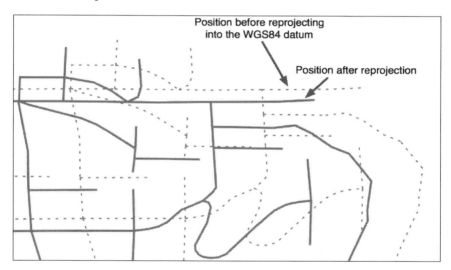

# Performing geospatial calculations

Shapely is a very capable library for performing various calculations on geospatial data. Let's put it through its paces with a complex, real-world problem.

# Task – identifying parks in or near urban areas

The US Census Bureau makes available a shapefile containing something called **Core Based Statistical Areas (CBSAs)**, which are polygons defining urban areas with a population of 10,000 or more. At the same time, the GNIS web site provides lists of place names and other details. Using these two data sources, we will identify any parks within or close to an urban area.

Because of the volume of data we are dealing with, we will limit our search to California. It would take a very long time to check all the CBSA polygon/place name combinations for the entire United States; it's possible to optimize the program to do this quickly, but this would make the example too complex for our current purposes.

Let's start by downloading the necessary data. We'll start by downloading a shapefile containing all the core-based statistical areas in the USA. Go to the TIGER web site:

```
http://census.gov/geo/www/tiger
```

Click on the **TIGER/Line Shapefiles** link, then follow the **Download** option for the latest version of the TIGER/Line shapefiles (as of this writing, it is the 2015 version). Select the **FTP Interface** option, and your computer will open an FTP session to the appropriate directory. Sign in as a guest, switch to the CBSA directory, and download the appropriate file you find there.

The file you want to download will have a name like `tl_XXXX_us_cbsa.zip`, where XXXX is the year the data file was created. Once the file has been downloaded, decompress it and place the resulting shapefile into a convenient location so that you can work with it.

You now need to download the GNIS place name data. Go to the GNIS web site, `http://geonames.usgs.gov/domestic`, and click on the **Download Domestic Names** hyperlink. Because we only need the data for California, choose this state from the **Select state for download** popup menu beneath the **States, Territories, Associated Areas of the United States** section of this page. This will download a file with a name like `CA_Features_XXX.txt`, where XXX is the date when the file was created. Place this file somewhere convenient, alongside the CBSA shapefile you downloaded earlier.

We're now ready to start writing our code. Let's start by reading through the CBSA urban area shapefile and extracting the polygons that define the outline of each urban area, as a Shapely geometry object:

```
shapefile = ogr.Open("tl_2015_us_cbsa.shp")
layer = shapefile.GetLayer(0)
```

```
for i in range(layer.GetFeatureCount()):
    feature = layer.GetFeature(i)
    geometry = feature.GetGeometryRef()
    wkt = geometry.ExportToWkt()
    outline = shapely.wkt.loads(wkt)
```

Next, we need to scan through the CA_Features_XXX.txt file to identify the features marked as parks. For each of these features, we want to extract the name of the feature and its associated latitude and longitude. Here's how we might do this:

```
f = open("CA_Features_XXX.txt", "r")
for line in f.readlines():
    chunks = line.rstrip().split("|")
    if chunks[2] == "Park":
        name = chunks[1]
        latitude = float(chunks[9])
        longitude = float(chunks[10])
```

Remember that the GNIS place name database is a "pipe-delimited" text file. That's why we have to split the line up using line.rstrip().split("|").

Now comes the fun part: we need to figure out which parks are within or close to each urban area. There are two ways we could do this, either of which will work:

• We could use the outline.distance() method to calculate the distance between the outline and a Point object representing the park's location:

- We could *dilate* the polygon using the `outline.buffer()` method, and then see whether the resulting polygon contained the desired point:

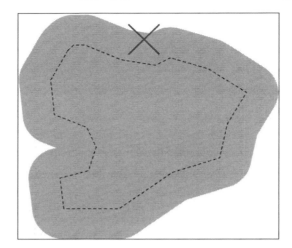

The second option is faster when dealing with a large number of points, as we can pre-calculate the dilated polygons and then use them to compare against each point in turn. Let's take this option:

```python
# findNearbyParks.py

from osgeo import ogr
import shapely.geometry
import shapely.wkt

MAX_DISTANCE = 0.1 # Angular distance; approx 10 km.

print("Loading urban areas...")

urbanAreas = {} # Maps area name to Shapely polygon.

shapefile = ogr.Open("tl_2015_us_cbsa.shp")
layer = shapefile.GetLayer(0)

for i in range(layer.GetFeatureCount()):
    print("Dilating feature {} of {}"
            .format(i, layer.GetFeatureCount()))
    feature = layer.GetFeature(i)
    name = feature.GetField("NAME")
    geometry = feature.GetGeometryRef()
```

```
    outline = shapely.wkt.loads(geometry.ExportToWkt())
    dilatedOutline = outline.buffer(MAX_DISTANCE)
    urbanAreas[name] = dilatedOutline

print("Checking parks...")

f = open("CA_Features_XXX.txt", "r")
for line in f.readlines():
    chunks = line.rstrip().split("|")
    if chunks[2] == "Park":
        parkName = chunks[1]
        latitude = float(chunks[9])
        longitude = float(chunks[10])

        pt = shapely.geometry.Point(longitude, latitude)

        for urbanName,urbanArea in urbanAreas.items():
            if urbanArea.contains(pt):
                print("{} is in or near {}"
                      .format(parkName, urbanName))
f.close()
```

Don't forget to change the name of the CA_Features_XXX.txt file to match the actual name of the file you downloaded. You should also add a path to the tl_2015_us_cbsa.shp and CA_Features_XXX.txt file references in your program if you placed these in a different directory.

It will take a few minutes to run this program, after which you will get a complete list of all the parks that are in or close to an urban area:

```
% python findNearbyParks.py
Loading urban areas...
Checking parks...
Imperial National Wildlife Refuge is in or near El Centro, CA
Imperial National Wildlife Refuge is in or near Yuma, AZ
Cibola National Wildlife Refuge is in or near El Centro, CA
Twin Lakes State Beach is in or near Santa Cruz-Watsonville, CA
Admiral William Standley State Recreation Area is in or near Ukiah, CA
...
```

> Our program takes a while to run because it includes urban areas throughout the USA, not just in California. An obvious optimization would be to only include urban areas in California, which would speed up the program significantly.

Note that our program uses **angular distances** to decide whether a park is in or near a given urban area. As we mentioned in *Chapter 2, GIS*, an angular distance is the angle between two lines going out from the center of the earth to its surface:

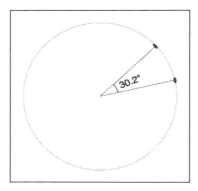

Because we are dealing with data for California, where one degree of angular measurement roughly equals 100 kilometers on the earth's surface, an angular measurement of 0.1 roughly equals a real-world distance of 10 km.

Using angular measurements makes the distance calculation easy and quick to calculate, though it doesn't give an exact distance on the earth's surface. If your application requires exact distances, you could start by using an angular distance to filter out the features obviously too far away and then obtain an exact result for the remaining features by calculating the point on the polygon's boundary that is closest to the desired point and calculating the linear distance between the two points. You would then discard the points that exceed your desired exact linear distance. Implementing this would be an interesting challenge, though not one we will examine in this book.

# Converting and standardizing units of geometry and distance

Imagine that you have two points on the earth's surface, with a straight line drawn between them:

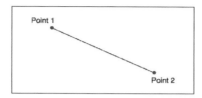

Each of these points can be described as a coordinate using some arbitrary coordinate system (for example, using latitude and longitude values), while the length of the straight line could be considered to be the distance between the two points.

 Of course, because the earth's surface is not flat, we aren't really dealing with straight lines at all. Rather, we are calculating geodetic or **great-circle** distances across the surface of the earth.

Given any two coordinates, it is possible to calculate the distance between them. Conversely, you can start with one coordinate, a desired distance and direction, and then calculate the coordinates for the other point.

The `pyproj` Python library allows you to perform these types of calculations for any given datum. You can also use `pyproj` to convert from projected coordinates back to geographic coordinates and vice versa, allowing you to perform these sorts of calculations for any desired datum, coordinate system, and projection.

Ultimately, a geometry such as a line or a polygon consists of nothing more than a list of connected points. This means that using the process we described earlier, you can calculate the geodetic distance between each connected pair of points in a polygon or LineString and sum the results to get the actual length for any geometry. Let's use this knowledge to solve a real-world problem.

# Task – calculating the length of the Thai-Myanmar border

To solve this problem, we will make use of the `common-border/border.shp` shapefile we created earlier. This shapefile contains a single feature, which is a LineString defining the border between these two countries. Let's start by taking a look at the individual line segments that make up this feature's geometry:

```python
import os.path
from osgeo import ogr

def getLineSegmentsFromGeometry(geometry):
    segments = []
    if geometry.GetPointCount() > 0:
        segment = []
        for i in range(geometry.GetPointCount()):
            segment.append(geometry.GetPoint_2D(i))
        segments.append(segment)
    for i in range(geometry.GetGeometryCount()):
        subGeometry = geometry.GetGeometryRef(i)
        segments.extend(
            getLineSegmentsFromGeometry(subGeometry))
    return segments

filename = os.path.join("common-border", "border.shp")
shapefile = ogr.Open(filename)
layer = shapefile.GetLayer(0)
feature = layer.GetFeature(0)
geometry = feature.GetGeometryRef()

segments = getLineSegmentsFromGeometry(geometry)

print(segments)
```

 Don't forget to change the `os.path.join()` statement to match the location of your `border.shp` shapefile.

Note that we use a recursive function, `getLineSegmentsFromGeometry()`, to pull the individual coordinates for each line segment out of the geometry. Because geometries are recursive data structures, we have to pull out the individual line segments before we can work with them.

Running this program produces a long list of points that make up the various line segments defining the border between these two countries:

```
% python calcBorderLength.py
[[(100.081322, 20.348841), (100.089432, 20.347218)],
 [(100.089432, 20.347218), (100.09137, 20.348606)],
 [(98.742752, 10.348608), (98.748871, 10.378054)], ...]
```

Each line segment consists of a list of points—in this case, you'll notice that each segment has only two points—and if you look closely, you will notice that each segment starts at the same point as the previous segment ended. There are a total of 459 segments defining the border between Thailand and Myanmar, that is, 459 point pairs that we can calculate the geodetic distance for.

 Remember that a geodetic distance is a distance measured on the surface of the earth.

Let's see how we can use `pyproj` to calculate the geodetic distance between any two points. We first create a `Geod` instance:

```
geod = pyproj.Geod(ellps='WGS84')
```

`Geod` is the `pyproj` class that performs geodetic calculations. Notice that we have to provide it with details of the datum used to describe the shape of the earth. Once our `Geod` instance has been set up, we can calculate the geodetic distance between any two points by calling `geod.inv()`, the inverse geodetic transformation method:

```
angle1,angle2,distance = geod.inv(long1, lat1, long2, lat2)
```

`angle1` will be the angle from the first point to the second measured in decimal degrees, `angle2` will be the angle from the second point back to the first (again in degrees), and `distance` will be the great-circle distance between the two points in meters.

Using this, we can iterate over the line segments, calculate the distance from one point to the next, and total up all the distances to obtain the total length of the border:

```
geod = pyproj.Geod(ellps='WGS84')

totLength = 0.0
for segment in segments:
    for i in range(len(segment)-1):
        pt1 = segment[i]
```

```
            pt2 = segment[i+1]

        long1,lat1 = pt1
        long2,lat2 = pt2

        angle1,angle2,distance = geod.inv(long1, lat1,
                                          long2, lat2)
        totLength += distance
```

Upon completion, `totLength` will be the total length of the border in meters.

Putting all this together, we end up with a complete Python program to read the `border.shp` shapefile and calculate and display the total length of the common border:

```
# calcBorderLength.py

import os.path
from osgeo import ogr
import pyproj

def getLineSegmentsFromGeometry(geometry):
    segments = []
    if geometry.GetPointCount() > 0:
        segment = []
        for i in range(geometry.GetPointCount()):
            segment.append(geometry.GetPoint_2D(i))
        segments.append(segment)
    for i in range(geometry.GetGeometryCount()):
        subGeometry = geometry.GetGeometryRef(i)
        segments.extend(
            getLineSegmentsFromGeometry(subGeometry))
    return segments

filename = os.path.join("common-border", "border.shp")
shapefile = ogr.Open(filename)
layer = shapefile.GetLayer(0)
feature = layer.GetFeature(0)
geometry = feature.GetGeometryRef()
segments = getLineSegmentsFromGeometry(geometry)

geod = pyproj.Geod(ellps='WGS84')
```

```
totLength = 0.0
for segment in segments:
    for i in range(len(segment)-1):
        pt1 = segment[i]
        pt2 = segment[i+1]

        long1,lat1 = pt1
        long2,lat2 = pt2

        angle1,angle2,distance = geod.inv(long1, lat1,
                                          long2, lat2)
        totLength += distance

    print("Total border length = {:.2f} km".format(totLength/1000))
```

Running this program tells us the total calculated length of the Thai-Myanmar border:

```
% python calcBorderLength.py
Total border length = 1730.55 km
```

In this program, we have assumed that the shapefile is in geographic coordinates using the WGS84 ellipsoid and only contains a single feature. Let's extend our program to deal with any supplied projection and datum and at the same time, process all the features in the shapefile rather than just the first. This will make our program more flexible and allow it to work with any arbitrary shapefile rather than just the common-border shapefile we created earlier.

Let's deal with the projection and datum first. We could change the projection and datum for our shapefile before we process it, just as we did with the LULC and roads shapefiles earlier in this chapter. That would work, but it would require us to create a temporary shapefile just to calculate the length, which isn't very efficient. Instead, let's make use of pyproj directly to reproject the shapefile back into geographic coordinates if necessary. We can do this by querying the shapefile's spatial reference:

```
shapefile = ogr.Open(filename)
layer = shapefile.GetLayer(0)
spatialRef = layer.GetSpatialRef()
if spatialRef == None:
    print("Shapefile has no spatial reference, using WGS84.")
    spatialRef = osr.SpatialReference()
    spatialRef.SetWellKnownGeogCS('WGS84')
```

Once we have the spatial reference, we can see whether the spatial reference is projected and if so, use pyproj to turn the projected coordinates back into lat/long values again, like this:

```
if spatialRef.IsProjected():
    # Convert projected coordinates back to lat/long values.
    srcProj = pyproj.Proj(spatialRef.ExportToProj4())
    dstProj = pyproj.Proj(proj='longlat', ellps='WGS84',
                          datum='WGS84')
    ...
    long,lat = pyproj.transform(srcProj, dstProj, x, y)
```

Using this, we can rewrite our program to accept data using any projection and datum. At the same time, we'll change it to calculate the overall length of every feature in the file rather than just the first, and also to accept the name of the shapefile from the command line. Finally, we'll add some error checking. Let's call our new program calcFeatureLengths.py.

 Remember that you can download a compete copy of this program as part of the example code for this chapter.

We'll start by copying the getLineSegmentsFromGeometry() function we used earlier:

```
import sys
from osgeo import ogr, osr
import pyproj

def getLineSegmentsFromGeometry(geometry):
    segments = []
    if geometry.GetPointCount() > 0:
        segment = []
        for i in range(geometry.GetPointCount()):
            segment.append(geometry.GetPoint_2D(i))
        segments.append(segment)
    for i in range(geometry.GetGeometryCount()):
        subGeometry = geometry.GetGeometryRef(i)
        segments.extend(
            getLineSegmentsFromGeometry(subGeometry))
    return segments
```

Next, we'll get the name of the shapefile to open from the command line:

```
if len(sys.argv) != 2:
    print("Usage: calcFeatureLengths.py <shapefile>")
    sys.exit(1)

filename = sys.argv[1]
```

We'll then open the shapefile and obtain its spatial reference, using the code we wrote earlier:

```
shapefile = ogr.Open(filename)
layer = shapefile.GetLayer(0)
spatialRef = layer.GetSpatialRef()
if spatialRef == None:
    print("Shapefile lacks a spatial reference, using WGS84.")
    spatialRef = osr.SpatialReference()
    spatialRef.SetWellKnownGeogCS('WGS84')
```

We'll then get the source and destination projections, again using the code we wrote earlier. Note that we only need to do this if we're using projected coordinates:

```
if spatialRef.IsProjected():
    srcProj = pyproj.Proj(spatialRef.ExportToProj4())
    dstProj = pyproj.Proj(proj='longlat', ellps='WGS84',
                          datum='WGS84')
```

We are now ready to start processing the shapefile's features:

```
for i in range(layer.GetFeatureCount()):
    feature = layer.GetFeature(i)
```

Now that we have the feature, we can borrow the code we used earlier to calculate the total length of that feature's line segments:

```
geometry = feature.GetGeometryRef()
segments = getLineSegmentsFromGeometry(geometry)

geod = pyproj.Geod(ellps='WGS84')

totLength = 0.0
for segment in segments:
    for j in range(len(segment)-1):
        pt1 = segment[j]
        pt2 = segment[j+1]

        long1,lat1 = pt1
        long2,lat2 = pt2
```

The only difference is that we need to transform the coordinates back to WGS84 if we are using a projected coordinate system:

```
if spatialRef.IsProjected():
    long1,lat1 = pyproj.transform(srcProj,
                                  dstProj,
                                  long1, lat1)
    long2,lat2 = pyproj.transform(srcProj,
                                  dstProj,
                                  long2, lat2)
```

We can then use `pyproj` to calculate the distance between the two points, as we did in our earlier example. This time, though, we'll wrap it in a `try...except` statement so that any failure to calculate the distance won't crash the program:

```
try:
    angle1,angle2,distance = geod.inv(long1, lat1,
                                      long2, lat2)
except ValueError:
    print("Unable to calculate distance from "
          + "{:.4f},{:.4f} to {:.4f},{:.4f}"
            .format(long1, lat1, long2, lat2))
    distance = 0.0

totLength += distance
```

 The `geod.inv()` call can raise a `ValueError` if the two coordinates are in a place where an angle can't be calculated, for example, if the two points are at the poles.

And finally, we can print out the feature's total length, in kilometers:

```
print("Total length of feature {} is {:.2f} km"
      .format(i, totLength/1000))
```

This program can be run over any shapefile, regardless of the projection and datum. For example, you could use it to calculate the border length for every country in the world by running it over the World Borders Dataset:

```
% python calcFeatureLengths.py TM_WORLD_BORDERS-0.3.shp
Total length of feature 0 is 127.28 km
Total length of feature 1 is 7264.69 km
Total length of feature 2 is 2514.76 km
Total length of feature 3 is 968.86 km
Total length of feature 4 is 1158.92 km
Total length of feature 5 is 6549.53 km
...
```

This program is a good example of converting geometry coordinates to distances. Let's now take a look at the inverse calculation: using distances to calculate new geometry coordinates.

# Task – finding a point 132.7 kilometers west of Shoshone, California

Using the CA_Features_XXX.txt file we downloaded earlier, it is possible to find the latitude and longitude of Shoshone, a small town in California west of Las Vegas:

```
f = open("CA_Features_XXXX.txt", "r")
for line in f.readlines():
    chunks = line.rstrip().split("|")
    if chunks[1] == "Shoshone" and \
        chunks[2] == "Populated Place" and \
        chunks[3] == "CA":
        latitude = float(chunks[9])
        longitude = float(chunks[10])
```

Given this coordinate, we can use pyproj to calculate the coordinate of a point a given distance away and at a given angle:

```
geod = pyproj.Geod(ellps="WGS84")
newLong,newLat,invAngle = geod.fwd(latitude, longitude,
                                   angle, distance)
```

For this task, we are given the desired distance and we know that desired point will be "due west" of Shoshone. pyproj uses azimuth angles, which are measured clockwise from the north. Thus, due west would correspond to an angle of 270 degrees.

Putting all this together, we can calculate the coordinates of the desired point:

```
# findShoshone.py

import pyproj

distance = 132.7 * 1000
angle    = 270.0

f = open("CA_Features_XXX.txt", "r")
for line in f.readlines():
    chunks = line.rstrip().split("|")
    if chunks[1] == "Shoshone" and \
        chunks[2] == "Populated Place" and \
```

```
chunks[3] == "CA":
 latitude = float(chunks[9])
 longitude = float(chunks[10])

geod = pyproj.Geod(ellps='WGS84')
newLong,newLat,invAngle = geod.fwd(longitude,
                                   latitude,
                                   angle, distance)

print("Shoshone is at {:.4f},{:.4f}"
      .format(latitude, longitude))
print("The point {:.2f} km west of Shoshone "
      .format(distance/1000.0) +
      "is at {:.4f}, {:.4f}".format(newLat, newLong))
```

```
f.close()
```

Running this program gives us the answer we want:

```
% python findShoshone.py
Shoshone is at 35.9730,-116.2711
The point 132.70 km west of Shoshone is at 35.9640,
-117.7423
```

# Exercises

If you are interested in exploring the techniques used in this chapter further, you might like to challenge yourself with the following tasks:

- Change the bounding box calculation to exclude outlying islands.

**Hint**

You can split each country's MultiPolygon into individual Polygon objects and then check the area of each polygon to exclude those that are smaller than a given total value.

- Use the World Borders Dataset to create a new shapefile, where each country is represented by a single Point geometry containing the geographical center of each country.

> **Hint**
>
> You can start with the country bounding boxes we calculated earlier and then calculate the midpoint using this:
>
> ```
> midLat = (minLat + maxLat) / 2
> midLong = (minLong + maxLong) / 2
> ```
>
> For an extra challenge, you could use Shapely's `centroid()` method to calculate a more accurate representation of each country's center. To do this, you would have to convert the country's outline into a Shapely geometry, calculate the centroid, and then convert the centroid back into an OGR geometry before saving it into the output shapefile.

- Extend the histogram example to only include height values that fall inside a selected country's outline.

> **Hint**
>
> Implementing this in an efficient way can be difficult. A good approach would be to identify the bounding box for each of the polygons that make up the country's outline and then iterate over the DEM coordinates within that bounding box. You could then check to see whether a given coordinate is actually inside the country's outline using `polygon.contains(point)` and only add the height to the histogram if the point is indeed within the country's outline.

- Optimize the example in the identify nearby parks section so that it can work quickly with larger data sets.

> **Hint**
>
> One possibility might be to calculate the rectangular bounding box around each urban area and then expand that bounding box north, south, east, and west by the desired angular distance. You could then quickly exclude all the points which aren't in that bounding box before making the time-consuming call to `polygon.contains(point)`.
>
> Another way of optimizing this program is to exclude urban areas outside of California. To do this, you would have to find a shapefile of US states, download the outline for California, and only include urban areas which lie (fully or partially) inside the state boundary.

- Calculate the total length of the coastline of the United Kingdom.

**Hint**

Remember that a country outline is a MultiPolygon, where each Polygon in the MultiPolygon represents a single island. You will need to extract the exterior ring from each of these individual island polygons and calculate the total length of the line segments within that exterior ring. You can then total the length of each individual island to get the length of the entire country's coastline.

- Design your own reusable library of geospatial functions that build on OGR, GDAL, Shapely, and `pyproj` to perform common operations such as those discussed in this chapter.

**Hint**

Writing your own reusable library modules is a common programming tactic. Think about the various tasks we solved in this chapter and how they can be turned into generic library functions. For example, you might like to write a function named `calcLineStringLength()`, which takes a LineString and returns the total length of the LineString's segments, optionally transforming the LineString's coordinates into lat/long values before calling `geod.inv()`.

You could then write a `calcPolygonOutlineLength()` function, which uses `calcLineStringLength()` to calculate the length of a polygon's outer ring.

# Summary

In this chapter, we looked at various techniques for using OGR, GDAL, Shapely, and `pyproj` within Python programs to solve a range of real-world problems. In doing so, we learned how to calculate the bounding box for a country, how to use Shapely to calculate the common border between two countries, how to analyze the contents of a DEM file, how to change projections and datums, how the `buffer()` function can be used to find points close to a polygon, how to use `pyproj` to calculate the length of a geometry, and how to calculate a point a given distance and bearing from a starting point.

Up to now, we have written programs that work directly with shapefiles and other data sources to load and then process geospatial data. In the next chapter, we will look at ways in which databases can be used to turbo-charge your geospatial development. Rather than having to read spatial data into memory one feature at a time, you can perform spatial queries directly in the database, allowing you to store and work with much more spatial data than would be feasible using the techniques we have covered so far.

# 6

# Spatial Databases

In this chapter, we will look at how you can use a PostGIS database to store and work with spatial data. In particular, we will cover:

- The concept of a spatially enabled database
- Spatial indexes and how they work
- How PostGIS acts as an extension to the PostgreSQL relational database
- How to install PostgreSQL, PostGIS, and the `psycopg2` Python database adapter onto your computer
- How to set up and configure a spatial database using PostGIS
- How to use the `psycopg2` database adapter to access a spatial database from your Python code
- How to create, import, and query against spatial data using Python
- Recommended best practices for storing spatial data in a database

This chapter is intended to be an introduction to using databases in a geospatial application. *Chapter 8, Working with Spatial Data,* will build on this to perform powerful spatial queries not possible using shapefiles and other geospatial data files.

## Spatially-enabled databases

In a sense, almost any database can be used to store geospatial data: simply convert a geometry to WKT format and store the results in a `text` column. But while this would allow you to store geospatial data in a database, it wouldn't let you query it in any useful way. All you could do is retrieve the raw WKT text and convert it back to a geometry object, one record at a time.

A spatially-enabled database, on the other hand, is aware of the notion of *space*, and allows you to work with spatial objects and concepts directly. In particular, a spatially-enabled database allows you to:

- Store **spatial data types** (points, lines, polygons, and so on) directly in the database in the form of a `geometry` column

- Perform **spatial queries** on your data, for example, `select all landmarks within 10 km of the city named "San Francisco"`

- Perform **spatial joins** on your data, for example, `select all cities and their associated countries by joining cities and countries on (city inside country)`

- Create new spatial objects using various **spatial functions**, for example, `set "danger_zone" to the intersection of the "flooded_area" and "urban_area" polygons`

As you can imagine, a spatially-enabled database is an extremely powerful tool for working with geospatial data. By using **spatial indexes** and other optimizations, spatial databases can quickly perform these types of operations and can scale to support vast amounts of data simply not feasible using other data-storage schemes.

# Spatial indexes

One of the defining characteristics of a spatial database is the ability to create and use "spatial" indexes to speed up geometry-based searches. These indexes are used to perform spatial operations, such as identifying all the features that lie within a given bounding box, identifying all the features within a certain distance of a given point, or identifying all the features that intersect with a given polygon.

Spatial indexes are one of the most powerful features of spatial databases, and it is worth spending a moment becoming familiar with how they work. Spatial indexes don't store the geometry directly; instead, they calculate the **bounding box** for each geometry and then index the geometries based on their bounding boxes. This allows the database to quickly search through the geometries based on their position in space:

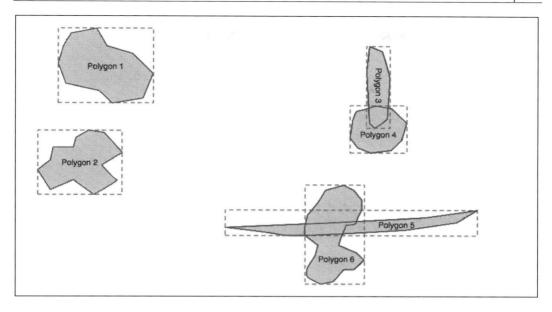

The bounding boxes are grouped into a nested hierarchy based on how close together they are, as shown in the following illustration:

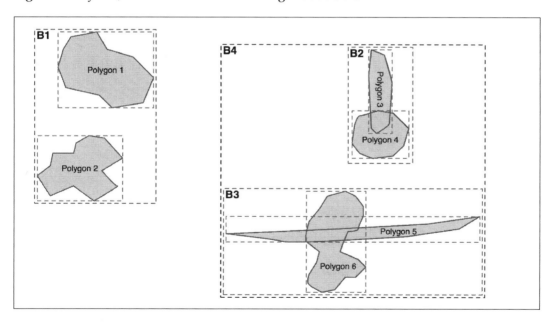

The hierarchy of nested bounding boxes is then represented using a tree-like data structure, as follows:

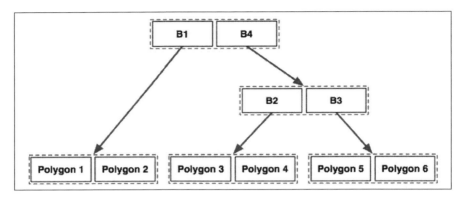

The computer can quickly scan through this tree to find a particular geometry or compare the positions or sizes of the various geometries. For example, the geometry containing the point represented by the X in the preceding diagram can be quickly found by traversing the tree and comparing the bounding boxes at each level. The spatial index will be searched in the following manner:

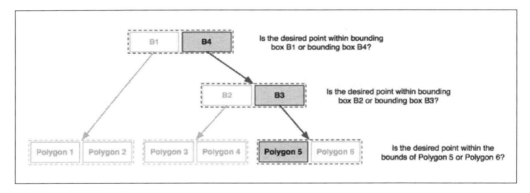

Using the spatial index, it only took three comparisons to find the desired polygon.

Because of their hierarchical nature, spatial indexes scale extremely well and can search through many tens of thousands of features using only a handful of bounding-box comparisons. And, because every geometry is reduced to a simple bounding box, spatial indexes can support any type of geometry, not just polygons.

Spatial indexes are not limited to only searching for enclosed coordinates; they can be used for all sorts of spatial comparisons and for spatial joins. We will be working with spatial indexes extensively throughout this book.

# Introducing PostGIS

In this book, we will be working with PostGIS. PostGIS is one of the most popular and powerful geospatial databases and has the bonus of being open source and freely available. PostGIS itself is actually an extension to the PostgreSQL relational database system—to use PostGIS from your Python programs, you first have to install and set up PostgreSQL, then install the PostGIS extension, and then finally install the `psycopg2` database adapter for Python. The following illustration shows how all these pieces fit together:

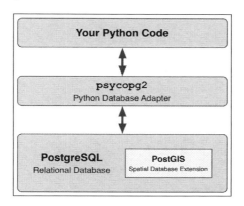

 Note that PostgreSQL is often referred to as **Postgres**. We will regularly use this more colloquial name throughout this book.

PostGIS allows you to store and query against various types of spatial data, including points, lines, polygons, and geometry collections. PostGIS provides two different types of spatial fields that can be used to store spatial data:

- The **geometry** field holds spatial data that is assumed to be in a projected coordinate system. All calculations and queries for geometry fields assume that the spatial data has been projected onto a flat Cartesian plane. This makes the calculations much simpler, but it will only work reliably if the spatial data is in a projected coordinate system.

- The **geography** field holds spatial data that uses geodetic (unprojected) coordinates. Calculations and queries against geography fields assume that the data is in angular units (that is, latitude and longitude values), using sophisticated mathematics to calculate lengths and areas using a spheroid model of the earth.

Because the mathematics involved is much more complicated, not all spatial functions are available for geography fields, and the operations often take a lot longer. However, geography fields are much easier to use if your spatial data uses an unprojected coordinate system such as WGS84.

Let's go ahead an install PostGIS onto your computer and then look at how we can use PostGIS to create and work with a spatial database using Python.

# Installing PostgreSQL

PostgreSQL is an extremely powerful open source relational database system. The main web site for Postgres can be found at `http://postgresql.org`. How you install the Postgres database will depend on which operating system your computer is running:

- For Linux, follow the instructions on the PostgreSQL download page (`http://postgresql.org/download`) to install Postgres onto your computer. Choose the appropriate link for your Linux distribution and you will be presented with the corresponding installation instructions.

- For Mac OS X, you can download an installer for Postgres from the KyngChaos web site (`http://www.kyngchaos.com/software/postgres`). Make sure you don't download the client-only version, as you'll need the Postgres server. Once it has been downloaded, open the disk image and double click on the `PostgreSQL.pkg` package file to install Postgres into your computer.

- For Microsoft Windows, you can download an installer for Postgres from `http://enterprisedb.com/products-services-training/pgdownload`. Select the appropriate installer for your version of Windows (32 or 64 bit), download the installer file, then simply double click on the installer and follow the instructions.

Once you have installed Postgres, you can check whether it is running by typing `psql` into a terminal or command-line window and pressing the *Return* key. All going well, you should see the Postgres command line:

```
psql (9.4.4)
Type "help" for help.


postgres=#
```

If the `psql` command-line client can't be found, you may have to add it to your path. For example, on a Mac, you can edit your `.bash_profile` file and add the following:

```
export PATH="$PATH:/usr/local/pgsql/bin"
```

If the `psql` command complains about user authentication, you may need to identify the user account to use when connecting to Postgres, for example:

```
% psql -U postgres
```

Many Postgres installations have a `postgres` user, which you need to select with the `-U` command-line option when accessing the database. Alternatively, you may need to use `sudo` to run `psql` as root, or open a command prompt as an administrator if you are running Microsoft Windows.

To exit the Postgres command-line client, type `\q` and press *Return*.

# Installing PostGIS

Our next task is to install the PostGIS spatial extension for Postgres. The main web site for PostGIS can be found at `http://postgis.net`. Once again, how you install PostGIS depends on which operating system you are running:

- For Linux-based computers, follow the instructions on the PostGIS installation page (`http://postgis.net/install`)

- For Mac OS X, you should download and run the PostGIS installer from the KyngChaos web site (`http://kyngchaos.com/software/postgres`)

Note that this PostGIS installer requires the **GDAL Complete** package, which you should have already installed while working through *Chapter 2, GIS*.

- For Microsoft Windows, you can download an installer from `http://download.osgeo.org/postgis/windows`

To check whether PostGIS has been successfully installed, try typing the following commands into your terminal window:

```
% createdb test_database
% psql -d test_database -c "CREATE EXTENSION postgis;"
% dropdb test_database
```

Don't forget to add the `-U postgres` option, or use `sudo` for each of these commands, if you need to run Postgres under a different user account.

The first command creates a new database, the second one enables the PostGIS extension for that database, and the third command deletes the database again. If this sequence of commands runs without any errors, then your PostGIS installation (and Postgres itself) is set up and running correctly.

# Installing psycopg2

`psycopg2` is the Python database adapter for Postgres. This is the Python library you use to access Postgres from within your Python programs. The main web site for `psycopg2` can be found at `http://initd.org/psycopg`.

As usual, how you install `psycopg2` will vary depending on which operating system you are using:

- For Linux, you will need to install `psycopg2` from source. For instructions on how to do this, refer to `http://initd.org/psycopg/docs/install.html`.

- For a Mac OS X machine, you can use pip, the Python package manager, to install `psycopg2` from the command line:

  ```
  pip install psycopg2
  ```

  Note that you will need to have the Xcode command-line tools installed so that `psycopg2` can compile.

- For MS Windows, you can download a double-clickable installer for `psycopg2` from `http://www.stickpeople.com/projects/python/win-psycopg`.

To check whether your installation worked, start up your Python interpreter and type the following:

```
>>> import psycopg2
>>>
```

If `psycopg2` was installed correctly, you should see the Python interpreter prompt reappear without any error messages, as shown in this example. If an error message does appear, you may need to follow the troubleshooting instructions on the `psycopg2` web site.

# Setting up a database

Now that we have installed the necessary software, let's see how we can use PostGIS to create and set up a spatial database. We will start by creating a Postgres user account, creating a database, and setting up the user to access that database, and then we will enable the PostGIS spatial extension for our database.

## Creating a Postgres user account

Our first task is to set up a Postgres user, who will own the database we create. While you might have a user account on your computer that you use for logging in and out, the PostgreSQL user is completely separate from this account and is used only within Postgres. You can set up a PostgreSQL user with the same name as your computer username, or you can give it a different name if you prefer.

 Note that a user is sometimes referred to as a "role" in the Postgres manual.

To create a new PostgreSQL user, type the following command:

```
% createuser -P <username>
```

 Obviously, replace <username> with whatever name you want to use for your new user. You may also need to add the -U postgres option or use sudo for these commands if you need to run Postgres under a different user account.

The -P command-line option tells Postgres that you want to enter a password for this new user. Don't forget the password that you enter, as you will need it when you try to access your database.

## Creating a database

You next need to create the database you want to use for storing your spatial data. Do this using the createdb command:

```
% createdb <dbname>
```

 Make sure you replace <dbname> with the name of the database you wish to create. Once again, add -U postgres or use sudo if required.

# Allowing the user to access the database

To let the user access this new database, type the following command into a terminal window, adding `-U postgres` if necessary:

```
% psql -c "GRANT ALL PRIVILEGES ON DATABASE <dbname> TO <user>;"
```

> Obviously, replace <dbname> with the name of your database and <user> with the name of your new user. Also, remember to add `-U postgres` or use `sudo` if you need to.

# Spatially enable the database

So far, we have created a Postgres database and an associated user. Our database is just a regular database; to turn it into a spatial database, we have to enable the PostGIS extension for it. To do this, type the following into a terminal window, replacing <dbname> with the name of your new database:

```
% psql -d <dbname> -c "CREATE EXTENSION postgis;"
```

# Using PostGIS

Now that we have a spatial database, let's see how to access it from Python. Using `psycopg2` to access a spatial database from Python is quite straightforward. For example, the following code shows how to connect to the database and issue a simple query:

```python
import psycopg2

connection = psycopg2.connect(database="...", user="...",
                              password="...")
cursor = connection.cursor()
cursor.execute("SELECT id,name FROM cities WHERE pop>100000")
for row in cursor:
    print(row[0],row[1])
```

The `psycopg2.connect()` statement opens up a connection to the database using the database name, user, and password you set up when you created and configured the database. Once you have a database connection, you then create a `Cursor` object against which you can execute queries. You can then retrieve the matching data, as shown in this example.

Let's use `psycopg2` to store the World Borders Dataset into a spatial database table and then perform some simple queries against that data. Place a copy of the World Borders Dataset into a suitable directory, and create a new Python program called `postgis_test.py` inside the same directory. Enter the following into your program:

```
import psycopg2
from osgeo import ogr

connection = psycopg2.connect(database="<dbname>", user="<user>",
                               password="<password>")
cursor = connection.cursor()
```

Don't forget to replace the `<dbname>`, `<user>`, and `<password>` values with the name of the database, the user account, and the password you set up earlier.

So far, we have simply opened a connection to the database. Let's create a table to hold the contents of the World Borders Dataset. To do this, add the following to the end of your program:

```
cursor.execute("DROP TABLE IF EXISTS borders")
cursor.execute("CREATE TABLE borders (" +
               "id SERIAL PRIMARY KEY," +
               "name VARCHAR NOT NULL," +
               "iso_code VARCHAR NOT NULL," +
               "outline GEOGRAPHY)")
cursor.execute("CREATE INDEX border_index ON borders " +
               "USING GIST(outline)")
connection.commit()
```

As you can see, we delete the database table if it exists already so that we can rerun our program without it failing. We then create a new table named `borders` with four fields: an `id`, a `name`, and an `iso_code`, all of which are standard database fields, and a spatial geography field named `outline`. Because we're using a geography field, we can use this field to store spatial data that uses unprojected lat/long coordinates.

The third statement creates a spatial index on the outline. In PostGIS, we use the `GIST` index type to define a spatial index.

Finally, because Postgres is a transactional database, we have to commit the changes we have made using the `connection.commit()` statement.

Now that we've defined our database table, let's add some data into it. Using the techniques we learned earlier, we'll read through the contents of the World Borders Dataset shapefile. Here is the relevant code:

```
shapefile = ogr.Open("TM_WORLD_BORDERS-0.3/TM_WORLD_BORDERS-0.3.shp")
layer = shapefile.GetLayer(0)

for i in range(layer.GetFeatureCount()):
    feature  = layer.GetFeature(i)
    name     = feature.GetField("NAME")
    iso_code = feature.GetField("ISO3")
    geometry = feature.GetGeometryRef()
    wkt      = geometry.ExportToWkt()
```

All of this should be quite straightforward. Our next task is to store this information into the database. To do this, we use the INSERT command. Add the following code to your program, inside the for loop:

```
cursor.execute("INSERT INTO borders (name, iso_code, outline) " +
               "VALUES (%s, %s, ST_GeogFromText(%s))",
               (name, iso_code, wkt))
```

Notice that psycopg2 automatically converts standard Python data types such as numbers, strings, and date/time values to the appropriate format for inserting into the database. Following the Python DB-API standard, %s is used as a placeholder to represent a value, and that value is taken from the list supplied as the second parameter to the execute() function. In other words, the first %s is replaced with the value of the name variable, the second with the value of the iso_code variable, and so on.

Because psycopg2 doesn't know about geometry data values, we have to convert the geometry into a WKT-format string and then use the ST_GeogFromText() function to convert that string back into a PostGIS geography object.

Now that we have imported all the data, we need to commit the changes we have made to the database. To do this, add the following statement to the end of your program (outside the for loop):

```
connection.commit()
```

If you run this program, it will take about 30 seconds to import all the data into the database, but nothing else will happen. To prove that it worked, let's perform a simple spatial query against the imported data—in this case, we want to find all countries that are within 500 kilometers of Zurich, in Switzerland. Let's start by defining the latitude and longitude for Zurich and the desired search radius in meters. Add the following to the end of your program:

```
start_long = 8.542
start_lat  = 47.377
radius     = 500000
```

We can now perform our spatial query using the ST_DWithin() query function, like this:

```
cursor.execute("SELECT name FROM borders WHERE ST_DWithin(" +
               "ST_MakePoint(%s, %s), outline, %s)",
               (start_long, start_lat, radius))
for row in cursor:
    print(row[0])
```

The ST_DWithin() function finds all records within the borders table that have an outline within radius meters of the given lat/long value. Notice that we use the ST_MakePoint() function to convert the latitude and longitude value to a Point geometry, allowing us to compare the outline against the given point.

Running this program will import all the data and show us the list of countries that are within 500 kilometers of Zurich:

```
Luxembourg
Monaco
San Marino
Austria
Czech Republic
France
Germany
Croatia
Italy
Liechtenstein
Belgium
Netherlands
Slovenia
Switzerland
```

While there is a lot more we could do, this program should show you how to use PostGIS to create a spatial database, insert data into it, and query against that data, all done using Python code.

# PostGIS documentation

Because PostGIS is an extension to PostgreSQL and you use `psycopg2` to access it, there are three separate sets of documentation you will need to refer to:

- The PostgreSQL manual: `http://postgresql.org/docs`

- The PostGIS manual: `http://postgis.refractions.net/docs`

- The `psycopg2` documentation: `http://initd.org/psycopg/docs`

Of these, the PostGIS manual is probably going to be the most useful, and you will also need to refer to the `psycopg2` documentation to find out the details of using PostGIS from Python. You will probably also need to refer to the PostgreSQL manual to learn the non-spatial aspects of using PostGIS, though be aware that this manual is *huge* and extremely complex, reflecting the complexity of PostgreSQL itself.

# Advanced PostGIS features

PostGIS supports a number of advanced features which you may find useful:

- On-the-fly transformations of geometries from one spatial reference to another.

- The ability to edit geometries by adding, changing, and removing points and by rotating, scaling, and shifting entire geometries.

- The ability to read and write geometries in GeoJSON, GML, KML, and SVG formats, in addition to WKT and WKB.

- A complete range of bounding-box comparisons, including `A overlaps B`, `A contains B`, and `A is to the left of B`. These comparison operators make use of spatial indexes to identify matching features extremely quickly.

- Proper spatial comparisons between geometries, including intersection, containment, crossing, equality, overlap, touching, and so on. These comparisons are done using the true geometry rather than just their bounding boxes.

- Spatial functions to calculate information such as the area, centroid, closest point, distance, length, perimeter, shortest connecting line, and so on. These functions take into account the geometry's spatial reference, if known.

PostGIS has a well-deserved reputation for being a geospatial powerhouse. While it is not the only freely available spatial database, it is easily the most powerful and useful, and we will be using it extensively throughout this book.

# Recommended best practices

In this section, we will look at a number of practical things you can do to ensure that your geospatial databases work as efficiently and effectively as possible.

## Best practice: use the database to keep track of spatial references

As we've seen in earlier chapters, different sets of geospatial data use different coordinate systems, datums, and projections. Consider, for example, the following two geometry objects:

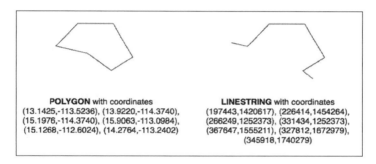

**POLYGON** with coordinates
(13.1425,-113.5236), (13.9220,-114.3740),
(15.1976,-114.3740), (15.9063,-113.0984),
(15.1268,-112.6024), (14.2764,-113.2402)

**LINESTRING** with coordinates
(197443,1420617), (226414,1454264),
(266249,1252373), (331434,1252373),
(367647,1555211), (327812,1672979),
(345918,1740279)

The geometries are represented as a series of coordinates, which are nothing more than numbers. By themselves, these numbers aren't particularly useful—you need to position these coordinates onto the earth's surface by identifying the **spatial reference** (coordinate system, datum, and projection) used by the geometry. In this case, the `Polygon` is using unprojected lat/long coordinates in the WGS84 datum, while the `LineString` is using coordinates defined in meters using the UTM zone 12N projection. Once you know the spatial reference, you can place the two geometries onto the earth's surface. This reveals that the two geometries actually overlap, even though the numbers they use are completely different:

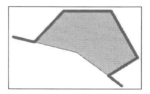

In all but the simplest databases, it is recommended that you store the spatial reference for each feature directly in the database itself. This makes it easy to keep track of which spatial reference is used by each feature. It also allows the queries and database commands you write to be aware of the spatial reference and enables you to transform geometries from one spatial reference to another as necessary in your spatial queries.

Spatial references are generally referred to using a simple integer value called a **spatial reference identifier (SRID)**. While you could choose arbitrary SRID values to represent various spatial references, it is strongly recommended that you use the **European Petroleum Survey Group (EPSG)** numbers as standard SRID values. Using this internationally recognized standard makes your data interchangeable with other databases and allows tools such as OGR and Mapnik to identify the spatial reference used by your data.

To learn more about EPSG numbers, and SRID values in general, refer to `http://epsg-registry.org`.

PostGIS automatically creates a table named `spatial_ref_sys` to hold the available set of SRID values. This table comes preloaded with a list of over 3,000 commonly used spatial references, all identified by EPSG number. Because the SRID value is the primary key for this table, tools that access the database can refer to this table to perform on-the-fly coordinate transformations using the `PROJ.4` library.

When you create a table, you can specify both the type of geometry (or geography) data to store and the SRID value to use for this data. Here's an example:

```
CREATE TABLE test (outline GEOMETRY(LINESTRING, 2193))
```

When defined in this way, the table will only accept geometries of the given type and with the given spatial reference.

When inserting a record into the table, you can also specify the SRID, like this:

```
INSERT INTO test (outline) VALUES (ST_GeometryFromText(wkt, 2193))
```

While the SRID value is optional, you should use this wherever possible to tell the database which spatial reference your geometry is using. In fact, PostGIS *requires* you to use the correct SRID value if a column has been set up to use a particular SRID. This prevents you from accidentally mixing spatial references within a table.

# Best practice: use the appropriate spatial reference for your data

Whenever you import spatial data into your database, it will be in a particular spatial reference. This doesn't mean, though, that it has to *stay* in that spatial reference. In many cases, it will be more efficient and accurate to transform your data into the most appropriate spatial reference for your particular needs. Of course, what you consider appropriate depends on what you want to achieve.

When you use the GEOMETRY field type, PostGIS assumes that your coordinates are projected onto a Cartesian plane. If you use this field type to store unprojected coordinates (latitude and longitude values) in the database, you will be limited in what you can do. Certainly, you can use unprojected geographic coordinates in a database to compare two features (for example, to see whether one feature intersects with another), and you will be able to store and retrieve geospatial data quickly. However, any calculation that involves area or distance will be all but meaningless.

Consider, for example, what would happen if you asked PostGIS to calculate the length of a LineString geometry stored in a GEOMETRY field:

```
# SELECT ST_Length(geom) FROM roads WHERE id=9513;
 ST_Length(geom)
-----------------
0.364491142657260
```

This "length" value is in decimal degrees, which isn't very useful. If you do need to perform length and area calculations on your geospatial data (and it is likely that you will need to do this at some stage), you have three options:

- Use a GEOGRAPHY field to store the data
- Transform the features into projected coordinates before performing the length or distance calculation
- Store your geometries in projected coordinates from the outset

Let's consider each of these options in more detail.

# Option 1: Using GEOGRAPHY fields

While the GEOGRAPHY field type is extremely useful and allows you to work directly with unprojected coordinates, it does have some serious disadvantages. In particular:

- Performing calculations on unprojected coordinates takes approximately an order of magnitude longer than performing the same calculations using projected (Cartesian) coordinates

- The GEOGRAPHY type only supports lat/long values on the WGS84 datum (SRID 4326)

- Many of the functions available for projected coordinates are not yet supported by the GEOGRAPHY type

Despite this, using GEOGRAPHY fields is an option you may want to consider.

# Option 2: Transforming features as required

Another possibility is to store your data in unprojected lat/long coordinates and transform the coordinates into a projected coordinate system before you calculate the distance or area. While this will work, and will give you accurate results, you should beware of doing this because you may well forget to transform the data to a projected coordinate system before making the calculation. In addition, performing on-the-fly transformations of large numbers of geometries is very time consuming. Despite these problems, there are situations where storing unprojected coordinates makes sense. We will look at this shortly.

# Option 3: Transforming features from the outset

Because transforming features from one spatial reference to another is rather time consuming, it often makes sense to do this once, at the time you import your data, and store it in the database already converted to a projected coordinate system.

By doing this, you will be able to perform your desired spatial calculations quickly and accurately. However, there are situations where this is not the best option, as we will see in the next section.

# When to use unprojected coordinates

As we saw in *Chapter 2, GIS*, projecting features from the three-dimensional surface of the earth onto a two-dimensional Cartesian plane can never be done perfectly. It is a mathematical truism that there will always be errors in any projection.

Different map projections are generally chosen to preserve values such as distance or area for a particular portion of the earth's surface. For example, the Mercator projection is accurate at the tropics but distorts features closer to the poles.

Because of this inevitable distortion, projected coordinates work best when your geospatial data only covers a part of the earth's surface. If you are only dealing with data for Austria, then a projected coordinate system will work very well indeed. But if your data includes features in both Austria and Australia, then using the same projected coordinates for both sets of features will once again produce inaccurate results.

For this reason, it is generally best to use a projected coordinate system for data that covers only a part of the earth's surface, but unprojected coordinates will work best if you need to store data covering large parts of the earth.

Of course, using unprojected coordinates leads to problems of its own, as we discussed earlier. This is why it is recommended that you use the *appropriate* spatial reference for your particular needs; what is appropriate for you depends on what data you need to store and how you intend to use it.

> The best way to find out what is appropriate would be to experiment: try importing your data in both spatial references, and write some test programs to work with the imported data. That will tell you which is the faster and easier spatial reference to work with, rather than having to guess.

# Best practice: avoid on-the-fly transformations within a query

Imagine that you have a `cities` table with a `geom` column containing `POLYGON` geometries in UTM 12N projection (EPSG number 32612). Being a competent geospatial developer, you have set up a spatial index on this column.

Now, imagine that you have a variable named `pt` that holds a `POINT` geometry in unprojected WGS84 coordinates (EPSG number 4326). You might want to find the city that contains this point, so you issue the following reasonable-looking query:

```
SELECT * FROM cities WHERE
    ST_Contains(ST_Transform(geom, 4326), pt);
```

This will give you the right answer, but it will take an extremely long time. Why? Because the `ST_Transform(geom, 4326)` expression is converting *every* polygon geometry in the table from UTM 12N to long/lat WGS84 coordinates before the database can check to see whether the point is inside the geometry. The spatial index is completely ignored, as it is in the wrong coordinate system.

Compare this with the following query:

```
SELECT * FROM cities WHERE
    Contains(geom, Transform(pt, 32612));
```

A very minor change, but a dramatically different result. Instead of taking hours, the answer should come back almost immediately. Can you see why? Since the `pt` variable does not change from one record to the next, the `ST_Transform(pt, 32612)` expression is being called just once, and the `ST_Contains()` call can then make use of your spatial index to quickly find the matching city.

The lesson here is simple: be aware of what you are asking the database to do, and make sure you structure your queries to avoid on-the-fly transformations of large numbers of geometries.

# Best practice: don't create geometries within a query

While we are discussing database queries that can cause the database to perform a huge amount of work, consider the following (where `poly` is a polygon):

```
SELECT * FROM cities WHERE
    NOT ST_IsEmpty(ST_Intersection(outline, poly));
```

In a sense, this is perfectly reasonable: identify all cities that have a non-empty intersection between the city's outline and the given polygon. And the database will indeed be able to answer this query—it will just take an *extremely* long time to do so. Hopefully, you can see why: the `ST_Intersection()` function creates a new geometry out of two existing geometries. This means that for every row in the database table, a new geometry is created and is then passed to `ST_IsEmpty()`. As you can imagine, these types of operations are extremely inefficient. To avoid creating a new geometry each time, you can rephrase your query like this:

```
SELECT * FROM cities WHERE ST_Intersects(outline, poly);
```

While this example may seem obvious, there are many cases where spatial developers have forgotten this rule and have wondered why their queries were taking so long to complete. A common example is using the ST_Buffer() function to see whether a point is within a given distance of a polygon, like this:

```
SELECT * FROM cities WHERE
    ST_Contains(ST_Buffer(outline, 100), pt);
```

Once again, this query will work, but it will be painfully slow. A much better approach would be to use the ST_DWithin() function:

```
SELECT * FROM cities WHERE ST_DWithin(outline, pt, 100);
```

As a general rule, remember that you *never* want to call any function that returns a GEOMETRY or GEOGRAPHY object within the WHERE portion of a SELECT statement.

# Best practice: use spatial indexes appropriately

Just like ordinary database indexes can make an immense difference to the speed and efficiency of your database, spatial indexes are also an extremely powerful tool for speeding up your database queries. Like all powerful tools, though, they have their limits:

- If you don't explicitly define a spatial index, the database can't use it. Conversely, if you have too many spatial indexes, the database will slow down because each index needs to be updated every time a record is added, updated, or deleted. Thus, it is crucial that you define the *right* set of spatial indexes: index the information you are going to search on, and nothing more.

- Because spatial indexes work on the geometries' bounding boxes, they can only tell you which bounding boxes actually overlap or intersect; they can't tell you whether the underlying points, lines, or polygons have this relationship. Thus, they are really only the first step in searching for the information you want. Once the possible matches have been found, the database still needs to check the geometries one at a time.

- Spatial indexes are most efficient when dealing with lots of relatively small geometries. If you have large polygons consisting of many thousands of vertices, a polygon's bounding box is going to be so large that it will intersect with lots of other geometries, and the database will have to revert to doing full polygon calculations rather than just using the bounding box. If your geometries are huge, these calculations can be very slow indeed — the entire polygon will have to be loaded into memory and processed one vertex at a time. If possible, it is generally better to split large geometries (and in particular, large Polygons and MultiPolygons) into smaller pieces so that the spatial index can work with them more efficiently.

# Best practice: know the limits of your database's query optimizer

When you send a query to the database, it automatically attempts to **optimize** the query to avoid unnecessary calculations and make use of any available indexes. For example, if you issued the following (non-spatial) query, the database would know that `Concat("John ","Doe")` yields a constant, and so would only calculate it once before issuing the query. It would also look for a database index on the `name` column and use it to speed up the operation.

```
SELECT * FROM people WHERE name=Concat("John ","Doe");
```

This type of query optimization is very powerful, and the logic behind it is extremely complex. In a similar way, spatial databases have a **spatial query optimizer** that looks for ways to precalculate values and make use of spatial indexes to speed up the query. For example, consider this spatial query from the previous section:

```
select * from cities where ST_DWithin(outline, pt, 12.5);
```

In this case, the PostGIS function `ST_DWithin()` is given one geometry taken from a table (`outline`) and a second geometry that is specified as a fixed value (`pt`), along with a desired distance (12.5 "units", whatever that means in the geometry's spatial reference). The query optimizer knows how to handle this efficiently, by first precalculating the bounding box for the fixed geometry plus the desired distance (`pt ±12.5`) and then using a spatial index to quickly identify the records that may have their `outline` geometry within that extended bounding box.

While there are times when the database's query optimizer seems to be capable of magic, there are many other times when it is incredibly stupid. Part of the art of being a good database developer is to have a keen sense of how your database's query optimizer works, when it doesn't, and what to do about it.

The PostGIS query optimizer looks at both the query itself and at the contents of the database to see how the query can be optimized. In order to work well, the PostGIS query optimizer needs to have up-to-date statistics on the databases' contents. It then uses a sophisticated *genetic algorithm* to determine the most effective way to run a particular query.

Because of this approach, you need to regularly run the VACUUM ANALYZE command, which gathers statistics on the database so that the query optimizer can work as effectively as possible. If you don't run VACUUM ANALYZE, the optimizer simply won't be able to work.

Here is how you can run this command from Python:

```
import psycopg2

connection = psycopg2.connect("dbname=... user=...")
cursor = connection.cursor()

old_level = connection.isolation_level
connection.set_isolation_level(0)
cursor.execute("VACUUM ANALYZE")
connection.set_isolation_level(old_level)
```

Don't worry about the isolation_level logic here; it just allows you to run the VACUUM ANALYZE command from Python using the transaction-based psycopg2 adapter.

 It is possible to set up an "autovacuum daemon" that runs automatically after a given period of time or after a table's contents have changed enough to warrant another vacuum. Setting up an autovacuum daemon is beyond the scope of this book.

Once you have run the VACUUM ANALYZE command, the query optimizer will be able to start optimizing your queries. To see how the query optimizer works, you can use the EXPLAIN SELECT command. For example:

```
psql> EXPLAIN SELECT * FROM cities
        WHERE ST_Contains(geom,pt);


                QUERY PLAN
```

```
----------------------------------------------------------
 Seq Scan on cities   (cost=0.00..7.51 rows=1 width=2619)
    Filter: ((geom &&
'0101000000000000000000000000000000000000000'::geometry) AND _st_
contains(geom, '0101000000000000000000000000000000000000000'::geometry))
(2 rows)
```

Don't worry about the `Seq Scan` part; there are only a few records in this table, so PostGIS knows that it can scan the entire table faster than it can read through an index. When the database gets bigger, it will automatically start using the index to quickly identify the desired records.

The `cost=` part is an indication of how much this query will cost, measured in arbitrary units that by default are relative to how long it takes to read a page of data from disk. The two numbers represent the start up cost (how long it takes before the first row can be processed) and the estimated total cost (how long it would take to process every record in the table). Since reading a page of data from disk is quite fast, a total cost of 7.51 is very quick indeed.

The most interesting part of this explanation is the `Filter`. Let's take a closer look at what the `EXPLAIN SELECT` command tells us about how PostGIS will filter this query. Consider the first part:

```
(geom && '0101000000000000000000000000000000000000000'::geometry)
```

This makes use of the `&&` operator, which searches for matching records using the bounding box defined in the spatial index. Now consider the second part of the filter condition:

```
_st_contains(geom,
'0101000000000000000000000000000000000000000'::geometry)
```

This uses the `ST_Contains()` function to identify the exact geometries that contain the desired point. This two-step process (first filtering by bounding box, then by the geometry itself) allows the database to use the spatial index to identify records based on their bounding boxes and then check the potential matches by doing an exact scan on the geometry itself. This is extremely efficient, and as you can see, PostGIS does this for us automatically, resulting in a quick but also accurate search for geometries that contain a given point.

# Summary

In this chapter, we took an in-depth look at the concept of storing spatial data in a database, using the freely available PostGIS database toolkit. We learned that spatial databases differ from ordinary relational databases in that they directly support spatial data types and use spatial indexes to perform queries and joins on spatial data. We saw that spatial indexes make use of the geometries' bounding boxes to quickly compare and find geometries based on their position in space.

We then looked at the PostGIS spatial extension to PostgreSQL and how the psycopg2 library can be used to access PostGIS spatial databases using Python. After installing the necessary software, we configured a spatial database and used psycopg2 to create the necessary database tables, import a set of spatial data, and perform useful queries against that data.

Next, we looked at some of the recommended best practices for working with spatial databases. We saw that it is important to store a spatial reference ID along with the data and looked at how you can select an appropriate spatial reference for your application.

We then looked at some of the mistakes that can kill the performance of a geospatial database, including creating geometries and performing transformations on the fly and using spatial indexes inappropriately so that the database cannot use them.

Finally, we learned about the PostGIS query optimizer and how we can use the EXPLAIN command to see exactly how PostGIS will execute a spatial query.

In the next chapter, we will learn how to use the Mapnik library to convert raw geospatial data into good-looking map images.

# 7
# Using Python and Mapnik to Generate Maps

Because geospatial data is almost impossible to understand until it is displayed, the use of maps to visually represent spatial data is an extremely important topic. In this chapter, we will look at **Mapnik**, a powerful Python library for transforming geospatial data into great-looking maps. In particular, we will look at:

- The underlying concepts Mapnik uses to generate maps
- An example program using Mapnik to generate a straightforward map
- Various data sources that you can use to add geospatial data to your map
- How to use rules, filters, and styles to control the map-generation process
- The "symbolizers" you can use to add points, lines, polygons, textual labels, and raster images to your maps
- How maps and map layers work together to create a map
- Ways of rendering a map into an image file

# Introducing Mapnik

We first looked at Mapnik in *Chapter 3, Python Libraries for Geospatial Development*. If you haven't already done so, please go back to the *Mapnik* section of that chapter and follow the instructions for installing it onto your computer.

Mapnik is a complex library with many different parts, and it is easy to get confused by the various names and concepts. Let's start our exploration of Mapnik by looking at a simple map:

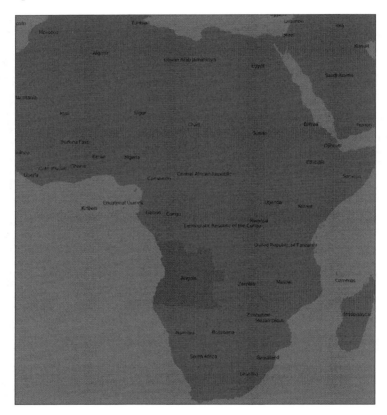

One thing that may not be immediately obvious is that the various elements within the map are *layered*, like this:

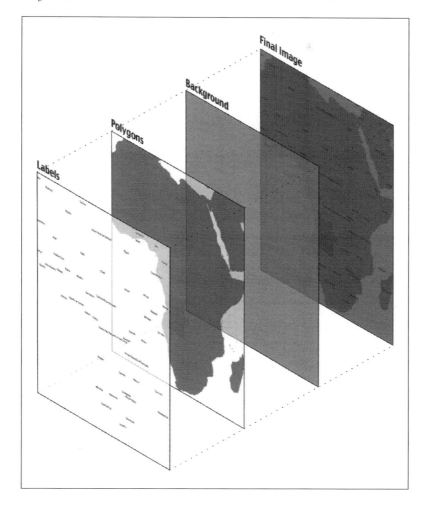

To generate this map, you have to tell Mapnik to initially draw the background, then the polygons, and finally the labels. This ensures that the polygons sit on top of the background and the labels appear in front of both the polygons and the background.

 Strictly speaking, the background isn't a layer. It's simply a color or image that Mapnik draws onto the map before it starts drawing the first layer.

Mapnik allows you to control the order in which the map elements are drawn through the use of **Layer** objects. A simple map may consist of just one layer, but most maps have multiple layers. The layers are drawn in a strict back-to-front order, so the first layer you define will appear behind all the others. In the example map we just looked at, the **Polygons** layer would be defined first, followed by the **Labels** layer. This ensures that the labels appear in front of the polygons. This layering approach is called the **painter's algorithm** because of its similarity to placing layers of paint onto an artist's canvas.

Each Layer has its own **data source**, which tells Mapnik where to load the data from. A data source can refer to a shapefile, a spatial database, a raster image file, or any number of other geospatial data sources. In most cases, setting up a Layer's data source is very easy.

Within each Layer, the visual display of the geospatial data is controlled through something called a **symbolizer**. While there are many different types of symbolizers available within Mapnik, three symbolizers are of interest to us here:

- A `PolygonSymbolizer` is used to draw filled polygons:

- A `LineSymbolizer` is used to draw the outline of polygons as well as to draw LineStrings and other linear features:

- A `TextSymbolizer` is used to draw labels and other text onto a map:

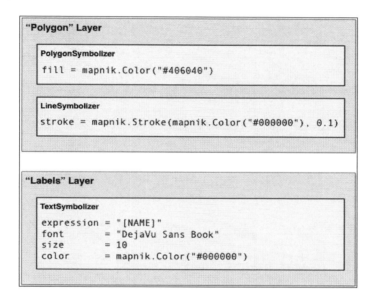

In many cases, these three symbolizers will be enough to draw an entire map. Indeed, almost all of the preceding map was produced using just one `PolygonSymbolizer`, one `LineSymbolizer`, and one `TextSymbolizer`, as shown here:

```
"Polygon" Layer

    PolygonSymbolizer
    fill = mapnik.Color("#406040")

    LineSymbolizer
    stroke = mapnik.Stroke(mapnik.Color("#000000"), 0.1)


"Labels" Layer

    TextSymbolizer
    expression = "[NAME]"
    font       = "DejaVu Sans Book"
    size       = 10
    color      = mapnik.Color("#000000")
```

Within each layer, the symbolizers are processed using the same painter's algorithm described earlier. In the case of the "Polygon" layer, the `LineSymbolizer` would be drawn on top of the `PolygonSymbolizer`.

Notice that the symbolizers aren't associated directly with a layer. Rather, there is an *indirect* association of symbolizers with a layer through the use of styles and rules. We'll look at styles in a minute, but for now, let's take a closer look at the concept of a Mapnik rule.

A **rule** allows a set of symbolizers to be applied only when a given condition is met. For example, the map at the start of this chapter displayed Angola in a different color. This was done by defining two rules within the "Polygons" layer, like this:

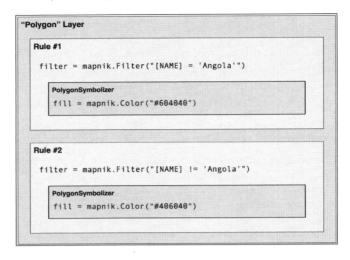

The first rule has a **filter** that only applies to features that have a NAME attribute equal to the value "Angola". For features that match this filter condition, the rule's PolygonSymbolizer will be used to draw the feature in dark red.

The second rule has a similar filter, this time checking for features that don't have a NAME attribute equal to "Angola". These features are drawn using the second rule's PolygonSymbolizer, which draws the features in dark green.

Obviously, rules are a very powerful tool for selectively changing the way features are displayed on a map. We'll be looking at rules in more detail in the *Rules, filters, and styles* section of this chapter.

When you define your symbolizers, you place them into rules. The rules themselves are grouped into **styles**, which can be used to organize and keep track of your various rules. Each map layer has a list of the styles that apply to that particular layer.

While the relationship between layers, styles, rules, filters, and symbolizers may seem complicated, it also provides much of Mapnik's power and flexibility. It is important that you understand how these various classes work together:

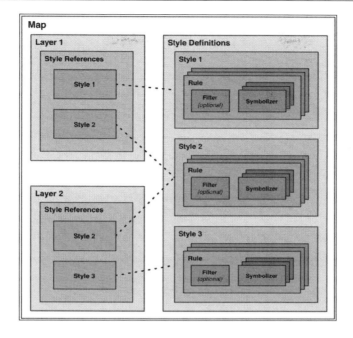

As you can see, the style definitions are stored directly within the map, while the various layers use style references to identify which of the defined styles each layer will use. This works in much the same way as a stylesheet in a word processing document, where you define styles and use them again and again. Note that the same style can be used in multiple layers.

 Mapnik provides an alternative way of defining your various styles, though the use of an XML-format map definition file. We will not be using map definition files in this book, however, as the XML-format files are rather hard to read. It is also easier to create your map definitions directly using Python code.

# Creating an example map

To better understand how the various parts of Mapnik work together, let's write a simple Python program to generate the map shown at the start of this chapter. This map makes use of the World Borders Dataset, which you downloaded in an earlier chapter; copy the TM_WORLD_BORDERS-0.3 shapefile directory into a convenient place, and create a new Python script in the same place. We'll call this program createExampleMap.py.

We'll start by importing the Mapnik toolkit and defining some constants the program will need:

```
import mapnik

MIN_LAT   = -35
MAX_LAT   = +35
MIN_LONG  = -12
MAX_LONG  = +50

MAP_WIDTH  = 700
MAP_HEIGHT = 800
```

The MIN_LAT, MAX_LAT, MIN_LONG, and MAX_LONG constants define the lat/long coordinates for the portion of the world to display on the map, while the MAP_WIDTH and MAP_HEIGHT constants define the size of the generated map image, measured in pixels. Obviously, you can change these if you want.

We're now ready to define the contents of the map. This map will have two layers, one for drawing the polygons and another for drawing the labels. We'll define a Mapnik Style object for each of these two layers. Let's start with the style for the Polygons layer:

```
polygonStyle = mapnik.Style()
```

As we discussed in the previous section, a Filter object lets you choose which particular features a rule will apply to. In this case, we want to set up two rules, one to draw Angola in dark red, and another to draw all the other countries in dark green:

```
rule = mapnik.Rule()
rule.filter = mapnik.Filter("[NAME] = 'Angola'")
symbol = mapnik.PolygonSymbolizer(mapnik.Color("#604040"))
rule.symbols.append(symbol)

polygonStyle.rules.append(rule)

rule = mapnik.Rule()
rule.filter = mapnik.Filter("[NAME] != 'Angola'")
symbol = mapnik.PolygonSymbolizer(mapnik.Color("#406040"))
rule.symbols.append(symbol)

polygonStyle.rules.append(rule)
```

Notice how we use a `PolygonSymbolizer` to fill each country's outline with an appropriate color and then add this symbolizer to our current rule. As we define the rules, we add them to our polygon style.

Now that we've filled the country polygons, we'll define an additional rule to draw the polygon outlines:

```
rule = mapnik.Rule()
symbol = mapnik.LineSymbolizer(mapnik.Color("#000000"), 0.1)
rule.symbols.append(symbol)

polygonStyle.rules.append(rule)
```

This is all that's required to display the country polygons on the map. Let's now go ahead and define a second Mapnik `Style` object for the "Labels" layer:

```
labelStyle = mapnik.Style()

rule = mapnik.Rule()
symbol = mapnik.TextSymbolizer(mapnik.Expression("[NAME]"),
                              "DejaVu Sans Book", 12,
                              mapnik.Color("#000000"))
rule.symbols.append(symbol)

labelStyle.rules.append(rule)
```

This style uses a `TextSymbolizer` to draw the labels onto the map. Notice that we create an `Expression` object to define the text to be displayed—in this case, we want to display the shapefile's NAME attribute; as you might expect, this attribute contains the name of the country.

> In this example, we are only using a single Mapnik style for each layer. When generating a more complex map, you will typically have a number of styles that can be applied to each layer, and styles may be shared between layers as appropriate. For this example, though, we are keeping the map definition as simple as possible.

Now that we have set up our styles, we can start to define our map's layers. Before we do this, though, we need to set up our data source:

```
datasource = mapnik.Shapefile(file="TM_WORLD_BORDERS-0.3/" +
                              "TM_WORLD_BORDERS-0.3.shp")
```

We can then define the two layers used by our map:

```
polygonLayer = mapnik.Layer("Polygons")
polygonLayer.datasource = datasource
polygonLayer.styles.append("PolygonStyle")

labelLayer = mapnik.Layer("Labels")
labelLayer.datasource = datasource
labelLayer.styles.append("LabelStyle")
```

 Notice that we refer to styles by name rather than inserting the style directly. This allows us to use a single style for multiple layers. We'll add the style definitions to our map shortly.

We can now finally create our `Map` object. A Mapnik `Map` object has a width and height, a projection, a background color, a list of styles, and a list of the layers that make up the map:

```
map = mapnik.Map(MAP_WIDTH, MAP_HEIGHT,
                 "+proj=longlat +datum=WGS84")
map.background = mapnik.Color("#8080a0")

map.append_style("PolygonStyle", polygonStyle)
map.append_style("LabelStyle", labelStyle)

map.layers.append(polygonLayer)
map.layers.append(labelLayer)
```

The last thing we have to do is tell Mapnik to zoom in on the desired area of the world and then render the map into an image file:

```
map.zoom_to_box(mapnik.Box2d(MIN_LONG, MIN_LAT,
                             MAX_LONG, MAX_LAT))
mapnik.render_to_file(map, "map.png")
```

If you run this program and open the resulting `map.png` file, you will see the map you generated:

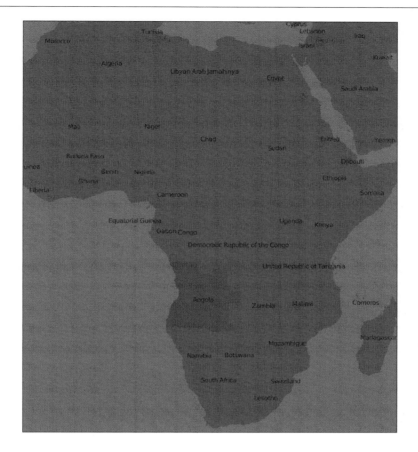

Obviously, there's a lot more that you can do with Mapnik, but this example covers the main points and should be enough to let you start generating your own maps. Make sure that you play with this example to become familiar with the way Mapnik works. Here are some things you might like to try:

- Adjusting the `MIN_LAT`, `MIN_LONG`, `MAX_LAT`, and `MAX_LONG` constants at the start of the program to zoom in on the country where you reside
- Changing the size of the generated image
- Altering the map's colors
- Adding extra rules to display the country name in different font sizes and colors based on the country's population

To do this, you'll need to define filters that look like this:
```
mapnik.Filter("[POP2005] > 1000000 and [POP2005]
<= 2000000")
```

# Mapnik concepts

In this section, we will examine the Python interface to the Mapnik toolkit in more detail. Since there are too many features to cover in their entirety, we will concentrate on the most important aspects of Mapnik that you are likely to use in your own programs. Feel free to refer to the Mapnik documentation (http://mapnik.org/docs) for anything not covered in this chapter.

# Data sources

A data source object acts as a "bridge" between Mapnik and your geospatial data. You typically create the data source using one of the following convenience constructors and then add that data source to any Mapnik `Layer` objects that use that data:

```
layer.datasource = datasource
```

There are many different types of data sources supported by Mapnik, though some are experimental or access data in commercial databases. Let's take a closer look at the types of data sources you are most likely to find useful.

# Shapefile

It is easy to use a shapefile as a Mapnik data source. All you need to do is supply the name and directory path for the desired shapefile to the `mapnik.Shapefile()` convenience constructor:

```
datasource = mapnik.Shapefile(file="path/to/shapefile.shp")
```

The optional `encoding` parameter can be used to specify the character encoding to use for the shapefile's attributes, like this, for example:

```
datasource = mapnik.Shapefile(file="shapefile.shp",
                              encoding="latin1")
```

If you don't set the `encoding` parameter, the shapefile is assumed to use UTF-8 character encoding.

# PostGIS

A PostGIS data source allows you to include data from a PostGIS database:

```
datasource = mapnik.PostGIS(user="..." password="...",
                            dbname="...", table="...")
```

Notice that you supply the username and password used to access the PostGIS database, the name of the database, and the name of the table that contains the spatial data you want to display on your map.

There are some performance issues to be aware of when retrieving data from a PostGIS database. If you use a `mapnik.Filter` object to selectively display features taken from a large database table, your map may take a long time to generate. This is because Mapnik needs to load every feature from the database table in turn to see whether it matches the filter expression. A much more efficient way to do this is to use what is called a **sub-select query** in order to limit the set of data that Mapnik retrieves from the database.

To use a sub-select query, you replace the table name with an SQL `SELECT` statement that does the filtering and returns the information needed by Mapnik to generate the map's layer. Here's an example:

```
query = "(SELECT geom FROM myBigTable WHERE level=1) AS data"
datasource = mapnik.PostGIS(user="...", password="...",
                            dbname="...", table=query)
```

We've replaced the table name with a PostGIS sub-select query that filters out all records with a `level` value not equal to `1` and returns just the `geom` field for the matching records.

Note that if you use a sub-select query, it is important that you include all the fields you want to refer to in your `SELECT` statement. If you don't include a field in the `SELECT` portion of the sub-select query, it won't be available for Mapnik to use.

# Gdal

The `Gdal` data source allows you to include any GDAL-compatible raster image data file within your map. It is straightforward to use:

```
datasource = mapnik.Gdal(file="myRasterImage.tiff")
```

Once you have a `Gdal` data source, you can use a `RasterSymbolizer` to draw it onto the map:

```
layer = mapnik.Layer("myLayer")
layer.datasource = datasource
layer.styles.append("myLayerStyle")

symbol = mapnik.RasterSymbolizer()

rule = mapnik.Rule()
rule.symbols.append(symbol)

style = mapnik.Style()
style.rules.append(rule)

map.append_style("myLayerStyle", style)
```

# MemoryDatasource

A `MemoryDatasource` allows you to manually define the geospatial data that appears on the map. To use a `MemoryDatasource`, you first create the data source object itself:

```
datasource = mapnik.MemoryDatasource()
```

You then define a `mapnik.Context` object that lists the attributes you want to associate with each of the data source's features:

```
context = mapnik.Context()
context.push("NAME")
context.push("ELEVATION")
```

Next, you create a `mapnik.Feature` object for each of the features you want to include on the map:

```
feature = mapnik.Feature(context, id)
```

Note that the `id` parameter should be a unique integer value identifying this feature within the memory data source.

Once the feature has been created, you then set the feature's attributes. This is done in the same way you define entries within a Python dictionary:

```
feature['NAME'] = "Hawkins Hill"
feature['ELEVATION'] = 1624
```

These attributes can be used by rules to select which features to display, and they can also be used by a `TextSymbolizer` to draw an attribute's value onto the map.

Each feature can have one or more geometries associated with it. The easiest way to set the feature's geometry is to use the `add_geometries_from_wkt()` method, like this:

```
feature.add_geometries_from_wkt("POINT (174.73 -41.33)")
```

Finally, you add the feature to the `MemoryDatasource` using the `add_feature()` method:

```
datasource.add_feature(feature)
```

Once your `MemoryDatasource` has been set up, you can add it to a map layer and use any of the vector-format symbolizers to draw the features onto the map.

# Rules, filters, and styles

As we saw earlier in this chapter, Mapnik uses rules to specify which particular symbolizers will be used to render a given feature. Rules are grouped together into a style, and the various styles are added to your map and then referred to by name when you set up your map layer. In this section, we will examine the relationship between rules, filters and styles, and see just what can be done with these various Mapnik classes.

Let's take a closer look at Mapnik's `Rule` class. A Mapnik rule has two parts: a set of conditions and a list of symbolizers. If the rule's conditions are met, then the symbolizers will be used to draw the matching features onto the map.

There are two main types of conditions supported by a Mapnik rule:

- A **filter** can be used to specify an expression that must be met by the feature if it is to be drawn
- The rule can have an **else** condition, which means that the rule will only be applied if no other rule in the style has had its conditions met

If the conditions for a rule have been met, then the associated list of symbolizers will be used to render the feature onto the map.

Let's take a look at filters and "else" conditions in more detail.

## Filters

Mapnik's `Filter()` constructor takes a single parameter, which is a string defining an expression that the feature must match if the rule is to apply. You then store the returned `Filter` object in the rule's `filter` attribute:

```
rule.filter = mapnik.Filter("...")
```

Let's consider a very simple filter expression, comparing a field or attribute against a specific value:

```
filter = mapnik.Filter("[level] = 1")
```

String values can be compared by putting single quote marks around the value, like this:

```
filter = mapnik.Filter("[type] = 'CITY'")
```

Notice that the field name and value are both case-sensitive and that you must surround the field or attribute name with square brackets.

Of course, simply comparing a field with a value is the most basic type of comparison you can do. Filter expressions have their own powerful and flexible syntax for defining conditions, similar in concept to an SQL WHERE expression. The following syntax diagram describes all the options for writing filter expression strings:

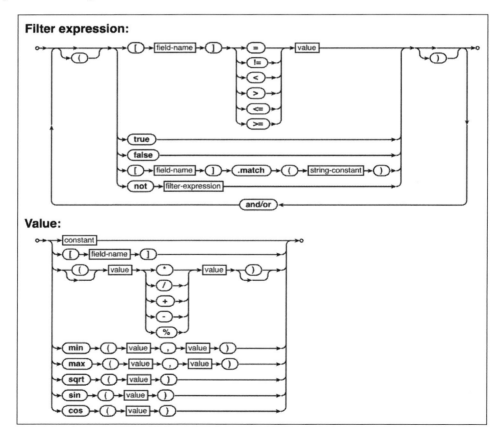

Mapnik also allows you to filter based on the type of geometry, using the following special syntax:

```
filter = mapnik.Filter("[mapnik::geometry_type] = point")
```

The following geometry type values are supported by this kind of filter expression:

- point
- linestring
- polygon
- collection

# "Else" rules

Imagine that you want to draw some features in one color and all other features in a different color. One way to achieve this is by using Mapnik filters, like this:

```
rule1.filter = mapnik.Filter("[level] = 1")
...
rule2.filter = mapnik.Filter("[level] != 1")
```

This is fine for simple filter expressions, but when the expressions get more complicated, it is a lot easier to use an "else" rule, like this:

```
rule.set_else(True)
```

If you call set_else(True) for a rule, then this rule is to be used if and only if no previous rule in the same style has had its filter conditions met.

Else rules are particularly useful if you have a number of filter conditions and want to have a catch-all rule at the end. This catch-all rule will apply if no other rule has been used to draw the feature, like this:

```
rule1.filter = mapnik.Filter("[type] = 'city'")
rule2.filter = mapnik.Filter("[type] = 'town'")
rule3.filter = mapnik.Filter("[type] = 'village'")
rule4.filter.set_else(True)
```

# Styles

A Mapnik style is nothing more than a list of rules. To define a style, create a new mapnik.Style object and add the rules to it one at a time, like this:

```
style = mapnik.Style()
style.rules.append(rule1)
style.rules.append(rule2)
...
```

For each feature, the rules are processed one after the other, with each rule's conditions being checked in turn to see whether the feature matches the rule. If it does, the rule's associated symbolizers will be used to draw that feature. If none of the rules match the feature, then the feature won't be displayed at all.

Once you have created the `Style` object, you add the style to your `mapnik.Map` object, giving the style a name. You then refer to that style by name from within your map layers, for example:

```
map.append_style("style_name", style)
layer.styles.append("style_name")
```

# Symbolizers

Symbolizers are used to draw features onto a map. In this section, we will look at the most common types of symbolizers you can use to draw points, lines, polygons, text, and raster images onto a map.

## Drawing points

To draw a point geometry, you use a **PointSymbolizer**. This draws an image at the specified point. The default constructor takes no arguments and displays each point as a black square of 4 x 4 pixels:

```
symbolizer = PointSymbolizer()
```

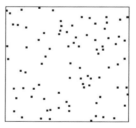

Alternatively, you can supply a path to an image file, which the `PointSymbolizer` will use to draw each point:

```
path = mapnik.PathExpression("path/to/image.png")
symbolizer = PointSymbolizer(path)
```

You can modify the behavior of the `PointSymbolizer` by setting the following attributes:

- `symbolizer.allow_overlap = True`: If you set this attribute to `True`, all points will be drawn even if the images overlap. The default (`False`) means that points will only be drawn if they don't overlap.

- `symbolizer.opacity = 0.75`: This attribute controls the amount of opaqueness or transparency used to draw the image. A value of `1.0` (the default) will draw the image completely opaque, while a value of `0.0` will draw the image completely transparent.

- `symbolizer.transform = "..."`: This is an SVG transformation expression that you can use to manipulate the image to be displayed. For example, `transform="rotate(45) scale(0.5, 0.5)"` will rotate the image clockwise by 45 degrees and then scale it to 50 percent of its original size.

# Drawing lines

A **LineSymbolizer** draws linear features and traces around the outline of polygons, as shown in the following diagram:

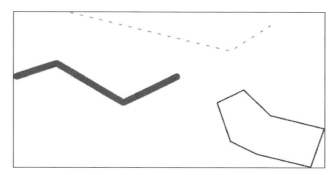

The `LineSymbolizer` is one of the most useful of the Mapnik symbolizers. For example, the dashed line in the previous image was created using the following Python code:

```
stroke = mapnik.Stroke()
stroke.color = mapnik.Color("#008000")
stroke.width = 1.0
stroke.add_dash(5, 10)
symbolizer = mapnik.LineSymbolizer(stroke)
```

As you can see, a LineSymbolizer uses a Mapnik Stroke object to define how the line will be drawn. To use a LineSymbolizer, you first create the Stroke object and set the various options for how you want the line to be drawn. You then create your LineSymbolizer instance, passing the Stroke object to the LineSymbolizer object's constructor:

```
symbolizer = mapnik.LineSymbolizer(stroke)
```

You can customize the Stroke object in the following ways:

- stroke.color = mapnik.Color("yellow"): This changes the color used to draw the line. Mapnik Color objects can be constructed using a color name, an HTML color code, or separate R, G, and B values, for example:

```
color1 = mapnik.Color("yellow")
color2 = mapnik.Color("#f0f028")
color3 = mapnik.Color(240, 240, 40)
```

> In addition to the RGB color values, you can include an optional fourth color value to specify the transparency of the color. For example, mapnik.Color(240, 240, 40, 128) will create a yellow-colored object with 50% transparency.

- stroke.width = 0.5: This sets the width of the line, measured in pixels. Note that because Mapnik uses antialiasing to draw lines, a line narrower than 1 pixel will often look better than a line with an integer width.

- stroke.opacity = 0.8: this sets how opaque or transparent the line is. The opacity can range from 0.0 (completely transparent) to 1.0 (completely opaque).

- stroke.line_cap = mapnik.line_cap.BUTT_CAP: This changes how the ends of the lines are to be drawn. Mapnik supports three standard line cap settings:

- stroke.line_join = mapnik.line_join.MITER_JOIN: This sets how a "corner" of the line is drawn when the line changes direction. Three standard line join options are supported:

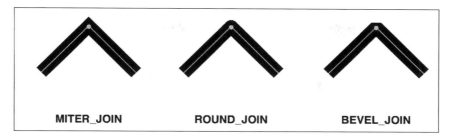

- `stroke.add_dash(5, 7)`: This lets you add a break to the line so that it appears dashed or dotted. The two parameters you supply are the *dash length* and the *gap length*; the line will be drawn for the given dash length and a gap of the specified length will then be left before the line continues:

Note that you can call `add_dash()` more than once. This allows you to create alternating patterns of dots or dashes, for example:

```
stroke.add_dash(10, 2)
stroke.add_dash(2, 2)
stroke.add_dash(2, 2)
```

This would result in the following repeating line pattern:

One thing that may not be immediately obvious when you start working with symbolizers is that you can use multiple symbolizers for a single feature. For example, consider the following code:

```
stroke = mapnik.Stroke()
stroke.color = mapnik.Color("#bf7a3a")
stroke.width = 7.0
roadEdgeSymbolizer = mapnik.LineSymbolizer(stroke)

stroke = mapnik.Stroke()
stroke.color = mapnik.Color("#ffd3a9")
stroke.width = 6.0
```

```
roadInteriorSymbolizer = mapnik.LineSymbolizer(stroke)

rule.symbols.append(roadEdgeSymbolizer)
rule.symbols.append(roadInteriorSymbolizer)
```

The two symbolizers will be laid on top of each other to draw a LineString feature that looks like a road on a street map:

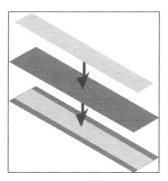

This technique can be used for more than just drawing roads; the creative use of symbolizers is one of the main tricks to achieving complex visual effects using Mapnik.

# Drawing polygons

A PolygonSymbolizer fills the interior of a polygon with a single color:

You can create a PolygonSymbolizer instance like this:

```
symbolizer = mapnik.PolygonSymbolizer()
```

Once it has been created, you can configure your `PolygonSymbolizer` instance by setting the following attributes:

- `symbolizer.fill = mapnik.Color("red")`: This sets the color to use for drawing the interior of the polygon.

- `symbolizer.opacity = 0.8`: This changes the opacity used to draw the polygon's interior.

- `symbolizer.gamma = 0.6`: The `gamma` value is used to control the amount of antialiasing used for drawing the edges of the polygon. If you try to draw adjacent polygons with the same color, the edges would normally be visible; reducing the `gamma` value slightly will allow the edges of adjacent polygons to disappear, merging the polygons together.

# Drawing text

A TextSymbolizer draws textual labels onto point, line, and polygon features:

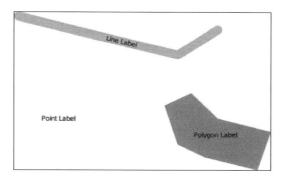

The basic usage of a `TextSymbolizer` is quite simple. For example, the polygon in the preceding illustration was labeled using the following code:

```
symbolizer = mapnik.TextSymbolizer(mapnik.Expression("[label]"),
"DejaVu Sans Book", 10, mapnik.Color("black"))
```

As you can see, the `TextSymbolizer` object's constructor takes four separate parameters:

- A `mapnik.Expression` object that defines the text to be displayed. In this example, the value to be displayed will be taken from the `label` attribute in the data source.

- The name of the font to use for drawing the text. To see which fonts are available, type the following into the Python command line:

```
import mapnik
for font in mapnik.FontEngine.face_names():
    print(font)
```

  You can also install custom fonts, as described on the web page at: https://github.com/mapnik/mapnik/wiki/UsingCustomFonts.

- The font size, measured in pixels.

- The `mapnik.Color` object to use for drawing the text.

Once it has been created, you can configure the `TextSymbolizer` object by setting the following attributes:

- `symbolizer.opacity = 0.5`: This changes the opacity used for drawing the text.

- `symbolizer.label_placement = mapnik.label_placement.LINE_PLACEMENT`: The `label_placement` attribute controls how the text is positioned. The default value, `POINT_PLACEMENT`, simply draws the text in the center of the geometry, like this:

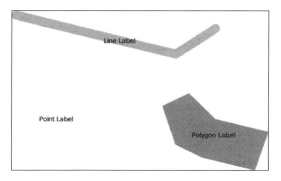

If you change this to `LINE_PLACEMENT`, the label will be drawn along the length of a LineString or along the perimeter of a polygon:

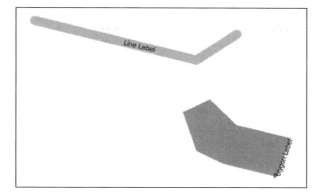

Note that the text won't be shown at all for a Point geometry when you use LINE_PLACEMENT, as there are no lines within a point.

- symbolizer.label_spacing = 30: By default, each label will only be drawn once for each feature. By setting label_spacing to a given pixel value, the label will be repeated, like this:

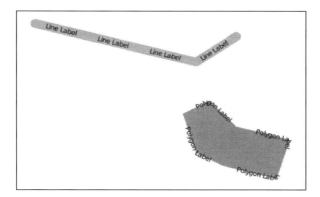

- symbolizer.allow_overlap = True: By default, Mapnik will avoid overlapping two labels by either shifting the labels slightly or by hiding one of the labels. Setting allow_overlap to True will disable this behavior, allowing multiple labels to be drawn on top of each other:

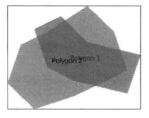

- `symbolizer.halo_radius = 1`: If you draw a label using dark text on a dark background, the label would normally be very hard to read. You can use this attribute to draw a "halo" effect around the label, making a dark label still visible against a dark background, for example:

  Note that the `halo_radius` value is specified in pixels; generally, a small value such as 1 or 2 is enough to ensure that the text is readable against a dark background.

- `symbolizer.halo_fill = mapnik.Color("white")`: This sets the color to use for drawing the halo effect around a label.

There are many more options for controlling how labels are drawn using a `TextSymbolizer`. For example, you can control how labels are split across multiple lines, specify character and line spacing, and even dynamically choose the attribute to display based on the length of the text and the available space. For more information on the available options, please consult the Mapnik documentation.

 In addition to a `TextSymbolizer`, there is a symbolizer called a **ShieldSymbolizer** which combines a `TextSymbolizer` object with a `PointSymbolizer` object, allowing you to draw both an image and a label at a given point. Due to its complexity, we will not be covering `ShieldSymbolizer` in this book; if you want to explore this symbolizer, you will find that it uses the same attributes as both the `TextSymbolizer` and the `PointSymbolizer`.

# Drawing raster images

Raster images are often used to draw a basemap onto which your vector data is displayed. To draw a raster image, you would typically use a **RasterSymbolizer**. For example:

```
symbolizer = mapnik.RasterSymbolizer()
```

A `RasterSymbolizer` draws the contents of the layer's raster-format data source onto the map. While there are some advanced options for controlling how the raster image is displayed, in most cases, the only option you are likely to be interested in is the `opacity` attribute. As you might expect, this sets the opacity for the image, allowing you to display multiple semi-transparent images one on top of the other.

# Maps and layers

Once you have set up your data sources, symbolizers, rules, and styles, you can combine them into Mapnik layers and place the various layers together onto a map. To do this, you first create a `mapnik.Map` object to represent the map as a whole:

```
map = mapnik.Map(width, height, srs)
```

You supply the width and height of the map image you want to generate, measured in pixels, and an optional Proj.4-format initialization string in the `srs` parameter. If you don't specify a spatial reference system, the map will use +proj=latlong +datum=WGS84, that is, unprojected lat/long coordinates on the WGS84 datum.

After creating the map, you set its background color and then add your various styles to the map by calling the `map.append_style()` method:

```
map.background_color = mapnik.Color('white')

map.append_style("countryStyle", countryStyle)
map.append_style("roadStyle", roadStyle)
map.append_style("pointStyle", pointStyle)
map.append_style("rasterStyle", rasterStyle)
...
```

You next need to create the various layers within the map. To do this, you create a `mapnik.Layer` object to represent each map layer:

```
layer = mapnik.Layer(layerName, srs)
```

Each layer is given a unique name and can optionally have a spatial reference associated with it. The `srs` string is once again a Proj.4-format initialization string; if no spatial reference is given, the layer will use +proj=latlong +datum=WGS84.

Once you have created your map layer, you assign it a data source and choose the style(s) that will apply to that layer, identifying each style by name:

```
layer.datasource = myDatasource

layer.styles.append("countryStyle")
layer.styles.append("rasterStyle")
...
```

Finally, you add your new layer to the map:

```
map.layers.append(layer)
```

While map layers can be used to combine multiple data sources into a single image, they can also be used to selectively show or hide information based on the current zoom level. For example, consider the following two maps:

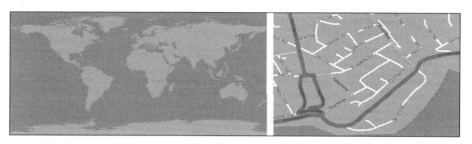

Obviously, there's no point in drawing streets onto a map of the entire world. Similarly, the country outlines shown on the world map are at too large a scale to draw detailed coastlines for an individual city. But if your application allows the user to zoom in from the world map right down to an individual street, you will need to use a single set of Mapnik styles to generate the map regardless of the scale at which you are drawing it.

The easiest way to do this is to set the minimum and maximum scale factor for a layer. For example:

```
layer.minzoom = 1/100000
layer.maxzoom = 1/200000
```

The layer will only be displayed when the map's current scale factor is within this range. This is useful if you have a data source that should only be used when displaying the map at a certain scale, for example, only using high-resolution shoreline data when the user has zoomed in.

# Map rendering

After creating your `mapnik.Map` object and setting up the various symbolizers, rules, styles, data sources, and layers within it, you are finally ready to convert your map into a rendered image.

Before rendering the map image, make sure that you have set the appropriate bounding box for the map so that the map will show the area of the world you are interested in. You can do this by either calling `map.zoom_to_box()` to explicitly set the map's bounding box to a given set of coordinates, or you can call `map.zoom_all()` to have the map automatically set its bounds based on the data to be displayed.

Once you have set the bounding box, you can generate your map image by calling the `render_to_file()` function, like this:

```
mapnik.render_to_file(map, 'map.png')
```

The parameters are the `mapnik.Map` object and the name of the image file to write the map to. If you want more control over the format of the generated image, you can add an extra parameter to specify the image format, like this:

```
mapnik.render_to_file(map, 'map.png', 'png256')
```

Supported image formats include the following:

| Image format | Description |
| --- | --- |
| `.png` | A 32-bit PNG-format image |
| `.png256` | An 8-bit PNG-format image |
| `.jpeg` | A JPEG-format image |
| `.svg` | An SVG-format image |
| `.pdf` | A PDF file |
| `.ps` | A PostScript-format file |

The `render_to_file()` function works well when you want to generate a single image from your entire map. Another useful way of rendering maps is to generate a number of "tiles", which can then be stitched together to display the map at a higher resolution:

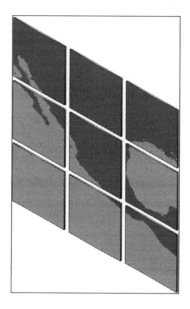

Mapnik provides a helpful function for creating tiles like this out of a single map:

```
mapnik.render_tile_to_file(map, xOffset, yOffset,
                           width, height, fileName, format)
```

The parameters for this function are as follows:

- `map` is the `mapnik.Map` object containing the map data
- `xOffset` and `yOffset` define the top-left corner of the tile, in map coordinates
- `width` and `height` define the size of the tile, in map coordinates
- `fileName` is the name of the file to save the tiled image to
- `format` is the file format to use for saving this tile

You can simply call this function repeatedly to create the individual tiles for your map. For example:

```
for x in range(NUM_TILES_ACROSS):
    for y in range(NUM_TILES_DOWN):
        xOffset = TILE_SIZE * x
        yOffset = TILE_SIZE * y
        tileName = "tile_{}_{}.png".format(x, y)
        mapnik.render_tile_to_file(map, xOffset, yOffset,
                                   TILE_SIZE, TILE_SIZE,
                                   tileName, "png")
```

# Summary

In this chapter, we explored the Mapnik map-generation toolkit in depth. We learned that maps are composed of multiple layers, drawn one on top of the other using the painter's algorithm. We saw that each layer has a data source and a list of styles that determine how the data is to be displayed. Styles are referred to by name, so they can be shared between the various map layers.

We learned that each style has a list of rules associated with it, where each rule can optionally have a filter limiting the set of features to be displayed as well as a list of symbolizers that control how the matching features are to be drawn.

We then saw how the mapnik.Map object combines the styles and map layers and how the map can be used to zoom in to a particular area of the world before rendering an image based on the map's contents.

We put all these concepts together into a simple map-generating program before delving deeper into the Mapnik library. We examined four of the major types of data sources: Shapefile, PostGIS, Gdal, and MemoryDatasource. We saw how rules, filters, and styles work together and examined the major types of symbolizers you are likely to use in your programs: the PointSymbolizer for drawing point geometries, the LineSymbolizer for drawing linear features and the outline of a polygon, the PolygonSymbolizer for filling the interior of a polygon, the TextSymbolizer for drawing textual labels, and the RasterSymbolizer for drawing raster images into a map.

We then looked at how the map and layer objects can work together, including how to use scale factors to selectively show or hide map layers, and finished by looking at the various ways in which a map image can be rendered.

In the next chapter, we will combine spatial databases with Mapnik to build a sophisticated geospatial application called DISTAL.

# 8
# Working with Spatial Data

In this chapter, we will apply and build on the knowledge that we gained in previous chapters to create a sophisticated web application called **DISTAL** (**Distance-based Identification of Shorelines, Towns, and Lakes**). In the process of building this application, we will learn:

- How to work with substantial amounts of geospatial data stored in a PostGIS database
- How to perform complex spatial database queries
- How to make accurate distance-based spatial queries
- How to integrate Mapnik into a web application to display results on a map

## About DISTAL

The DISTAL application will have the following basic workflow:

1. The user starts by selecting the country they wish to work with:

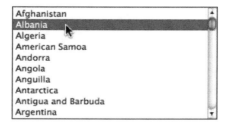

2. A simple map of the country is then displayed:

3. The user selects a desired radius in miles and clicks on a point within the country:

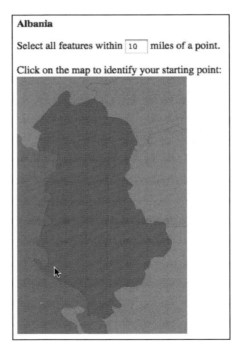

4. The system identifies all the cities and towns within the given radius of that point:

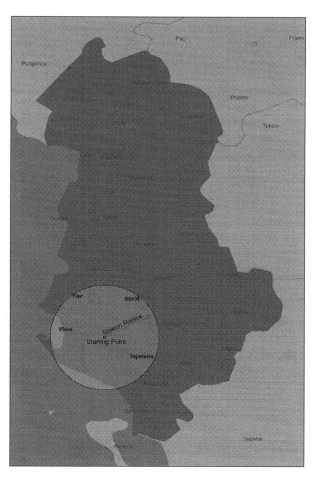

5.  Finally, the resulting features are displayed at a higher resolution for the user to view or print:

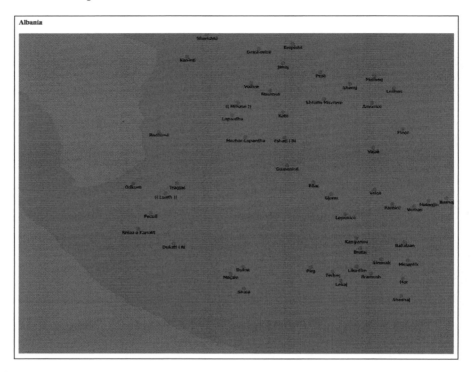

We are going to implement the DISTAL system as a series of CGI scripts. While this is simplistic and lacks the look and feel of a proper Google Maps-like "slippy map" interface, it allows us to concentrate on the core geospatial aspects of this application without getting bogged down in the complexity of building a full web application.

# Designing and building the database

Let's start our design of the DISTAL application by thinking about the various pieces of data it will require:

*   A list of all the countries. Each country needs to include a simple boundary map, which can be displayed to the user.

*   Detailed shoreline and lake boundaries worldwide. A list of all major cities and towns worldwide.

*   For each city/town, we need to have the name of the city/town and a point representing the location of that town or city.

Fortunately, this data is readily available:

- The list of countries and their outlines are included in the World Borders Dataset

- Shoreline and lake boundaries (as well as other land-water boundaries, such as islands within lakes) are readily available using the GSHHG shoreline database

- City and town data can be found in two places: The GNIS Database provides official place-name data for the United States, while the GEOnet Names Server provides similar data for the rest of the world

Looking at these data sources, we can start to design the database schema for the DISTAL system, which will look like this:

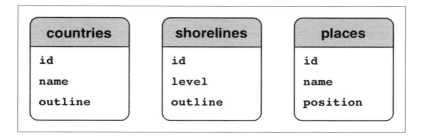

 The `level` field in the `shorelines` table corresponds to the level value in the GSHHG database: a value of 1 represents a coastline, 2 represents a lake, 3 represents an island within a lake, and 4 represents a pond on an island in a lake.

While this is very simple, it's enough to get us started. Let's use this schema to create our spatial database and set up our database schema. This involves the following steps:

1. Open a terminal or command-line window and enter the following command:

   ```
   createdb distal
   ```

 Don't forget to add the `-U postgres` option or to use `sudo` for this command and the ones that follow if you need to run Postgres under a different user account.

2. Create a new user to access this database by entering the following command:

```
createuser -P distal_user
```

You'll be asked to enter a password for this new user. Make sure you remember the password you enter.

3. Run the Postgres command-line interface by typing the following:

```
psql distal
```

4. Allow the distal_user user to access the distal database by entering the following:

```
GRANT ALL PRIVILEGES ON DATABASE distal TO distal_user;
```

5. Spatially-enable our new database by typing the following command:

```
CREATE EXTENSION postgis;
```

You can now exit the Postgres command-line client by typing \q and pressing *Return*. We're next going to write a Python script to create our various database tables. Before we can do this, though, we're going to need somewhere to store the source code to the DISTAL system. Create a new directory called DISTAL in a convenient location. Inside this directory, create a new Python script named create_db.py, and enter the following into this file:

```python
import psycopg2

connection = psycopg2.connect(database="distal",
                              user="distal_user",
                              password="...")
cursor = connection.cursor()

cursor.execute("DROP TABLE IF EXISTS countries")
cursor.execute("""
    CREATE TABLE countries (
        id       SERIAL,
        name     VARCHAR(255),
        outline GEOMETRY(GEOMETRY, 4326),

        PRIMARY KEY (id))
""")
cursor.execute("""
    CREATE INDEX countryIndex ON countries
        USING GIST(outline)
""")

cursor.execute("DROP TABLE IF EXISTS shorelines")
cursor.execute("""
```

```
CREATE TABLE shorelines (
    id    SERIAL,
    level INTEGER,
    outline GEOMETRY(GEOMETRY, 4326),

    PRIMARY KEY (id))
""")
cursor.execute("""
    CREATE INDEX shorelineIndex ON shorelines
        USING GIST(outline)
""")

cursor.execute("DROP TABLE IF EXISTS places")
cursor.execute("""
    CREATE TABLE places (
        id      SERIAL,
        name    VARCHAR(255),
        position GEOGRAPHY(POINT, 4326),

        PRIMARY KEY (id))
""")
cursor.execute("""
    CREATE INDEX placeIndex ON places
        USING GIST(position)
""")

connection.commit()
```

There is a lot of source code in this chapter, but you don't need to type it all in by hand. You can download a complete copy of the DISTAL application as a part of the sample code that comes with this chapter.

Notice that we define the outlines to have a column type of GEOMETRY(GEOMETRY, 4326). The first occurrence of the word GEOMETRY defines the column type; we are using geometry columns rather than geography columns to avoid problems with calculating bounding boxes and other values, which unfortunately doesn't work with geography columns. Within the parentheses, the second occurrence of the word GEOMETRY tells PostGIS that we can hold any type of geometry value we want; this allows us to store either a Polygon or a MultiPolygon for the outline, depending on the type of outline we want to store. We're also following the recommended best practice of specifying the spatial reference ID (SRID) value for our data. We'll use the WGS84 datum and unprojected lat/long coordinates for our data, which corresponds to an SRID value of 4326.

For the `places` table, we are using `GEOGRAPHY(POINT, 4326)`, which does use the `GEOGRAPHY` column type so that we can perform accurate distance-based queries within the database. This time, we're constraining the place to hold a single Point value, and we again use the SRID value of 4326 for this data.

Go ahead and run the `create_db.py` program; it should run without any errors, leaving you with a properly set up database schema.

# Downloading and importing the data

As described in the previous section, the DISTAL application will make use of four separate sets of freely available geospatial data:

- The World Borders Dataset
- The high-resolution GSHHG shoreline database
- The GNIS Database of US place names
- The GEONet Names Server's list of non-US place names

 For more information on these sources of data, refer to *Chapter 4, Sources of Geospatial Data*.

Let's work through the process of downloading and importing each of these datasets in turn.

## The World Borders Dataset

You downloaded a copy of this dataset earlier. Create a subdirectory named `data` within your DISTAL directory, and place a copy of the `TM_WORLD_BORDERS-0.3` directory into the `data` directory. Then, create a new Python program named `import_world_borders.py` within your DISTAL directory, and enter the following into it:

```
import os.path
import psycopg2
import osgeo.ogr

connection = psycopg2.connect(database="distal",
                              user="distal_user",
                              password="...")
cursor = connection.cursor()

cursor.execute("DELETE FROM countries")
```

```
srcFile = os.path.join("data", "TM_WORLD_BORDERS-0.3",
                       "TM_WORLD_BORDERS-0.3.shp")
shapefile = osgeo.ogr.Open(srcFile)
layer = shapefile.GetLayer(0)
num_done = 0

for i in range(layer.GetFeatureCount()):
    feature = layer.GetFeature(i)
    name    = feature.GetField("NAME")
    wkt     = feature.GetGeometryRef().ExportToWkt()

    cursor.execute("INSERT INTO countries (name,outline) " +
                   "VALUES (%s, ST_GeometryFromText(%s, 4326))",
                   (name, wkt))

    num_done = num_done + 1

connection.commit()

print("Imported {} countries".format(num_done))
```

This program should be pretty easy to understand; we're simply making use of OGR to load the contents of the shapefile and `psycopg2` to copy the data into the `countries` table. When you run this program, the contents of the World Borders Dataset should be imported into your database.

# The GSHHG shoreline database

Download a copy of the GSHHG shoreline database (`http://www.ngdc.noaa.gov/mgg/shorelines/gshhs.html`) if you haven't already done so. Make sure you download the full database in Shapefile format. Place the resulting `GSHHS_shp` directory into your `data` subdirectory.

> Remember that the GSHHG database used to be called GSHHS, which is why the GSHHS abbreviation still appears in a few places, such as the name of this shapefile.

The GSHHG shoreline database consists of separate shapefiles defining land/water boundaries at five different resolutions. For the DISTAL application, we want to import four of these levels (coastline, lake, island-in-lake, and pond-in-island-in-lake) at full resolution. This shapefile is stored in a subdirectory named `f`, which stands for full resolution.

To import this data into the DISTAL database, create a new program named
`import_gshhg.py` within your DISTAL directory, and enter the following
Python code into this file:

```python
import os.path
import psycopg2
import osgeo.ogr

connection = psycopg2.connect(database="distal",
                              user="distal_user",
                              password="...")
cursor = connection.cursor()

cursor.execute("DELETE FROM shorelines")

for level in [1, 2, 3, 4]:
    num_done = 0

    srcFile = os.path.join("data", "GSHHS_shp", "f",
                           "GSHHS_f_L{}.shp".format(level))
    shapefile = osgeo.ogr.Open(srcFile)
    layer = shapefile.GetLayer(0)

    for i in range(layer.GetFeatureCount()):
        feature = layer.GetFeature(i)
        geometry = feature.GetGeometryRef()
        if geometry.IsValid():
            cursor.execute("INSERT INTO shorelines " +
                           "(level,outline) VALUES " +
                           "(%s, ST_GeometryFromText(%s, 4326))",
                           (level, geometry.ExportToWkt()))

        num_done = num_done + 1

    connection.commit()

    print("Imported {} shorelines at level {}".format(num_done,
    level))
```

Don't forget to enter the password you set up for your
distal_user user in the call to psycopg2.connect().

Notice that we have to check that the geometry is valid before inserting it into the database. This is because of some problems with a few of the geometries in the GSHHG database. It is theoretically possible to fix these invalid records, but doing so is quite complicated, so we're simply skipping them.

When you run this program, it will take a few minutes to complete as there are over 180,000 high-resolution polygons to be imported.

# US place names

You can download the list of US place names from `http://geonames.usgs.gov/domestic`. Click on the **Download Domestic Names** hyperlink, and choose the **Download all national features in one .zip file** option. This will download a file named `NationalFile_YYYYMMDD.zip`, where `YYYYMMDD` is the datestamp identifying when the file was last updated. Once again, decompress the resulting `.zip` archive and move the `NationalFile_YYYYMMDD.txt` file into your `data` subdirectory.

The file you have just downloaded is a *pipe-delimited* text file, meaning that each column is separated by a | character, like this:

```
FEATURE_ID|FEATURE_NAME|FEATURE_CLASS|...|DATE_EDITED
399|Agua Sal Creek|Stream|AZ|...|02/08/1980
400|Agua Sal Wash|Valley|AZ|...|02/08/1980
```

The first line contains the names of the various fields. While there are a lot of fields in the file, there are four fields that we are particularly interested in:

- The `FEATURE_NAME` field contains the name of the location, in UTF-8 character encoding.

- The `FEATURE_CLASS` field tells us what type of feature we are dealing with, in this case, a `Stream` or a `Valley`. There are a lot of features we don't need for the DISTAL application, for example, the names of bays, beaches, bridges, and oilfields. In fact, there is only one feature class we are interested in: `Populated Place`.

- The `PRIM_LONG_DEC` and `PRIM_LAT_DEC` fields contain the longitude and latitude of the location, in decimal degrees. According to the documentation, these coordinates use the NAD83 datum rather than the WGS84 datum used by the other data we are importing.

We are going to import the data from this file into our `places` database table. Because the latitude and longitude values use the NAD83 datum, we will use `pyproj` to convert the coordinates into WGS84 so that it is compatible with the other data we are using.

Strictly speaking, this step isn't necessary. We will be using pyproj to transform coordinates from NAD83 to WGS84. However, the data we are importing is all within the United States, and these two datums happen to be identical for points within the United States. Because of this, pyproj won't actually change the coordinates at all. But we will do this anyway, following the recommended practice of knowing the spatial reference for our data and transforming when necessary — even if that transformation is a no-op at times.

Let's write the program to import this data into the database. Create a new file named import_gnis.py in your main DISTAL directory, and enter the following Python code into this file:

```
import psycopg2
import os.path
import pyproj

connection = psycopg2.connect(database="distal",
                              user="distal_user",
                              password="...")
cursor = connection.cursor()

cursor.execute("DELETE FROM places")

srcProj = pyproj.Proj(proj='longlat', ellps='GRS80',
                      datum='NAD83')
dstProj = pyproj.Proj(proj='longlat', ellps='WGS84',
                      datum='WGS84')

f = file(os.path.join("data",
                      "NationalFile_YYYYMMDD.txt"), "r")
heading = f.readline() # Ignore field names.

num_inserted = 0

for line in f:
    parts = line.rstrip().split("|")
    featureName = parts[1]
    featureClass = parts[2]
    lat = float(parts[9])
    long = float(parts[10])
```

```
    if featureClass == "Populated Place":
        long,lat = pyproj.transform(srcProj, dstProj,
                                    long, lat)
        cursor.execute("INSERT INTO places " +
                       "(name, position) VALUES (%s, " +
                       "ST_SetSRID(" +
                       "ST_MakePoint(%s,%s), 4326))",
                       (featureName, long, lat))

        num_inserted += 1
        if num_inserted % 1000 == 0:
            connection.commit()

connection.commit()
f.close()

print("Inserted {} placenames".format(num_inserted))
```

>  Make sure you enter the password for `distal_user` in the call to `psycopg2.connect()`. Also make sure that you use the correct name for the `NationalFile_YYYYMMDD.txt` file you downloaded, according to its datestamp.

Note that we're committing the changes to the database for every 1,000 records. This speeds up the importing process. We're also using the `ST_SetSRID()` function to specify the SRID for the Point geometry before we insert it—we need to do this because we've told PostGIS to only accept geometries which have an SRID value of `4326`.

When you run this program, it will take a few minutes to complete. Once it's finished, you will have imported over 200,000 US place names into the `places` table.

# Non-US place names

If you haven't already done so, download the list of non-US place names from `http://geonames.nga.mil/gns/html/namefiles.html` by clicking on the **Entire country files dataset** hyperlink. Note that this is a large download—over 450 megabytes in compressed form—so it may take a while to download.

Once it has finished downloading, you will end up with a file named `geonames_YYYYMMDD.zip` where once again YYYMMDD is the datestamp identifying when the file was last updated. Decompress this file, which will result in a directory containing two text files: `Countries.txt` and `Countries_disclaimer.txt`. We want the file named `Countries.txt`, so copy this file into your data subdirectory.

The `Countries.txt` file is probably too big to open up in a text editor. If you could, however, you'd see that this is a tab-delimited text file that uses UTF-8 character encoding. The first few lines of this file look something like this:

```
RC   UFI      ... FULL_NAME_ND_RG   NOTE        MODIFY_DATE
1   -1307834  ... Pavia                         1993-12-21
1   -1307889  ... Santa Anna        gjgscript   1993-12-21
```

As with the US place name data, there are many more features here than we need for the DISTAL application. Since we are only interested in the official names of towns and cities, we need to filter this data in the following way:

- The FC (**feature classification**) field tells us which type of feature we are dealing with. We want features with an FC value of "P" (populated place).

- The NT (**name type**) field tells us the status of this feature's name. We want names with an NT value of "N" (approved name).

- The DSG (**feature designation code**) field tells us the type of feature, in more detail than the FC field. For the DISTAL application, we are interested in features with a DSG value of "PPL" (populated place), "PPLA" (administrative capital), or "PPLC" (capital city).

> If you want to see a full list of all the feature designation codes, go to `http://geonames.nga.mil/namesgaz` and click on the **Designation Codes** link in the sidebar on the left, under **Lookup Tables**. This brings up a page where you can search for a particular feature designation code; if you leave all the fields blank and click on the **Search Designation Codes** button, a window will appear showing you all the various feature designation codes and what they mean.

There are also several different versions of each place name; we want the full name in normal reading order, which is in the field named FULL_NAME_RO.

This tells us everything we need to know to import the non-US place names into our `places` database table. Create a new Python script named `import_geonames.py` inside your `DISTAL` directory, and enter the following into this file:

```python
import psycopg2
import os.path

connection = psycopg2.connect(database="distal",
                              user="distal_user",
                              password="...")
cursor = connection.cursor()

f = open(os.path.join("data", "Countries.txt"), "r")

heading = f.readline() # Ignore field names.

num_inserted = 0

for line in f:
    parts = line.rstrip().split("\t")
    lat = float(parts[3])
    long = float(parts[4])
    featureClass = parts[9]
    featureDesignation = parts[10]
    nameType = parts[17]
    featureName = parts[22]

    if (featureClass == "P" and nameType == "N" and
        featureDesignation in ["PPL", "PPLA", "PPLC"]):
        cursor.execute("INSERT INTO places " +
                       "(name, position) VALUES (%s, " +
                       "ST_SetSRID(" +
                       "ST_MakePoint(%s,%s), 4326))",
                       (featureName, long, lat))

        num_inserted = num_inserted + 1
        if num_inserted % 1000 == 0:
            connection.commit()

f.close()
connection.commit()

print("Inserted {} placenames".format(num_inserted))
```

Notice that we don't delete the existing contents of the `places` table. This is because we've already imported some data into that table. If you need to re-import the data, you'll need to run both the `import_gnis.py` script and the `import_geonames.py` script, in that order.

Go ahead and run this program. It will take a while to complete—maybe 10 to 15 minutes, depending on the speed of your computer—as you're adding over three million place names to the database.

# Implementing the DISTAL application

Now that we have the data, we can start to implement the DISTAL application itself. To keep things simple, we will use CGI scripts to implement the user interface.

**What is a CGI Script?**

While the details of writing CGI scripts are beyond the scope of this book, the basic concept is to print the raw HTML output to `stdout` and to process the incoming CGI parameters from the browser using the built-in `cgi` module.

To run a Python program as a CGI script on Mac OS X or Linux, you have to do two things: first, you have to add a "shebang" line to the start of the script, like this:

```
#!/usr/bin/python
```

The exact path you use will depend on where you have Python installed on your computer. The second thing you need to do is make your script executable, like this:

```
chmod +x selectCountry.py
```

On MS Windows computers, the file extension (`.py`) will automatically cause the CGI scripts to call the Python interpreter, so you shouldn't need to do either of these things.

For more information on CGI scripts, take a look at one of the CGI tutorials available on the Internet, for example `http://wiki.python.org/moin/CgiScripts`.

CGI scripts aren't the only way we could implement the DISTAL application. Other possible approaches include using web application frameworks such as TurboGears or Django, using AJAX to write your own dynamic web application, using CherryPy (`http://cherrypy.org`), or even using tools such as Pyjamas (`http://pyjs.org`) to compile Python code into JavaScript. All of these approaches, however, are more complicated than CGI, and we will be making use of CGI scripts in this chapter to keep the code as straightforward as possible.

Let's take a look at how our CGI scripts will implement the DISTAL application's workflow:

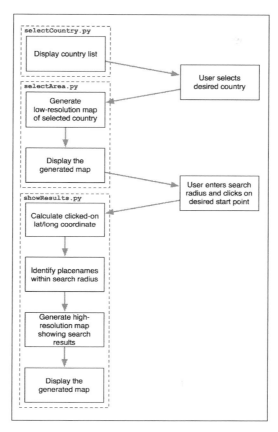

As you can see, there are three separate CGI scripts, selectCountry.py, selectArea.py, and showResults.py, each implementing a distinct part of the DISTAL application.

Let's start by creating a simple web server capable of running our CGI scripts. With Python, this is easy; simply create the following program, which we will call webServer.py:

```
import http.server

address = ('', 8000)
handler = http.server.CGIHTTPRequestHandler
server = http.server.HTTPServer(address, handler)
server.serve_forever()
```

Place this file into your main DISTAL directory. Next, create a new subdirectory named cgi-bin in the same directory. This subdirectory will hold the various CGI scripts you create.

Running webServer.py will start up a web server at http://127.0.0.1:8000 which will execute any CGI scripts you place into the cgi-bin subdirectory. So, for example, you could access the selectCountry.py script by entering the following URL into your web browser:

http://127.0.0.1:8000/cgi-bin/selectCountry.py

# The "select country" script

The task of the selectCountry.py script is to display a list of countries to the user. This allows the user to choose a desired country, which is then passed on to the selectArea.py script for further processing.

Here is what the selectCountry.py script's output will look like:

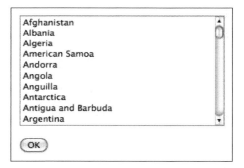

 We're not worrying too much about the visual appearance of our program. It would be easy to use a CSS stylesheet, or even a library such as Bootstrap, to make the DISTAL system look more professional. In this chapter, however, we're concentrating on functionality rather than how to make our program look good.

This CGI script is very basic—we simply print out the contents of the HTML page that lets the user choose a country from a list of country names:

```
#!/usr/bin/python

import psycopg2

connection = psycopg2.connect(database="distal",
```

```
                              user="distal_user",
                              password="...")
cursor = connection.cursor()

print('Content-Type: text/html; charset=UTF-8')
print()
print()
print('<html>')
print('<head><title>Select Country</title></head>')
print('<body>')
print('<form method="POST" action="selectArea.py">')
print('<select name="countryID" size="10">')

cursor.execute("SELECT id,name FROM countries " +
                "ORDER BY name")
for id,name in cursor:
    print('<option value="'+str(id)+'">'+name+'</option>')

print('</select>')
print('<p>')
print('<input type="submit" value="OK">')
print('</form>')
print('</body>')
print('</html>')
```

Make sure you name this script `selectCountry.py` and place it inside your `cgi-bin` directory. If you are running this on Mac OS X or Linux, you will need to change the shebang line at the start of the script if you need to use a different Python interpreter. You should also use the `chmod` command, as described earlier, to make the script executable.

**Understanding HTML forms**

If you haven't used HTML forms before, don't panic. They are quite straightforward, and if you want, you can just copy the code from the examples given here. To learn more about HTML forms, check out one of the many tutorials available online. A good example can be found at `http://www.pagetutor.com/form_tutor`.

You should now be able to run this script by starting up the `webserver.py` program and typing the following URL into your web browser:

`http://127.0.0.1:8000/cgi-bin/selectCountry.py`

All going well, you should see the list of countries and be able to select one. If you click on the **OK** button, you should see a 404 error, indicating that the selectArea.py script doesn't exist yet—which is perfectly correct, as we haven't implemented it yet.

# The "select area" script

The next part of the DISTAL application is selectArea.py. This script generates a web page that displays a simple map of the selected country. The user can enter a desired search radius and click on the map to identify the starting point for the DISTAL search:

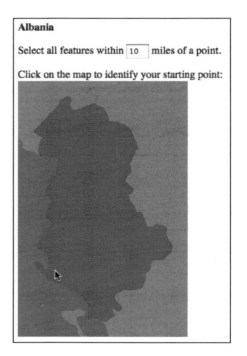

Because this script involves displaying a map, we are going to have to learn how to access Mapnik from a CGI script. We've already seen how Mapnik works in *Chapter 7, Using Python and Mapnik to Generate Maps*; for the DISTAL application, we're going to write a standalone mapGenerator.py module that generates the map and stores the resulting image into a temporary file so that it can be displayed.

Here is the full source code for the `mapGenerator.py` module. Even though this isn't a CGI script, it should be placed in your `cgi-bin` directory so that our various CGI scripts can access it.

```python
# mapGenerator.py

import os, os.path, sys, tempfile
import mapnik

def generateMap(tableName, minX, minY, maxX, maxY,
                mapWidth, mapHeight,
                hiliteExpr=None, points=None):

    extent = "{},{},{},{}".format(minX, minY, maxX, maxY)

    layer = mapnik.Layer("Layer")
    layer.datasource = mapnik.PostGIS(dbname="distal",
                                      table=tableName,
                                      user="distal_user",
                                      password="...",
                                      extent=extent,
                                      geometry_field="outline",
                                      srid=4326)

    map = mapnik.Map(mapWidth, mapHeight,
                     '+proj=longlat +datum=WGS84')
    map.background = mapnik.Color("#8080a0")

    style = mapnik.Style()

    rule = mapnik.Rule()
    if hiliteExpr != None:
        rule.filter = mapnik.Filter(hiliteExpr)

    rule.symbols.append(mapnik.PolygonSymbolizer(
        mapnik.Color("#408000")))
    rule.symbols.append(mapnik.LineSymbolizer(
        mapnik.Stroke(mapnik.Color("#000000"), 0.1)))

    style.rules.append(rule)

    rule = mapnik.Rule()
    rule.set_else(True)
```

```
rule.symbols.append(mapnik.PolygonSymbolizer(
    mapnik.Color("#a0a0a0")))
rule.symbols.append(mapnik.LineSymbolizer(
    mapnik.Stroke(mapnik.Color("#404040"), 0.1)))

style.rules.append(rule)

map.append_style("Map Style", style)
layer.styles.append("Map Style")
map.layers.append(layer)

if points != None:
    memoryDatasource = mapnik.MemoryDatasource()
    context = mapnik.Context()
    context.push("name")
    next_id = 1
    for long,lat,name in points:
        wkt = "POINT (%0.8f %0.8f)" % (long,lat)
        feature = mapnik.Feature(context, next_id)
        feature['name'] = name
        feature.add_geometries_from_wkt(wkt)
        next_id = next_id + 1
        memoryDatasource.add_feature(feature)

    layer = mapnik.Layer("Points")
    layer.datasource = memoryDatasource

    style = mapnik.Style()
    rule = mapnik.Rule()

    pointImgFile = os.path.join(os.path.dirname(__file__),
                                "point.png")

    shield = mapnik.ShieldSymbolizer(
            mapnik.Expression('[name]'),
            "DejaVu Sans Bold", 10,
            mapnik.Color("#000000"),
            mapnik.PathExpression(pointImgFile))
    shield.displacement = (0, 7)
    shield.unlock_image = True
    rule.symbols.append(shield)

    style.rules.append(rule)
```

```
        map.append_style("Point Style", style)
        layer.styles.append("Point Style")

        map.layers.append(layer)

    map.zoom_to_box(mapnik.Envelope(minX, minY, maxX, maxY))

    scriptDir = os.path.dirname(__file__)
    cacheDir = os.path.join(scriptDir, "..", "mapCache")
    if not os.path.exists(cacheDir):
        os.mkdir(cacheDir)
    fd,filename = tempfile.mkstemp(".png", dir=cacheDir)
    os.close(fd)

    mapnik.render_to_file(map, filename, "png")

    return "../mapCache/" + os.path.basename(filename)
```

 Don't forget to specify the password for your `distal_user` so the program can access the database.

Most of this should be pretty easy to understand, given the concepts covered in *Chapter 7, Using Python and Mapnik to Generate Maps*. There are three things you may not have encountered before:

- Using a `ShieldSymbolizer` to display the points.

- The extra parameters passed to the `PostGIS` data source, which are required because Mapnik can't automatically handle `Geography` columns.

- The way we use a temporary file to hold the generated map image so it can be displayed on a web page. As you can see, we're returning the path (relative to our main `DISTAL` directory) for the generated map image.

Note that to use this module, you will need to download or create a small image file to represent the position of a place name on the map. This 9 x 9 pixel image looks like this:

A copy of this image is available as a part of the example source code that comes with this book. If you don't have access to the example code, you can create or search for an image that looks like this; make sure the image is named `point.png` and is placed in the same directory as the `mapGenerator.py` module.

We're now ready to start writing the `selectArea.py` script. We'll start with our shebang line and import the various modules we'll need:

```
#!/usr/bin/python

import cgi, os.path, sys
import psycopg2
import mapGenerator
```

Next, we will define some useful constants to make the HTML generation easier:

```
HEADER = "Content-Type: text/html; charset=UTF-8\n\n" \
       + "<html><head><title>Select Area</title>" \
       + "</head><body>"
FOOTER = "</body></html>"
HIDDEN_FIELD = '<input type="hidden" name="{}" value="{}">'

MAX_WIDTH = 600
MAX_HEIGHT = 400
```

We next open up a connection to the database:

```
connection = psycopg2.connect(database="distal",
                              user="distal_user",
                              password="...")
cursor = connection.cursor()
```

Our next task is to extract the ID of the country the user clicked on:

```
form = cgi.FieldStorage()
if "countryID" not in form:
    print(HEADER)
    print('<b>Please select a country</b>')
    print(FOOTER)
    sys.exit(0)

countryID = int(form['countryID'].value)
```

Now that we have the ID of the selected country, we're ready to start generating the map. Doing this is a three-step process:

1.  Calculating the bounding box that defines the portion of the world to be displayed.
2.  Calculating the map's dimensions.
3.  Rendering the map image.

Let's look at each of these in turn.

# Calculating the bounding box

Before we can show the selected country on a map, we need to calculate the bounding box for that country, that is, the minimum and maximum latitude and longitude values. Knowing the bounding box allows us to draw a map centered over the desired country.

Add the following to the end of your selectArea.py script:

```
cursor.execute("SELECT name," +
               "ST_YMin(ST_Envelope(outline))," +
               "ST_XMin(ST_Envelope(outline))," +
               "ST_YMax(ST_Envelope(outline))," +
               "ST_XMax(ST_Envelope(outline)) " +
               "FROM countries WHERE id=%s",
               (countryID,))

row = cursor.fetchone()
if row != None:
    name     = row[0]
    min_lat  = row[1]
    min_long = row[2]
    max_lat  = row[3]
    max_long = row[4]
else:
    print(HEADER)
    print('<b>Missing country</b>')
    print(FOOTER)
    sys.exit(0)

minLong = minLong - 0.2
minLat = minLat - 0.2
maxLong = maxLong + 0.2
maxLat = maxLat + 0.2
```

As you can see, we extract the country's bounding box from the database and then increase the bounds slightly so that the country won't butt up against the edge of the map. We also grab the name of the country at the same time, as we'll need this shortly.

## Calculating the map's dimensions

Because countries aren't square, we can't simply draw the country onto a map of a fixed size. Instead, we have to calculate the **aspect ratio** of the country's bounding box (its width as a proportion of its height) and then calculate the size of the map image based on this aspect ratio, while limiting the overall size of the image so that it can fit within our web page. Here's the necessary code, which you should add to the end of your `selectArea.py` script:

```
width = float(maxLong - minLong)
height = float(maxLat - minLat)
aspectRatio = width/height

mapWidth = MAX_WIDTH
mapHeight = int(mapWidth / aspectRatio)

if mapHeight > MAX_HEIGHT:
    # Scale the map to fit.
    scaleFactor = float(MAX_HEIGHT) / float(mapHeight)
    mapWidth = int(mapWidth * scaleFactor)
    mapHeight = int(mapHeight * scaleFactor)
```

Doing this means that the map is correctly sized to reflect the dimensions of the country we are displaying.

## Rendering the map image

With the bounding box, the map's dimensions, and the data source all set up, we are finally ready to render the map into an image file. This is done using a single function call, as follows:

```
hilite = "[id] = " + str(countryID)
imgFile = mapGenerator.generateMap("countries",
                                   minLong, minLat,
                                   maxLong, maxLat,
                                   mapWidth, mapHeight,
                                   hiliteExpr=hilite)
```

Notice that we set the `hiliteExpr` parameter to the value `[id] = "+str(countryID)`. This visually highlights the country with the given ID.

The `mapGenerator.generateMap()` function returns a reference to a PNG-format image file containing the generated map. This image file is stored in a temporary directory, and the file's relative pathname is returned to the caller. This allows us to use the returned `imgFile` directly within our CGI script, like this:

```
print(HEADER)
print('<b>' + name + '</b>')
print('<p>')
print('<form method="POST" action="showResults.py">')
print('Select all features within')
print('<input type="text" name="radius" value="10" size="2">')
print('miles of a point.')
print('<p>')
print('Click on the map to identify your starting point:')
print('<br>')
print('<input type="image" src="' + imgFile + '" ismap>')
print(HIDDEN_FIELD.format("countryID", countryID))
print(HIDDEN_FIELD.format("countryName", name))
print(HIDDEN_FIELD.format("mapWidth", mapWidth))
print(HIDDEN_FIELD.format("mapHeight", mapHeight))
print(HIDDEN_FIELD.format("minLong", minLong))
print(HIDDEN_FIELD.format("minLat", minLat))
print(HIDDEN_FIELD.format("maxLong", maxLong))
print(HIDDEN_FIELD.format("maxLat", maxLat))
print('</form>')
print(FOOTER)
```

The HIDDEN_FIELD template generates lines that look like the following:

`<input type="hidden" name="..." value="...">`

These lines define *hidden form fields* that pass the various values we calculate on to the next CGI script. We'll discuss how this information is used in the next section.

The use of `<input type="image" src="..." ismap>` in this CGI script has the interesting effect of making the map **clickable**: when the user clicks on the image, the enclosing HTML form will be submitted with two extra parameters named `x` and `y`. These contain the coordinate within the image that the user clicked on.

This completes the `selectArea.py` CGI script. If you are running this on Mac OS X or a Linux machine, you will need to make sure you added an appropriate shebang line to the start of your program and made it executable, as described earlier, so that it can run as a CGI script.

All going well, you should be able to point your web browser to `http://127.0.0.1:8000/cgi-bin/selectCountry.py`.

When you select a country, you should see a map of that country displayed within your web browser. If you click within the map, you'll get a 404 error, indicating that the final CGI script hasn't been written yet.

# The "show results" script

The final CGI script is where the real work is done. Start by creating your `showResults.py` file, and type the following into this file:

```python
#!/usr/bin/env python

import psycopg2
import cgi

import mapGenerator

##############################################################

MAX_WIDTH = 800
MAX_HEIGHT = 600

METERS_PER_MILE = 1609.344

##############################################################

connection = psycopg2.connect(database="distal",
                              user="distal_user",
                              password="...")
cursor = connection.cursor()
```

> Make sure you enter the password for your `distal_user` database user in the `psycopg2.connect()` statement. Also, don't forget to mark this file as executable and enter the appropriate shebang value if you are running this on Mac OS X or Linux.

In this script, we will take the (*x*, *y*) coordinate the user clicked on along with the entered search radius, convert the (*x*, *y*) coordinate into a longitude and latitude, and identify all the place names within that search radius. We will then generate a high-resolution map showing the shorelines and place names within the search radius and display that map to the user.

 Remember that *x* corresponds to a longitude value and *y* to a latitude value. (*x*, *y*) equals (longitude, latitude), not (latitude, longitude).

Let's examine each of these steps in turn.

# Identifying the clicked-on point

The `selectArea.py` script generates an HTML form that is submitted when the user clicks on the low-resolution country map. The `showResults.py` script receives the form parameters, including the *x* and *y* coordinates of the point the user clicked on.

By itself, this coordinate isn't very useful, as it's simply the *x* and *y* offset, measured in pixels, of the point the user clicked on. We need to translate the submitted (*x*, *y*) pixel coordinate into a latitude and longitude value corresponding to the clicked-on point on the earth's surface.

To do this, we need to have the following information:

- The map's bounding box in geographic coordinates: `minLong`, `minLat`, `maxLong`, and `maxLat`
- The map's size in pixels: `mapWidth` and `mapHeight`

These variables were all calculated in the previous section and passed to us using hidden form variables, along with the country name and ID, the desired search radius, and the (*x*,*y*) coordinate of the clicked-on point. We can retrieve all of these using the `cgi` module. To do this, add the following to the end of your `showResults.py` file:

```
form = cgi.FieldStorage()

countryID   = int(form['countryID'].value)
radius      = int(form['radius'].value)
x           = int(form['x'].value)
y           = int(form['y'].value)
mapWidth    = int(form['mapWidth'].value)
mapHeight   = int(form['mapHeight'].value)
countryName = form['countryName'].value
```

```
minLong      = float(form['minLong'].value)
minLat       = float(form['minLat'].value)
maxLong      = float(form['maxLong'].value)
maxLat       = float(form['maxLat'].value)
```

With this information, we can now calculate the latitude and longitude that the user clicked on. We start by calculating how far across the image the user clicked, as a number in the range from 0 to 1:

```
xFract = float(x)/float(mapWidth)
```

An xFract value of 0.0 corresponds to the left side of the image, while an xFract value of 1.0 corresponds to the right side of the image. We then combine this with the minimum and maximum longitude values to calculate the longitude of the clicked-on point:

```
longitude = minLong + xFract * (maxLong-minLong)
```

We then do the same to convert the Y coordinate into a latitude value:

```
yFract = float(y)/float(mapHeight)
latitude = minLat + (1-yFract) * (maxLat-minLat)
```

Notice that we are using (1-yFract) rather than yFract in the preceding calculation. This is because the minLat value refers to the latitude of the *bottom* of the image, while a yFract value of 0.0 corresponds to the *top* of the image. By using (1-yFract), we flip the values vertically so that the latitude is calculated correctly.

# Identifying matching place names

Let's review what we have achieved so far: the user has selected a country, viewed a simple map of the country's outline, entered the desired search radius, and clicked on a point on the map to identify the origin for the search. We then converted this clicked-on point into a latitude and longitude value.

All of this provides us with three numbers: the desired search radius and the latitude and longitude of the point at which to start the search. Our task now is to identify which place names are within the given search radius of the clicked-on point:

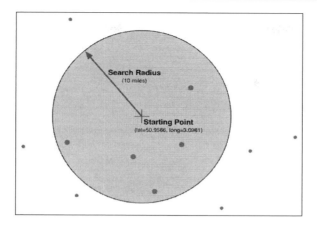

Fortunately, because our `places` table uses the GEOGRAPHY column type, we can ask PostGIS to do all the hard work for us. Here is the necessary code to find the matching place names:

```
cursor.execute("SELECT ST_X(position::geometry)," +
               "ST_Y(position::geometry),name " +
               "FROM places WHERE " +
               "ST_DWithin(position, ST_MakePoint(%s, %s), %s)",
               (longitude, latitude, radius * METERS_PER_MILE))

points = []
for name,long,lat in cursor:
    points.append([long, lat, name])
```

> Notice that we have to use `position::geometry` to extract the *X* and *Y* values from the place names. This syntax converts the `position` value from a geography value back into a geometry one—we have to do this because the `ST_X()` and `ST_Y()` functions don't accept geography values.

The matching place names will be stored in the `points` variable, as a list of (`longitude`, `latitude`, `name`) tuples.

# Displaying the results

Now that we have calculated the list of place names within the desired search radius, we can use the `mapGenerator.py` module to display them. To do this, we're going to have to calculate the bounding box for the area to display, based on the clicked-on point, the supplied search radius, and a *margin* to ensure that we don't draw place names right on the edge of the map:

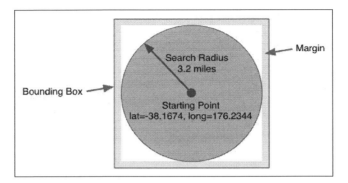

To do this, we'll use `pyproj` to calculate the position of four coordinates directly north, south, east, and west of the starting point:

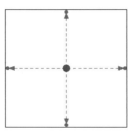

How far north, south, east, or west we go depends on the search radius, but we'll also add a 10% margin to this distance. Using `pyproj`, this calculation is quite straightforward:

```
geod = pyproj.Geod(ellps="WGS84")
distance = radius * METERS_PER_MILE * 1.1
```

```
x,y,angle = geod.fwd(longitude, latitude, 0, distance)
maxLat = y

x,y,angle = geod.fwd(longitude, latitude, 90, distance)
maxLong = x

x,y,angle = geod.fwd(longitude, latitude, 180, distance)
minLat = y

x,y,angle = geod.fwd(longitude, latitude, 270, distance)
minLong = x
```

Once this has been done, we can use our `mapGenerator.py` module to generate a map showing the results we have found:

```
imgFile = mapGenerator.generateMap("shorelines",
                                   minLong, minLat,
                                   maxLong, maxLat,
                                   600, 600,
                                   points=points)
```

When we called the map generator previously, we used a filter expression to highlight particular features. In this case, we don't need to highlight anything. Instead, we pass it the list of place names to display on the map in the keyword parameter named `points`.

The map generator creates a PNG-format file and returns a reference to that file. Let's finish our program by displaying the map so the user can see it:

```
print(HEADER)
print('<b>' + countryName + '</b>')
print('<p>')
print('<img src="' + imgFile + '">')
print(FOOTER)
```

This completes our first attempt at the entire DISTAL application. Let's now see how it runs.

# Using DISTAL

To run the DISTAL system, simply start up the `webserver.py` script you wrote earlier, and use your web browser to go to the following URL: `http://127.0.0.1:8000/cgi-bin/selectCountry.py`. Select the country you are interested in, and then click on the **OK** button. Then, enter a search radius and click on a point within the map of that country. All going well, you should see a detailed map of the area you clicked on, with its various place names displayed on the map. The following image shows what the results should look like:

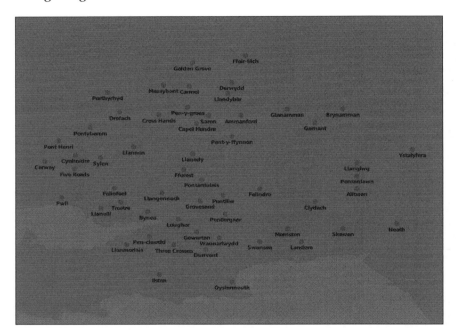

There's a lot more we could do with our program, and if you dig deep enough, you'll start to notice a few problems with it. Don't worry, though; we'll look further into these problems in the next chapter.

# Summary

In this chapter, we implemented a sophisticated web-based application that displays shorelines, towns, and lakes within a given radius of a starting point. This application was the impetus for exploring a number of important concepts within geospatial application development, including storing large amounts of spatial information in a database, performing distance-based queries against spatial data, and using Mapnik to display maps on a web page. In the next chapter, we will examine the DISTAL application in more detail and look at ways in which we can improve the usability and performance of this application.

# 9

# Improving the DISTAL Application

In the previous chapter, we wrote a complete implementation of the DISTAL system that works as advertised: a user can choose a country, enter a search radius in miles, click on a starting point, and see a high-resolution map showing all the place names within the desired search radius. Unfortunately, the DISTAL application is lacking in a number of areas, and even a cursory look at it will reveal some major problems. In this chapter, we will work on solving these problems. Along the way, we will:

- Learn about the anti-meridian and solve the problems it can cause when working with latitude and longitude-based coordinates

- See how to add a zoom feature to our CGI scripts

- Discover the consequences of working with huge polygons, and how you can improve performance by breaking these polygons down into smaller pieces

- Make huge improvements to the speed of our DISTAL application by splitting the shoreline data into tiles and displaying a single tile rather than the entire shoreline

Let's work through these issues one at a time.

# Dealing with the anti-meridian line

If you explore the DISTAL application, you will soon discover a major usability problem with some of the countries. For example, if you click on **United States** in the **Select Country** page, you will be presented with the following map to click on:

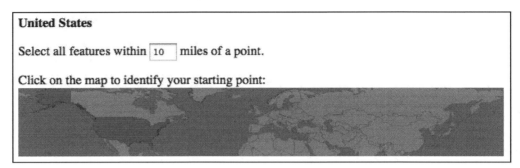

Accurately clicking on a desired point using this map would be almost impossible because it covers most of the earth's surface.

The problem is that Alaska crosses the **anti-meridian line**. The anti-meridian line is the line where the left and right sides of the world map join, that is, at ±180 degrees of longitude. Because of the way longitude values wrap around the globe, -180 degrees of longitude is the same as +180 degrees of longitude. The ±180 degree line is called the anti-meridian line and is the cause of many problems when dealing with geospatial data.

In the case of the USA, part of the Alaskan peninsula extends beyond 180 degrees west and continues across the Aleutian Islands to finish at Attu Island, which has a longitude of 172 degrees east. Because it crosses the anti-meridian line, Alaska appears on both the left and right sides of the world map:

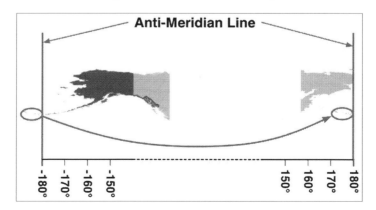

Because the portion of Alaska that sits to the left of the -180 degree line is shifted to the right-hand side of the map, the DISTAL application thinks that Alaska, and hence the entire USA, spans almost the entire globe. This is why we get strange results when we draw a map covering the bounds of the USA.

To solve this problem, we are going to have to identify the countries that cross the anti-meridian line and adjust them so they only appear on one side of the line.

We can do this for the DISTAL application because we only show a single country's outline at a time. If we had to show multiple countries at once, we'd have to create two versions of every country's outline: one in its original place and another shifted by 180 degrees. We could then choose which of the two sets of outlines to display based on which country the user selected.

This adjustment is done by moving the individual polygons that make up the country's outline so they all sit on the same side of the map. The resulting polygons will sit on either side of the anti-meridian line, with some polygons on one side and some on the other:

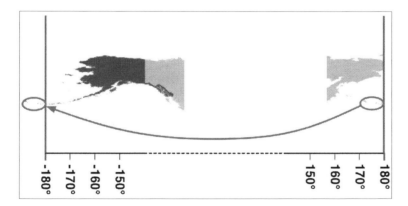

Note that this adjustment moves the overall bounds of the country's polygons beyond ±180 degrees. This isn't a problem, as both PostGIS and Mapnik treat the coordinates as real numbers that can have any value.

To support adjusting the polygons that cross the anti-meridian line, we will need to update the `import_world_borders.py` script we wrote in the previous chapter. Go back to this script, and add the following highlighted line to this file:

```
for i in range(layer.GetFeatureCount()):
    feature = layer.GetFeature(i)
    name = feature.GetField("NAME")
```

```
wkt = feature.GetGeometryRef().ExportToWkt()
wkt = adjust_for_antimeridian(name, wkt)

cursor.execute("INSERT INTO countries (name,outline) " +
               "VALUES (%s, ST_GeometryFromText(%s, 4326))",
               (name, wkt))

num_done = num_done + 1

connection.commit()

print("Imported {} countries".format(num_done))
```

As you can see, we're calling a new function called `adjust_for_antimeridian()` to do the hard work. Before we start writing this function, add the following `import` statements to the top of your program:

```
import shapely.wkt
from shapely.geometry import MultiPolygon
from shapely.affinity import translate
```

Our function is going to use these imported modules. Next, we want to define the function itself. Add the following to your program, immediately after the `import` statements:

```
def adjust_for_antimeridian(name, wkt):
```

As you can see, we're passing in the name of the country as well as the country's outline in WKT format. We need the name of the country so that we can tell the user which country's outline we have adjusted. Upon completion, our function will return either the original WKT outline unchanged or a new WKT outline representing the adjusted outline for the country.

Let's start by creating a Shapely `Geometry` object from the supplied WKT text and then checking to see whether it is a MultiPolygon. If the outline isn't a MultiPolygon, then the country doesn't have multiple parts and so we can't do any adjusting. Here is the relevant code, which you should enter immediately after the function definition:

```
outline = shapely.wkt.loads(wkt)

if outline.geom_type != "MultiPolygon":
    print("Importing {}".format(name))
    return wkt
```

Notice that we're printing out the name of the country, so the user knows which country we're importing. We then return the original outline unchanged.

Next, we want to skip any countries that don't sit close to the anti-meridian line on both sides. If a country doesn't sit close to the anti-meridian line on both sides, then it won't span that line, and we can skip it. Here is the relevant code:

```
minLong,minLat,maxLong,maxLat = outline.bounds
if minLong >= -160 or maxLong <= 160:
    print("Importing {}".format(name))
    return wkt
```

Our next task is to split the country's outline up into individual parts, where each part is a single Polygon within the outline's MultiPolygon. For each part, we record whether the Polygon is closer to the anti-meridian line on the left side or the right. Add the following to the end of your adjust_for_antimeridian() function:

```
parts = []

for geom in outline.geoms:
    left = geom.bounds[0]
    right = geom.bounds[2]
    if left == -180 and right == +180:
        print("{} spans the entire world, so we can't shift it."
              .format(name))
        return wkt

    distance_to_left_side = -(-180 - left)
    distance_to_right_side = 180 - right

    if distance_to_left_side < distance_to_right_side:
        side = "left"
    else:
        side = "right"

    parts.append({'side' : side,
                  'geom' : geom})
```

Notice that we check to see whether a single Polygon within the outline spans the entire world. If so, we return the original outline unchanged, as we have no way of adjusting it. Note that this only applies to Antarctica.

Now that we've split the country's outline up into separate parts, let's use this information to decide whether to shift the entire country to the left or right side of the map. To do this, we'll count how many parts are on each side of the map and shift the whole country to the side with the most parts. To do this, add the following to the end of your function:

```
num_on_left = 0
num_on_right = 0

for part in parts:
    if part['side'] == "left":
        num_on_left = num_on_left + 1
    else:
        num_on_right = num_on_right + 1

if num_on_left > num_on_right:
    print("Shifting {} to left".format(name))
    shift_direction = "left"
else:
    print("Shifting {} to right".format(name))
    shift_direction = "right"
```

We next want to shift the parts to the appropriate side. That is, if we are shifting the entire country to the right, we will shift any parts that are on the left across to the right by adding 360 degrees to the part's longitude. Similarly, if we are shifting the country to the left, we shift any parts that are on the right over to the left by subtracting 360 degrees from the part's longitude. Here is the relevant code:

```
for part in parts:
    old_bounds = part['geom'].bounds
    if part['side'] == "left" and shift_direction == "right":
        part['geom'] = translate(part['geom'], 360)
    elif part['side'] == "right" and shift_direction == "left":
        part['geom'] = translate(part['geom'], -360)
```

Finally, we need to combine the various parts back into a single combined outline, which we can return back to the caller in WKT format:

```
polygons = []
for part in parts:
    polygons.append(part['geom'])
combined = MultiPolygon(polygons)

return combined.wkt
```

This completes our `adjust_for_antimeridian()` function. You should now be able to re-import the country outlines by running the updated `import_world_borders.py` script. If you then run the DISTAL application, you will see that the outline of the USA no longer spans the entire globe:

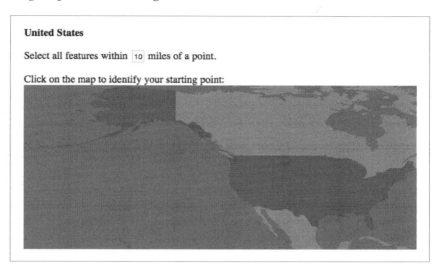

**United States**

Select all features within [10] miles of a point.

Click on the map to identify your starting point:

# Dealing with the scale problem

The preceding illustration reveals a second problem with the DISTAL system: because the USA including Alaska is over 4,000 miles wide, accurately selecting a 10-mile search radius by clicking on a point on this map would be an exercise in frustration.

To solve this problem, we will implement a **zoom** feature so that the user can click more accurately on the desired starting point. Because the DISTAL system is implemented as a series of CGI scripts, our zoom feature is going to be rather basic: if the user holds down the *Shift* key while clicking, we zoom in on the clicked-on point. If the *Shift* key is not held down when the user clicks, we proceed with the search as usual.

In a real web application, we would implement a complete **slippy map** interface that supports click-and-drag as well as on-screen controls to zoom both in and out. Doing this is way beyond what we can do with simple CGI scripts, however. We will return to the topic of slippy maps in *Chapter 10, Tools for Web-based Geospatial Development*.

To implement zooming, we will need to update the `selectArea.py` script we wrote earlier. We will make use of some rudimentary JavaScript code to detect whether the user held down the *Shift* key and, if so, reload the "select area" page with additional CGI parameters that allow us to zoom in. In particular, we are going to modify our CGI script to accept the following additional parameters:

| CGI parameter(s) | Description |
|---|---|
| x and y | The coordinates of the point on which the user clicked. |
| zoom | The zoom level to use, where 0 equals no zoom. |
| minLat, minLong, maxLat, maxLong | The lat/long bounding box that was used to draw the map at the previous zoom level. |

All of these parameters are optional—if they are not supplied, default values will be calculated.

Let's modify our script to use these parameters to zoom in on the map. Start by deleting the block of code that calculated the lat/long bounding box, that is, the lines of code starting with the `cursor.execute("SELECT name, ...")` statement and ending with the line `maxLat = maxLat + 0.2`. Replace these with the following code:

```
if "x" in form:
    click_x = int(form['x'].value)
else:
    click_x = None

if "y" in form:
    click_y = int(form['y'].value)
else:
    click_y = None

if "zoom" in form:
    zoom = int(form['zoom'].value)
else:
    zoom = 0

if ("minLat" in form and "minLong" in form and
    "maxLat" in form and "maxLong" in form):
    # Use the supplied bounding box.
    minLat  = float(form['minLat'].value)
```

```
        minLong = float(form['minLong'].value)
        maxLat  = float(form['maxLat'].value)
        maxLong = float(form['maxLong'].value)
    else:
        # Calculate the bounding box from the country outline.

        cursor.execute("SELECT " +
                "ST_YMin(ST_Envelope(outline))," +
                "ST_XMin(ST_Envelope(outline))," +
                "ST_YMax(ST_Envelope(outline))," +
                "ST_XMax(ST_Envelope(outline)) " +
                "FROM countries WHERE id=%s", (countryID,))

        row = cursor.fetchone()
        if row != None:
            minLat  = row[0]
            minLong = row[1]
            maxLat  = row[2]
            maxLong = row[3]
        else:
            print(HEADER)
            print('<b>Missing country</b>')
            print(FOOTER)
            sys.exit(0)

        minLong = minLong - 0.2
        minLat = minLat - 0.2
        maxLong = maxLong + 0.2
        maxLat = maxLat + 0.2

    # Get the country's name.

    cursor.execute("SELECT name FROM countries WHERE id=%s",
                (countryID,))
    name = cursor.fetchone()[0]
```

As you can see, we extract the x, y, and zoom CGI parameters, setting them to default values if they are not supplied. We then check whether the minLat, minLong, maxLat, and maxLong parameters are supplied. If not, we ask the database to calculate these values based on the country's outline and then add a margin of 0.2 degrees to each one. Finally, we load the name of the country from the database.

Now that we have our CGI parameters and are still calculating default values when required, we can use these parameters to zoom in on the map as required. Fortunately, this is quite easy: we simply modify the bounding box to show a smaller area of the world if the user has zoomed in. To do this, add the following code immediately before the `hilite = "[id] = " + str(countryID)` line:

```
if zoom != 0 and click_x != None and click_y != None:
    xFract = float(click_x)/float(mapWidth)
    longitude = minLong + xFract * (maxLong-minLong)

    yFract = float(click_y)/float(mapHeight)
    latitude = minLat + (1-yFract) * (maxLat-minLat)

    width = (maxLong - minLong) / (2**zoom)
    height = (maxLat - minLat) / (2**zoom)

    minLong = longitude - width / 2
    maxLong = longitude + width / 2
    minLat = latitude - height / 2
    maxLat = latitude + height / 2
```

In this section of the script, we first calculate the latitude and longitude of the point where the user clicked. We will zoom in on this point. We then use the zoom level to calculate the width and height of the area to display, and we then recalculate the bounding box so that it has the given width and height but is centered on the clicked-on point.

We next need to write the JavaScript code to detect when the user clicks with the *Shift* key held down, and call our script again with the appropriate parameters. To do this, replace the HEADER definition near the top of the file with the following:

```
HEADER = "\n".join([
    "Content-Type: text/html; charset=UTF-8",
    "",
    "",
    "<html><head><title>Select Area</title>",
    "<script type='text/javascript'>",
    "  function onClick(e) {",
    "    e = e || window.event;",
    "    if (e.shiftKey) {",
    "      var target = e.target || e.srcElement;",
    "      var rect = target.getBoundingClientRect();",
    "      var offsetX = e.clientX - rect.left;",
    "      var offsetY = e.clientY - rect.top;",
```

```
     "         var countryID = document.getElementsByName('countryID')[0].
value;",
     "         var minLat = document.getElementsByName('minLat')[0].
value;",
     "         var minLong = document.getElementsByName('minLong')[0].
value;",
     "         var maxLat = document.getElementsByName('maxLat')[0].
value;",
     "         var maxLong = document.getElementsByName('maxLong')[0].
value;",
     "         var zoom = document.getElementsByName('zoom')[0].value;",
     "         var new_zoom = parseInt(zoom, 10) + 1;",
     "         window.location.href = 'selectArea.py'",
     "                            + '?countryID=' + countryID",
     "                            + '&minLat=' + minLat",
     "                            + '&minLong=' + minLong",
     "                            + '&maxLat=' + maxLat",
     "                            + '&maxLong=' + maxLong",
     "                            + '&zoom=' + new_zoom",
     "                            + '&x=' + offsetX",
     "                            + '&y=' + offsetY;",
     "       return false;",
     "    } else {",
     "       return true;",
     "    }",
     "  }",
     "</script>",
     "</head><body>"])
```

We won't go into the details of this code, as writing JavaScript is beyond the scope of this book. In this JavaScript code, we define a function called `onClick()` which checks to see whether the user held down the *Shift* key and, if so, calculates the various CGI parameters and sets `window.location.href` to the URL used to reload the CGI script with those parameters.

There are just two more things we need to do to complete our new zoom feature: we need to add a new hidden form field to store the `zoom` value, and we need to call our `onClick()` function when the user clicks on the map. Add the following line to the list of `print(HIDDEN_FIELD.format(...))` statements near the bottom of the script:

```
print(HIDDEN_FIELD.format("zoom", zoom))
```

Finally, change the `print('<input type="image"...>')` line to the following:

```
print('<input type="image" src="' + imgFile + '" ismap ' +
    'onClick="return onClick()">')
```

This completes the changes required to support zooming. If you now run the DISTAL program and select a country, you should be able to hold down the *Shift* key while clicking to zoom in on the map. This should make it much easier to select the desired point within a larger country.

 To zoom back out again, click on the **Back** button in your web browser.

We have now corrected the two major usability issues in the DISTAL system. There is, however, one other area we need to look at: performance. Let's do this now.

# Performance

Our DISTAL application is certainly working, but its performance leaves something to be desired. While the `selectCountry.py` and `selectArea.py` scripts run quickly, it can take two seconds or more for the `showResults.py` script to complete. Clearly, this isn't good enough: a delay like this is annoying to the user but would be disastrous for the server if it started to receive more requests than it could process.

# Finding the problem

Adding some timing code to the `showResults.py` script soon shows where the bottleneck lies:

```
Calculating lat/long coordinate took 0.0110 seconds

Identifying place names took 0.0088 seconds

Generating map took 3.0208 seconds

Building HTML page took 0.0000 seconds
```

Clearly, the map-generation process is the problem here. Since it only took a fraction of a second to generate a map within the `selectArea.py` script, there's nothing inherent in the map-generation process that takes this long. So what has changed?

It could be that displaying the place names takes a while, but that's unlikely. It's far more likely to be caused by the amount of map data that we are displaying: the `showResults.py` script is using high-resolution shoreline outlines taken from the GSHHG dataset rather than the low-resolution country outlines taken from the World Borders Dataset. To test this theory, we can change the map data being used to generate the map, altering `showResults.py` to use the low-resolution `countries` table instead of the high-resolution `shorelines` table.

The result is a dramatic improvement in speed:

```
Generating map took 0.1729 seconds
```

So, how can we make the map generation in `showResults.py` faster? The answer lies in the nature of the shoreline data and how we are using it. Consider the situation where you are identifying points within 10 miles of Le Havre in France:

The high-resolution shoreline image would look like this:

But this section of coastline is actually part of the following GSHHG shoreline feature:

This shoreline polygon is enormous, consisting of over 1.1 million points, and we're only displaying a very small part of it.

Because these shoreline polygons are so big, the map generator needs to read in the entire huge polygon and then discard 99 percent of it to get the desired section of shoreline. Also, because the polygon bounding boxes are so large, many irrelevant polygons are being processed (and then filtered out) to generate the map. This is why `showResults.py` is so slow.

 Because large and complex polygons are a common challenge when dealing with geospatial data, you will quite likely need to use the techniques we cover here to improve performance in your own systems.

# Improving performance

It is certainly possible to improve the performance of the `showResults.py` script. As was mentioned in the *Best practices* section of *Chapter 6, Spatial Databases*, spatial indexes work best when working with relatively small geometries—and our shoreline polygons are anything but small. However, because the DISTAL application only shows points within a certain distance, we can split these enormous polygons into **tiles** that are then precalculated and stored in the database.

Let's say that we're going to impose a limit of 100 kilometers to the search radius. We'll also arbitrarily define the tiles to be one whole degree of latitude tall and one whole degree of longitude wide:

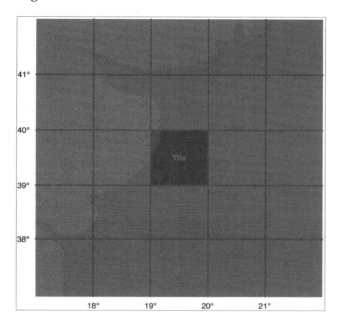

Note that we could choose any tile size we like but have selected whole degrees of longitude and latitude to make it easy to calculate which tile a given lat/long coordinate is inside. Each tile will be given an integer latitude and longitude value, which we'll call iLat and iLong. We can then calculate the tile to use for any given latitude and longitude like this:

```
iLat = int(round(latitude))
iLong = int(round(longitude))
```

We can then simply look up the tile with the given iLat and iLong value.

For each tile, we will calculate the bounds of a rectangle 100 kilometers north, east, west, and south of the tile:

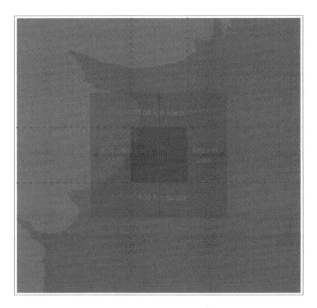

Using the bounding box, we can calculate the intersection of the shoreline data with this bounding box:

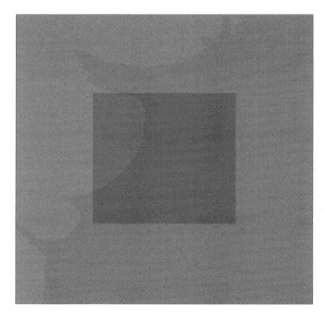

Any search done within the tile's boundary, up to a maximum of 100 kilometers in any direction, will only display shorelines within this bounding box. We will store this intersected shoreline into the database along with the lat/long coordinates for the tile, and tell the map generator to use the appropriate tile's outline to display the desired shoreline rather than using the original GSHHG polygons.

# Calculating the tiled shorelines

Let's write the program that calculates these tiled shorelines. We'll call this program `tileShorelines.py`. Start by entering the following into this file:

```
import math

import pyproj
from shapely.geometry import Polygon
from shapely.ops import cascaded_union
import shapely.wkt
import psycopg2

MAX_DISTANCE = 100000 # Maximum search radius, in meters.
```

We next need a function to calculate the tile bounding boxes. This function, `expandRect()`, should take a rectangle defined using lat/long coordinates and expand it in each direction by a given number of meters. Using the techniques we have learned, this is straightforward: we can use `pyproj` to perform an inverse great-circle calculation to calculate four points the given number of meters north, east, south, and west of the original rectangle. This will give us the desired bounding box. Here's what our function will look like:

```
def expandRect(minLat, minLong, maxLat, maxLong, distance):

    geod = pyproj.Geod(ellps="WGS84")
    midLat  = (minLat + maxLat) / 2.0
    midLong = (minLong + maxLong) / 2.0

    try:
        availDistance = geod.inv(midLong, maxLat, midLong,
                                 +90)[2]
        if availDistance >= distance:
            x,y,angle = geod.fwd(midLong, maxLat, 0, distance)
            maxLat = y
        else:
            maxLat = +90
    except:
```

```
        maxLat = +90 # Can't expand north.

    try:
        availDistance = geod.inv(maxLong, midLat, +180,
                                 midLat)[2]
        if availDistance >= distance:
            x,y,angle = geod.fwd(maxLong, midLat, 90,
                                 distance)
            maxLong = x
        else:
            maxLong = +180
    except:
        maxLong = +180 # Can't expand east.

    try:
        availDistance = geod.inv(midLong, minLat, midLong,
                                 -90)[2]
        if availDistance >= distance:
            x,y,angle = geod.fwd(midLong, minLat, 180,
                                 distance)
            minLat = y
        else:
            minLat = -90
    except:
        minLat = -90 # Can't expand south.

    try:
        availDistance = geod.inv(maxLong, midLat, -180,
                                 midLat)[2]
        if availDistance >= distance:
            x,y,angle = geod.fwd(minLong, midLat, 270,
                                 distance)
            minLong = x
        else:
            minLong = -180
    except:
        minLong = -180 # Can't expand west.

    return (minLat, minLong, maxLat, maxLong)
```

 Notice that we've added error-checking here, to allow for rectangles close to the North or South Pole.

Using this function, we will be able to calculate the bounding rectangle for a given tile in the following way:

```
minLat,minLong,maxLat,maxLong = expandRect(iLat, iLong,
                                           iLat+1, iLong+1,
                                           MAX_DISTANCE)
```

Enter the `expandRect()` function into your `tileShorelines.py` script, placing it immediately below the last `import` statement.

We are now ready to start implementing the tiling algorithm. We'll start by opening a connection to the database:

```
connection = psycopg2.connect(database="distal",
                              user="distal_user",
                              password="...")
cursor = connection.cursor()
```

> Don't forget to enter the password you entered for the `distal_user` when you set up the database.

We next need to load the shoreline polygons into memory. Here is the necessary code:

```
shorelines = []

cursor.execute("SELECT ST_AsText(outline) " +
               "FROM shorelines WHERE level=1")

for row in cursor:
    outline = shapely.wkt.loads(row[0])
    shorelines.append(outline)
```

> This implementation of the shoreline tiling algorithm uses a lot of memory. If your computer has less than 2 gigabytes of RAM, you may need to store temporary results in the database. Doing this will of course slow down the tiling process, but it will still work.

Now that we've loaded the shoreline polygons, we can start calculating the contents of each tile. Let's create a list-of-lists that will hold the (possibly clipped) polygons that appear within each tile; add the following to the end of your tileShorelines.py script:

```
tilePolys = []
for iLat in range(-90, +90):
    tilePolys.append([])
    for iLong in range(-180, +180):
        tilePolys[-1].append([])
```

For a given iLat/iLong combination, tilePolys[iLat][iLong] will contain a list of the shoreline polygons that appear inside that tile.

We now want to fill the tilePolys array with the portions of the shorelines that will appear within each tile. The obvious way to do this would be to calculate the polygon intersections in the following way:

```
shorelineInTile = shoreline.intersection(tileBounds)
```

Unfortunately, this approach would take a *very* long time to calculate—just as the map generation takes about 2-3 seconds to calculate the visible portion of a shoreline, it takes about 2-3 seconds to perform this intersection on a huge shoreline polygon. Because there are 360 x 180 = 64,800 tiles, it would take several days to complete this calculation using this naive approach.

A much faster solution would be to "divide and conquer" the large polygons. We first split the huge shoreline polygon into vertical strips, like this:

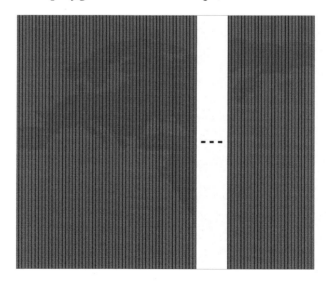

We then split each vertical strip horizontally to give us the individual parts of the polygon, which can be merged into the individual tiles:

By dividing the huge polygons into strips and then further dividing each strip, the intersection process is much faster. Here is the code that performs this intersection; we start by iterating over each shoreline polygon and calculating the polygon's bounds expanded to the nearest whole number:

```
for shoreline in shorelines:
    minLong,minLat,maxLong,maxLat = shoreline.bounds
    minLong = int(math.floor(minLong))
    minLat  = int(math.floor(minLat))
    maxLong = int(math.ceil(maxLong))
    maxLat  = int(math.ceil(maxLat))
```

We then split the polygon into vertical strips:

```
vStrips = []
for iLong in range(minLong, maxLong+1):

    stripMinLat  = minLat
    stripMaxLat  = maxLat
    stripMinLong = iLong
    stripMaxLong = iLong + 1

    bMinLat,bMinLong,bMaxLat,bMaxLong = \
            expandRect(stripMinLat, stripMinLong,
                       stripMaxLat, stripMaxLong,
                       MAX_DISTANCE)

    bounds = Polygon([(bMinLong, bMinLat),
                      (bMinLong, bMaxLat),
                      (bMaxLong, bMaxLat),
                      (bMaxLong, bMinLat),
                      (bMinLong, bMinLat)])

    strip = shoreline.intersection(bounds)
    vStrips.append(strip)
```

Next, we process each vertical strip, splitting the strip into tile-sized blocks and storing the polygons within each block into `tilePolys`:

```
stripNum = 0
for iLong in range(minLong, maxLong+1):
    vStrip = vStrips[stripNum]
    stripNum = stripNum + 1

    for iLat in range(minLat, maxLat+1):
        bMinLat,bMinLong,bMaxLat,bMaxLong = \
            expandRect(iLat, iLong, iLat+1, iLong+1,
                       MAX_DISTANCE)

        bounds = Polygon([(bMinLong, bMinLat),
                          (bMinLong, bMaxLat),
                          (bMaxLong, bMaxLat),
                          (bMaxLong, bMinLat),
                          (bMinLong, bMinLat)])

        polygon = vStrip.intersection(bounds)
        if not polygon.is_empty:
            tilePolys[iLat][iLong].append(polygon)
```

We have now stored the tiled polygons into `tilePolys` for every possible `iLat`/`iLong` value.

We're now ready to save the tiled shorelines back into the database. Before we can do that, however, we have to create a new database table to hold the tiled shoreline polygons. Here is the necessary code:

```
cursor.execute("DROP TABLE IF EXISTS tiled_shorelines")
cursor.execute("CREATE TABLE tiled_shorelines (" +
               "  intLat  INTEGER," +
               "  intLong INTEGER," +
               "  outline GEOMETRY(GEOMETRY, 4326)," +
               "  PRIMARY KEY (intLat, intLong))")
cursor.execute("CREATE INDEX tiledShorelineIndex "+
               "ON tiled_shorelines USING GIST(outline)")
```

Finally, we can save the tiled shoreline polygons into the `tiled_shorelines` table:

```
for iLat in range(-90, +90):
    for iLong in range(-180, +180):
        polygons = tilePolys[iLat][iLong]
        if len(polygons) == 0:
            outline = Polygon()
        else:
            outline = shapely.ops.cascaded_union(polygons)
        wkt = shapely.wkt.dumps(outline)

        cursor.execute("INSERT INTO tiled_shorelines " +
                       "(intLat, intLong, outline) " +
                       "VALUES (%s, %s, " +
                       "ST_GeomFromText(%s))",
                       (iLat, iLong, wkt))
    connection.commit()

connection.close()
```

This completes our program to tile the shorelines. You can run it by typing the following into a terminal or command-line window:

```
python tileShorelines.py
```

Note that it may take several hours for this program to complete because of all the shoreline data that needs to be processed. You may want to leave it running overnight.

The first time you run the program, you might want to replace this line:

```
for shoreline in shorelines:
```

with the following:

```
for shoreline in shorelines[1:2]:
```

This will let the program finish in only a minute or two so that you can make sure it's working before removing the [1:2] and running it on the entire shoreline database.

## Using the tiled shorelines

All this gives us a new database table, tiled_shorelines, that holds the shoreline data split into partly overlapping tiles:

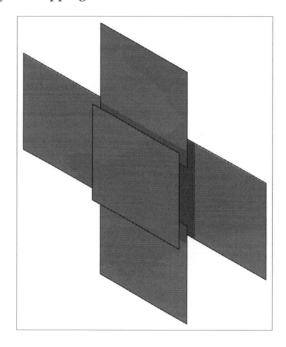

Since we can guarantee that all the shoreline data for a given set of search results will be within a single tiled_shoreline record, we can modify our showResults.py script to use the tiled shoreline rather than the raw shoreline data.

To use the tiled shorelines, we are going to make use of a clever feature built into the `mapnik.PostGIS` data source. The `table` parameter passed to this data source is normally the name of the database table holding the data to be displayed. However, instead of just supplying a table name, you can pass in an SQL `SELECT` command to choose the particular subset of records to display. We're going to use this to identify the particular tiled shoreline record to display.

Fortunately, our `mapGenerator.generateMap()` function accepts a `tableName` parameter, which is passed directly to the `mapnik.PostGIS` data source. This allows us to modify the table name passed to the map generator so that the appropriate tiled shoreline record will be used.

To do this, edit the `showResults.py` script and find the statement that calls the `mapGenerator.generateMap()` function. This statement currently looks like this:

```
imgFile = mapGenerator.generateMap("shorelines",
                                   minLong, minLat,
                                   maxLong, maxLat,
                                   MAX_WIDTH, MAX_HEIGHT,
                                   points=points)
```

Replace this statement with the following:

```
iLat = int(round(latitude))
iLong = int(round(longitude))

subSelect = "(SELECT outline FROM tiled_shorelines" \
        + " WHERE (intLat={})".format(iLat) \
        + " AND (intLong={})".format(iLong) \
        + ") AS shorelines"

imgFile = mapGenerator.generateMap(subSelect,
                                   minLong, minLat,
                                   maxLong, maxLat,
                                   MAX_WIDTH, MAX_HEIGHT,
                                   points=points)
```

With these changes, the `showResults.py` script will use the tiled shorelines rather than the full shoreline data downloaded from GSHHG. Let's now take a look at how much of a performance improvement these tiled shorelines give us.

# Analyzing the performance improvement

As soon as you run this new version of the DISTAL application, you should notice an improvement in speed: showResults.py now seems to return its results almost instantly rather than taking a second or more to generate the map. Adding timing code back into the showResults.py script shows how quickly it is running now:

```
Generating map took 0.1074 seconds
```

Compare this with how long it took when we were using the full high-resolution shoreline:

```
Generating map took 3.0208 seconds
```

As you can see, this is a dramatic improvement in performance: the map generator is now 15-20 times faster than it was, and the total time taken by the showResults.py script is now less than a quarter of a second. That's not bad for a relatively simple change to our underlying map data.

# Summary

In this chapter, we made a number of improvements to the DISTAL application, fixing various usability and performance issues. Along the way, we learned about the anti-meridian line and how to deal with country outlines that span it. We saw how to add a zoom feature to our CGI scripts so that the user can accurately click on a desired search point, and we saw the effect that having huge polygons can have on the performance of our system. We then learned how to split those large polygons into smaller overlapping tiles that can be used to display a small portion of the high-resolution shoreline without affecting performance.

We now have a fully functioning version of the DISTAL system. If you wanted to, you could publish the DISTAL system on a public web server, making it available for anyone to use. However, DISTAL is implemented as a series of CGI scripts, which is a very rudimentary way of implementing a web application. In the next chapter, we will look at a web framework called GeoDjango, which is ideal for developing more sophisticated web-based geospatial applications.

# 10
# Tools for Web-based Geospatial Development

In this chapter, we will learn about various tools and techniques that can be used to develop geospatial applications that run in a user's web browser. Web-based applications are becoming increasingly popular, and there is a huge potential for geospatial development based on this technology.

We will start our examination of web-based geospatial development with an overview of the tools and techniques that can be used both for web application development in general and geospatial web application development in particular. We will look at web applications, web services, the concept of a "slippy map", and a number of standard protocols for sharing and manipulating geospatial data across the Internet.

We will then turn our attention to three particular tools and techniques that will be used to develop a complete geospatial web application in the final three chapters of this book: the TMS protocol, OpenLayers, and the GeoDjango web application framework.

## Tools and techniques for geospatial web development

While web browsers were initially designed to show static HTML pages, they are now a sophisticated programming environment in their own right. Complex applications can now be implemented in JavaScript running on the user's web browser, interacting with server-side APIs and web services to perform tasks that previously could only be implemented using complex standalone systems.

Web application development has transformed the programming landscape, and geospatial developers have not been left behind. In this section, we will learn about web application development and see how these technologies can be applied to build sophisticated geospatial systems that run within the user's web browser.

# Web applications

There are many ways in which you can develop a web-based application. You can write your own code by hand, for example as a series of CGI scripts or you can use one of the many web application frameworks available. In this section, we will look at the different ways in which web applications can be structured so that the different parts work together to implement the application's functionality.

# A bare-bones approach

In *Chapter 8, Working with Spatial Data*, we created a simple web application named DISTAL. This web application was built using CGI scripts to provide distance-based identification of towns and other features. DISTAL is a good example of a bare-bones approach to web application development, using nothing more than a web server, a database, and a collection of CGI scripts:

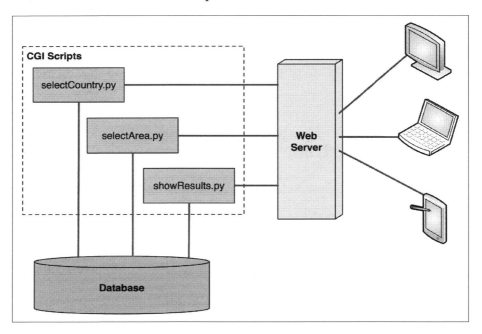

The advantage of this approach is that you don't need special tools or knowledge to write a web application in this way. The disadvantage is that you have to do all the low-level coding by hand. It's a tedious and slow way of building a web application, especially a complex one with lots of features.

# Web application stacks

To make the job of building web-based applications easier, you generally use existing tools that allow you to write your application at a higher level. For example, you might choose to implement a complex web application in the following way:

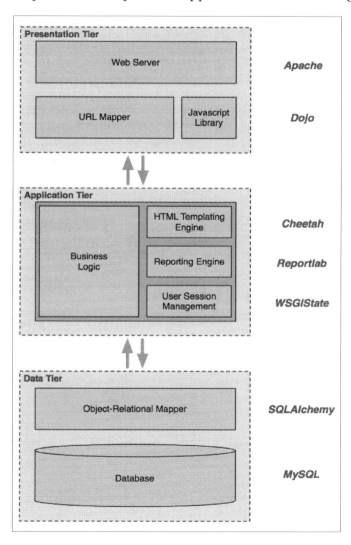

This stack of tools works together to implement your application: at the lowest level, you have a **Data Tier** that deals with the storage of data. In this case, the application uses MySQL for the database and SQLAlchemy as an object-relational mapper to provide an object-oriented interface to this database. The **Application Tier** contains the application's business logic as well as various libraries to simplify the job of building a stateful and complex web application. Finally, the **Presentation Tier** deals with the user interface, serving web pages to the users, mapping incoming URLs to the appropriate calls to your business logic, and using a sophisticated JavaScript library to build complex user interfaces within the user's web browser.

Different terms are sometimes used for these three tiers. For example, the data tier is sometimes called the **data access layer**, and the application tier is sometimes referred to as the **business logic layer**. The concept is the same, however.

Note that the only parts of this application that a developer would create from scratch are the business logic, the URL mappings, and the database schema used by the object-relational mapper. The rest is all just a collection of off-the-shelf components.

Don't be too concerned about the details of this particular application's architecture — the main thing to realize is that there is a **stack** of tools all working together, where each tool makes use of the tools below it. Also, notice the complexity of this system: this application depends on a *lot* of different tools and libraries. Developing, deploying, and upgrading an application like this can be challenging because it has so many different parts.

# Web application frameworks

To avoid the complexity of mixing and matching so many different parts, web developers have created various **frameworks** that combine tools to provide a complete web development system. Instead of having to select, install, and deploy ten different libraries, you can simply choose a complete framework that brings a known good set of libraries together and adds its own logic to provide a complete "batteries included" web-development experience. Most of these toolkits provide you with built-in logic to handle tasks such as:

- Defining and migrating your database schema
- Keeping track of user sessions and handling user authentication
- Building sophisticated user interfaces, often using AJAX to handle complex widgets within the user's browser

- Automatically allowing users to create, read, update, and delete records in the database (the so-called CRUD interface)
- Simplifying the creation of database-driven applications through standard templates and recipes

There is a lot more to these frameworks, but the important thing to remember is that they aim to provide a "full stack" of features in order to allow developers to quickly implement the most common aspects of a web application with minimum fuss. They aim to provide **rapid application development (RAD)** for web-based systems.

There are a number of Python-based web application frameworks available, including three that support the building of geospatial applications: Django with its built-in GeoDjango extension, Pyramid with the Mapfish extension, and Turbogears with its `tgext.geo` extension. We will take a closer look at GeoDjango later in this chapter.

# User interface libraries

While it is easy to build a simple web-based interface in HTML, users are increasingly expecting web applications to compete with desktop applications in terms of their user interface. Selecting objects by clicking on them, drawing images with the mouse, and dragging and dropping are no longer actions restricted to desktop applications.

**AJAX** (short for **asynchronous JavaScript and XML**) is the technology typically used to build complex user interfaces in a web application. In particular, running JavaScript code on the user's web browser allows the application to dynamically respond to user actions and make the web page behave in ways that simply can't be achieved with static HTML pages.

While JavaScript is ubiquitous, it can also be tricky to program in. The various web browsers in which JavaScript code can run all have their own quirks and limitations, making it hard to write code that runs the same way on every browser. JavaScript code is also very low level, requiring detailed manipulation of the web page contents to achieve a given effect. For example, implementing a pop-up menu requires creating a `<DIV>` element that contains the menu, formatting it appropriately (typically using CSS), and making it initially invisible. When the user clicks on the appropriate part of the page, the pop-up menu should be shown by making the associated `<div>` element visible. You then need to respond to the user mousing over each item in the menu by visually highlighting that item and un-highlighting the previously highlighted item. Then, when the user clicks on an item, you have to hide the menu again before responding to the user's action.

All this detailed low-level coding can take weeks to get right—especially when dealing with multiple types of browsers and different browser versions. Since all you want to do in this case is create a pop-up menu that lets the user choose an action, it just isn't worth doing all this low-level coding yourself. Instead, you would typically make use of one of the available **user interface libraries** to do all the hard work for you.

These user interface libraries are written in JavaScript, and you typically add them to your web site by making the JavaScript library file(s) available for download and then adding a line like the following to your HTML page to import the JavaScript library:

```
<script type="text/javascript" src="library.js">
```

If you are writing your own web application from scratch, you would then make calls to the library to implement the user interface for your application. However, many of the web application frameworks that include a user interface library will write the necessary code for you, making even this step unnecessary.

There are many different user interface libraries that you can choose to include in your web applications. JQuery UI, AngularJS, and Bootstrap are three of the more popular examples. When writing geospatial web applications, it is easy to forget that geospatial web applications are, first and foremost, ordinary web applications that also happen to work with geospatial data. Much of a geospatial web application's functionality is rather mundane: providing a consistent look and feel, implementing menus or toolbars to navigate between pages, user signup, login and logout, entry of ordinary (non-geospatial) data, reporting, and so on. All of this functionality can be handled by one of these general-purpose user interface libraries, and you are free to either choose one or more libraries of your liking or make use of the UI library built into whatever web application framework you have chosen to use.

In addition to these general-purpose UI libraries, there are other libraries specifically designed for implementing geospatial web applications. We will explore one of these libraries, OpenLayers, later in this chapter.

# Web services

A **web service** is a piece of software that has an application programming interface (API) which is accessed via the HTTP protocol. Web services implement the behind-the-scenes functionality used by other systems; they don't generally interact with end users at all.

Web services are accessed via a URL; other parts of the system send a request to this URL along with a number of parameters and receive back a response, often in the form of XML or JSON encoded data, which is then used for further processing.

There are two main types of web services you are likely to encounter: RESTful web services, which use parts of the URL itself to tell the web service what to do, and "big web services", which typically use the SOAP protocol to communicate with the outside world.

**REST** stands for **REpresentational State Transfer**. This protocol uses sub-paths within the URL to define the request to be made. For example, a web service might use the following URL to return information about a customer:

```
http://myserver.com/webservice/customer/123
```

In this example, `customer` defines what type of information you want (the "resource"), and `123` is the internal ID of the desired customer. RESTful web services are easy to implement and use, and are becoming increasingly popular with web application developers.

A "big web service", on the other hand, has just one URL for the entire web service. A request is sent to this URL, usually in the form of an XML-format message, and the response is sent back, also as an XML-formatted message. The SOAP protocol is often used to describe the message format and how the web service should behave. Big web services are popular in large commercial systems, despite being more complex than their RESTful equivalents.

## An example web service

Let's take a look at a simple but useful web service. The following CGI script, called `greatCircleDistance.py`, calculates and returns the great-circle distance between two coordinates on the earth's surface. Here is the full source code for this web service:

```python
#!/usr/bin/python

import cgi
import pyproj

form = cgi.FieldStorage()

lat1 = float(form['lat1'].value)
long1 = float(form['long1'].value)
lat2 = float(form['lat2'].value)
long2 = float(form['long2'].value)
```

```
geod = pyproj.Geod(ellps="WGS84")
angle1,angle2,distance = geod.inv(long1, lat1, long2, lat2)

print('Content-Type: text/plain')
print()
print("{:.4f}".format(distance))
```

Because this is intended to be used by other systems rather than end users, the two coordinates are passed as query parameters, and the resulting distance (in meters) is returned as the body of the HTTP response. Because the returned value is a single number, there is no need to encode the results using XML or JSON; instead, the distance is returned as plain text.

You can use the webserver.py script we wrote in *Chapter 8, Working with Spatial Data,* to make the greatCircleDistance. py script available for other programs to use. Simply make the greatCircleDistance.py script executable and place it inside your cgi-bin directory, then type python webserver.py to make your web service available for other programs.

Let's now look at a simple Python program that calls this web service:

```
import urllib

URL = "http://127.0.0.1:8000/cgi-bin/greatCircleDistance.py"

params = urllib.urlencode({'lat1'  : 53.478948, # Manchester.
                           'long1' : -2.246017,
                           'lat2'  : 53.411142, # Liverpool.
                           'long2' : -2.977638})

f = urllib.urlopen(URL, params)
response = f.read()
f.close()

print(response)
```

Running this program tells us the distance in meters between these two coordinates, which happen to be the locations of Manchester and Liverpool in England:

```
% python callWebService.py
49194.4632
```

While this might not seem very exciting, web services are an extremely important part of web-based development. When developing your own web-based geospatial applications, you may well make use of existing web services, and potentially implement your own web services as part of your web application development.

# Map rendering using a web service

We saw in *Chapter 8, Working with Spatial Data*, how Mapnik can be used to generate great-looking maps. Within the context of a web application, map rendering is usually performed by a web service that takes a request and returns the rendered map as an image file. For example, your application might include a map renderer at the relative URL /render that accepts the following query-string parameters:

| Parameter(s) | Description |
| --- | --- |
| minX, maxX, minY, maxY | The minimum and maximum latitude and longitude of the area to include on the map. |
| width, height | The pixel width and height for the generated map image. |
| layers | A comma-separated list of the layers that are to be included on the map. The available predefined layers are "coastline", "forest", "waterways", "urban", and "street". |
| format | The desired image format. Available formats are "PNG", "JPEG", and "GIF". |

This hypothetical /render web service would return the rendered map back to the caller as an image file. Once this has been set up, the web service would act as a black box providing map images upon request for other parts of your web application.

As an alternative to hosting and configuring your own map renderer, you can choose to use an openly available external renderer. For example, OpenStreetMap provides a freely available map renderer for OpenStreetMap data at http://staticmap. openstreetmap.de.

# Tile caching

Because creating an image out of raw map data is a time- and processor-intensive operation, your entire web application can become overloaded if you get too many requests for map images at any one time. As we saw with the DISTAL application in *Chapter 7, Using Python and Mapnik to Generate Maps* there is a lot you can do to improve the speed of the map-generation process, but there are still limits on how many maps your application can render in a given time period.

Because the map data is generally quite static, you can make a huge improvement to your application's performance by **caching** the generated images. This is generally done by dividing the world up into **tiles**, rendering tile images as required, and then stitching the tiles together to produce the entire map:

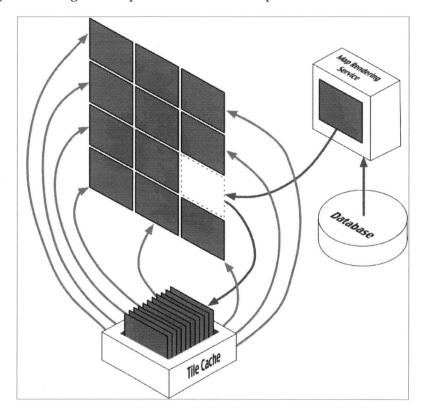

Tile caches work in exactly the same way as any other cache:

- When a tile is requested, the tile cache checks to see whether it contains a copy of the rendered tile. If it does, the cached copy is returned right away.

- Otherwise, the map rendering service is called to generate the tile, and the newly rendered tile is added to the cache before it is returned to the caller.

- As the cache grows too big, tiles that haven't been requested for a long time are removed to make room for new tiles.

Of course, tile caching will only work if the underlying map data doesn't change. As we saw when building the DISTAL application, you can't use a tile cache where the rendered image varies from one request to the next.

One interesting use of a tile cache is combining it with **map overlays** to improve performance even when the map data does change. Because the outlines of countries and other physical features on a map don't change, it is possible to use a map generator with a tile cache to generate the "base map", onto which changing features are then drawn as an overlay:

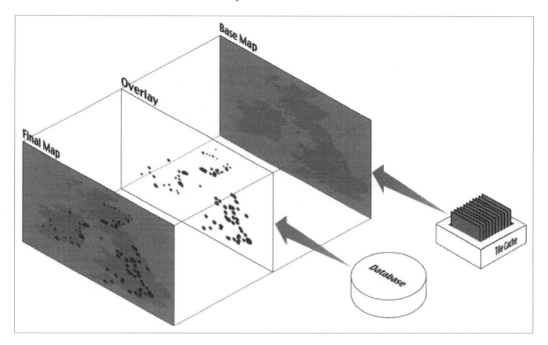

The final map could be produced using Mapnik by drawing the overlay onto the base map, which is accessed using a `RasterDataSource` and displayed using a `RasterSymbolizer`. If you have enough disk space, you could even pre-calculate all of the base map tiles and have them available for quick display. Using Mapnik in this manner is a fast and efficient way of combining changing and non-changing map data onto a single view—though there are other ways of overlaying data onto a map, for example, using OpenLayers to display multiple map layers at once.

# The "slippy map" stack

The "slippy map" is a concept popularized by Google Maps: a zoomable map where the user can click and drag to scroll around and double-click to zoom in. Here is an example of a Google Maps slippy map showing a portion of Europe:

Image copyright Google; map data copyright Europa Technologies, PPWK, and Tele Atlas

Slippy maps have become extremely popular, and much of the work done on geospatial web application development has been focused on creating and working with slippy maps.

The slippy map experience is typically implemented using a custom software stack, like this:

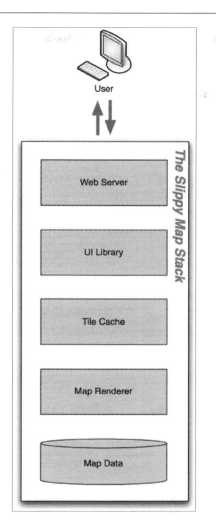

Starting at the bottom, the raw map data is typically stored in a spatial database. This is then rendered using a tool such as Mapnik, and a tile cache is used to speed up repeated access to the same map images. A user-interface library such as OpenLayers is then used to display the map in the user's web browser and to respond when the user clicks on the map. Finally, a web server is used to allow web browsers to access and interact with the slippy map.

# Geospatial web protocols

Because web-based applications are generally broken into multiple components, the way these components communicate becomes extremely important. It's quite likely that your web application will use off-the-shelf components or rely on existing components running on a remote server. In these cases, the **protocols** used to communicate between the various components is crucial to allowing these various components to work together.

In terms of geospatial web applications, a number of standard protocols have been developed to allow different components to communicate. Some of the more common web protocols relating to geospatial development include:

- The **Web Map Service (WMS)** protocol, which provides a standard way for a web service to receive a map-generation request and return the map image back to the caller. The complete specification for the WMS protocol can be found at `http://www.opengeospatial.org/standards/wms`.

- The **Web Map Tile Service (WMTS)** protocol, which allows a web service to provide map tiles on request. The specification for the WMTS protocol can be found at `http://www.opengeospatial.org/standards/wmts`.

- The **Tile Map Service (TMS)**, which is a simpler protocol for providing map tiles on demand. More information about the TMS protocol can be found at `http://wiki.osgeo.org/wiki/Tile_Map_Service_Specification`.

- The **Web Coverage Service (WCS)** protocol, which provides *coverages* on demand. A coverage is a set of data collected across an area, for example, soil moisture levels, elevation, or type of vegetation. The specification for the WCS protocol can be found at `http://www.opengeospatial.org/standards/wcs`.

- The **Web Feature Service (WFS)** protocol, which stores geospatial features and allows callers to issue queries and manipulate those features. In many ways, a WFS acts like a spatial database sitting behind a web service. The complete specification for the WFS protocol can be found at `http://www.opengeospatial.org/standards/wfs`.

Many of these protocols have been developed by the Open Geospatial Consortium, an international standards organization that developed these protocols so that different geospatial systems and services could interact.

# A closer look at three specific tools and techniques

In the final three chapters of this book, we will build a complete sophisticated geospatial web application called **ShapeEditor**. The ShapeEditor is built on top of a number of existing technologies; before we can start implementing it, we need to become familiar with these technologies. In this section, we will learn about three of the key tools and techniques used to implement the ShapeEditor: the Tile Map Service protocol, OpenLayers, and GeoDjango.

# The Tile Map Service protocol

The **Tile Map Service** (**TMS**) protocol defines the interface for a web service that returns map tile images upon request. The TMS protocol is similar to WMS, except that it is simpler and more oriented towards the storage and retrieval of map tiles rather than arbitrarily-specified complete maps.

The TMS protocol uses RESTful principles, which means that the URL used to access the web service includes all of the information needed to complete a request. Unlike WMS, there is no need to create and submit complex XML documents to retrieve a map tile—all of the information is contained within the URL itself.

Within the TMS protocol, a **Tile Map Service** is a mechanism for providing access to rendered map images at a given set of scale factors and using a predetermined set of spatial reference systems.

A single **TMS Server** can host multiple Tile Map Services:

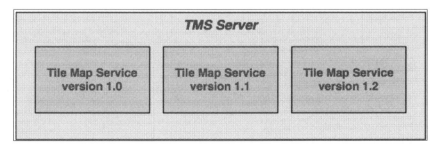

This is typically used to provide different versions of a TMS so that new versions of it can be implemented without breaking clients that depend on features in an older version.

Each Tile Map Service within a TMS server is identified by a URL that is used to access that particular service. For example, if a TMS server is running at `http://tms.myserver.com`, version 1.2 of the Tile Map Service running on that server would generally reside at the sub-URL `http://tms.myserver.com/1.2/`. Accessing the top-level URL (`http://tms.myserver.com`) will return a list of all the Tile Map Services available on that server:

```
<?xml version="1.0" encoding="UTF-8"/>
<Services>
  <TileMapService title="MyServer TMS" version="1.0"
   href="http://tms.myserver.com/1.0/"/>
  <TileMapService title="MyServer TMS" version="1.1"
   href="http://tms.myserver.com/1.1/"/>
  <TileMapService title="MyServer TMS" version="1.2"
   href="http://tms.myserver.com/1.2/"/>
</Services>
```

Each Tile Map Service provides access to one or more **Tile Maps**:

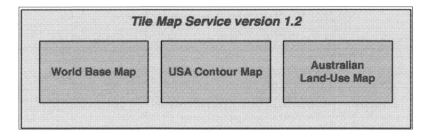

A Tile Map: is a complete map of all or part of the Earth, displaying particular sets of features or styled in a particular way. The examples given in the figure, of a world base map, a usa contour map, and an australian land-use map, show how different Tile Maps might contain different sorts of map data or cover different areas of the Earth's surface. Different Tile Maps may also be used to make maps available in different image formats or to provide maps in different spatial reference systems.

If a client system accesses the URL for a particular Tile Service, the Tile Service will return more detailed information about that service, including a list of the Tile Maps available within that service:

```
<?xml version="1.0" encoding="UTF-8"/>
<TileMapService version="1.2" services="http://tms.myserver.com">
  <Title>MyServer TMS</Title>
  <Abstract>TMS Service for the myserver.com server</Abstract>
  <TileMaps>
```

```
    <TileMap title="World Base Map"
            srs="EPSG:4326"
            profile="none"
            href="http://tms.myserver.com/1.2/baseMap"/>
    <TileMap title="USA Contour Map"
            srs="EPSG:4326"
            profile="none"
            href="http://tms.myserver.com/1.2/usaContours"/>
    <TileMap title="Australian Land-Use Map"
            srs="EPSG:4326"
            profile="none"
            href="http://tms.myserver.com/1.2/ausLandUse"/>
    </TileMap>
  </TileMaps>
</TileMapService>
```

Client systems accessing rendered maps via a TMS server will generally want to be able to display that map at various resolutions. For example, a world base map might initially be displayed as a complete map of the world, and the user could zoom in to see a more detailed view of a desired area:

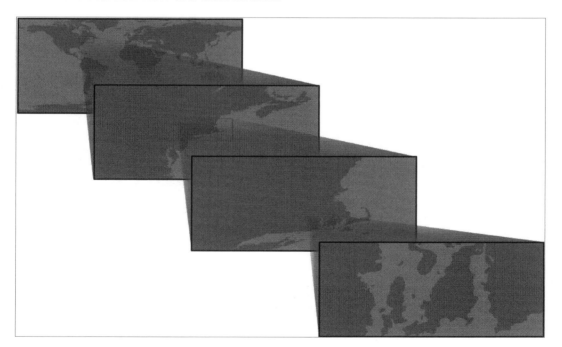

This zooming-in process is done through the use of appropriate **scale factors**. Each Tile Map consists of a number of **Tile Sets**, where each Tile Set depicts the map at a given scale factor. For example, the first figure in the preceding illustration was drawn at a scale factor of approximately 1:100,000,000, the second at a scale factor of 1:10,000,000, the third at a scale factor of 1:1,000,000, and the last at a scale factor of 1:100,000. Thus, there would be four Tile Sets within this Tile Map, one for each of the scale factors.

If a client system accesses the URL for a given Tile Map, the server will return information about that map, including a list of the available Tile Sets:

```
<?xml version="1.0" encoding="UTF-8">
<TileMap version="1.2"
         tilemapservice="http://tms.myserver.com/1.2">
  <Title>World Base Map</Title>
  <Abstract>Base map of the entire world</Abstract>
  <SRS>ESPG:4326</SRS>
  <BoundingBox minx="-180" miny="-90" maxx="180" maxy="90"/>
  <Origin x="-180" y="-90"/>
  <TileFormat width="256"
              height="256"
              mime-type="image/png"
              extension="png"/>
  <TileSets profile="none">
    <TileSet href="http://tms.myserver.com/1.2/basemap/0"
             units-per-pixel="0.703125"
             order="0"/>
    <TileSet href="http://tms.myserver.com/1.2/basemap/1"
             units-per-pixel="0.3515625"
             order="1"/>
    <TileSet href="http://tms.myserver.com/1.2/basemap/2"
             units-per-pixel="0.17578125"
             order="2"/>
    <TileSet href="http://tms.myserver.com/1.2/basemap/3"
             units-per-pixel="0.08789063"
             order="3"/>
  </TileSets>
</TileMap>
```

Notice how each Tile Set has its own unique URL. This URL will be used to retrieve the individual **Tiles** within the tile set. Each Tile is given an x and y coordinate value indicating its position within the overall map. For example, using the preceding Tile Map covering the entire world, the third Tile Set would consist of 32 Tiles arranged as follows:

| x = 0 y = 3 | x = 1 y = 3 | x = 2 y = 3 | x = 3 y = 3 | x = 4 y = 3 | x = 5 y = 3 | x = 6 y = 3 | x = 7 y = 3 |
|---|---|---|---|---|---|---|---|
| x = 0 y = 2 | x = 1 y = 2 | x = 2 y = 2 | x = 3 y = 2 | x = 4 y = 2 | x = 5 y = 2 | x = 6 y = 2 | x = 7 y = 2 |
| x = 0 y = 1 | x = 1 y = 1 | x = 2 y = 1 | x = 3 y = 1 | x = 4 y = 1 | x = 5 y = 1 | x = 6 y = 1 | x = 7 y = 1 |
| x = 0 y = 0 | x = 1 y = 0 | x = 2 y = 0 | x = 3 y = 0 | x = 4 y = 0 | x = 5 y = 0 | x = 6 y = 0 | x = 7 y = 0 |

This arrangement of Tiles is defined by the following information taken from the Tile Map and the selected Tile Set:

- The Tile Map uses the ESPG:4326 spatial reference system, which equates to longitude/latitude coordinates based on the WGS84 datum. This means that the map data is using latitude/longitude coordinate values, with longitude values increasing from left to right and latitude values increasing from bottom to top.

- The map's bounds range from -180 to +180 in the $x$ (longitude) direction and from -90 to +90 in the $y$ (latitude) direction.

- The map's origin is at (-180,-90) — that is, the bottom-left corner of the map.

- Each Tile in the Tile Map is 256 pixels wide and 256 pixels high.

- The third Tile Set has a `units-per-pixel` value of 0.17578125.

Multiplying the units-per-pixel value by the tile's size, we can see that each Tile covers 0.17578125 x 256 = 45 degrees of latitude and longitude. Since the map covers the entire earth, this yields eight tiles across and four tiles high, with the origin in the bottom-left corner.

Once the client software has decided on a particular Tile Set to use and has calculated the x and y coordinates of the desired tile, retrieving that tile's image is a simple matter of concatenating the Tile Set's URL, the x and y coordinates, and the image file suffix:

```
url = tileSetURL + "/" + x + "/" + y + "." + imgFormat
```

For example, to retrieve the tile at the coordinate (3, 2) from the preceding Tile Set, you would use the following URL:

```
http://tms.myserver.com/1.2/basemap/2/3/2.png
```

Notice how this URL (and indeed, every URL used by the TMS protocol) looks as if it is simply retrieving a file from the server. Behind the scenes, the TMS server may indeed be running a complex set of map-generation and map-caching tools to generate these tiles on demand—but the entire TMS server could just as easily be defined by a series of hardwired XML files and a number of directories containing pre-generated image files.

This notion of a **static tile map server** is a deliberate design feature of the TMS protocol. If you don't need to generate too many map tiles, or if you have a particularly large hard disk, you could easily pre-generate all the tile images and create a static TMS server by creating a few XML files and serving the whole thing behind a standard web server such as Apache.

In the final chapter of this book, we will implement a Python-based TMS server as part of the ShapeEditor system. You may also wish to make use of TMS servers in your own web applications, possibly by creating a static Tile Map Server or by using an existing software library that implements the TMS protocol. There are two popular open source libraries that implement tile caching: TileCache (`http://tilecache.org`) and MapProxy (`http://mapproxy.org`), both of which are implemented in Python.

# OpenLayers

OpenLayers (`http://openlayers.org`) is a sophisticated JavaScript library for building mapping applications. It includes a JavaScript API for building slippy maps, combining data from multiple layers, and including various widgets for manipulating maps as well as viewing and editing vector-format data.

OpenLayers version 2 has been available for many years, while a complete rewrite called OpenLayers 3 has only recently become available. You should use OpenLayers 3 as it employs a much more modern design and is actively supported. As of the time of writing this, the latest version of OpenLayers is version 3.10.1.

To use OpenLayers in your web application, you first need to create an HTML file to be loaded into the user's web browser and then write some JavaScript code that uses the OpenLayers API to build the desired map. OpenLayers then builds your map and allows the user to interact with it, loading map data from the data source(s) you have specified. OpenLayers can read from a variety of geospatial data sources, including TMS, WMS, and WFS servers. All these parts work together to produce the user interface for your web application in the following way:

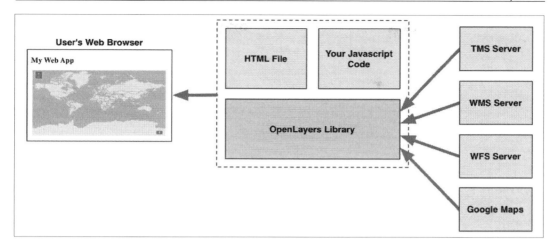

 To use OpenLayers, you have to be comfortable writing JavaScript code. This is almost a necessity when creating your own web applications. Fortunately, the OpenLayers API is quite high level, and makes map-creation relatively simple.

Here is the code for an example HTML page that displays a slippy map using OpenLayers:

```html
<html>
  <head>
    <link rel="stylesheet"
          href="http://openlayers.org/en/v3.10.1/css/ol.css"
          type="text/css">
    <script src="http://openlayers.org/en/v3.10.1/build/ol.js"
            type="text/javascript">
    </script>
    <script type="text/javascript">
      function initMap() {
        var source = new ol.source.OSM();

        var layer = new ol.layer.Tile({source: source});

        var origin = ol.proj.fromLonLat([0, 0]);

          var view = new ol.View({center: origin,
                                  zoom: 1});
```

```
         var map = new ol.Map({target: "map",
                                layers: [layer],
                                view: view});
      }
    </script>
  </head>
  <body onload="initMap()">
    <div style="width:100%; height:100%" id="map"></div>
  </body>
</html>
```

Notice the following line:

```
<div style="width:100%; height:100%" id="map"></div>
```

This `<div>` element will contain the slippy map. We use inline styles to make this element take up the entire width and height of the page, and we also give this element an `id` of "map".

The `onload="initMap()"` attribute in the page's `<body>` tag tells the web browser to run the `initMap()` JavaScript function when the page is loaded. All of the actual work takes place inside this function, which defines five separate values that are used to create the slippy map:

- `source` represents the data source to use for obtaining the underlying map data. In our example, we will display data from OpenStreetMap.

- `layer` is the map layer to be displayed. In this example, we are using a tiled layer to display the map data using map tiles.

- `origin` represents the point on which the map will be centered. Because the OpenStreetMap data source uses Spherical Mercator, we have to ask OpenLayers to convert our unprojected (long/lat) coordinate into this projection when we calculate the origin.

- `view` represents the portion of the map to be displayed when the page first loads. In this case, the map will be centered on the origin we calculated and will be zoomed out as much as possible.

- Finally, the `map` object represents the OpenLayers slippy map. The `target` value is the ID of the `<div>` element where the map is to be displayed, and we set up the map to use the `layer` and `view` objects we calculated earlier.

If you load this HTML page on your web browser, you should see a slippy map showing the OpenStreetMap map data:

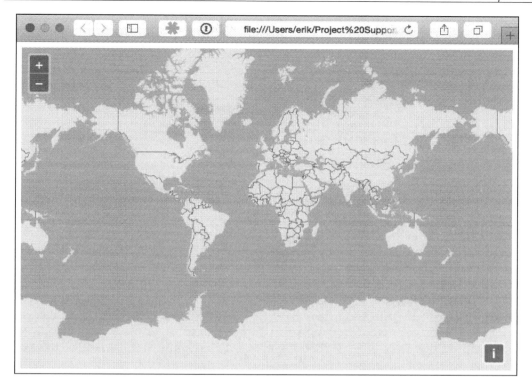

This map is still quite basic, but by using the various OpenLayers features, you could do a lot more with it. For example:

- You could display multiple map layers, including raster-format base images and dynamically generated vector-format data

- You could add more controls to the map

- You could use various *interactions* to define how the user can manipulate the contents of the map

- You could allow the user to edit vector-format map data directly within the map

OpenLayers is a powerful tool for building geospatial web interfaces. Even if you don't use it directly in your own code, many of the web application frameworks that support geospatial web development (including GeoDjango) use OpenLayers internally to display and edit map data.

# GeoDjango

GeoDjango is a built-in extension to the popular Django web application framework. Using GeoDjango, you can develop sophisticated web-based applications that let the user view and edit geospatial data. Before we can work with GeoDjango, however, we need to understand Django itself.

Let's start with a hands-on tutorial to get you working with Django. Once you understand the basic concepts and have built a simple web application, we will look at how GeoDjango builds on the Django framework to let you create your own geospatial web applications. We won't go into too much detail about GeoDjango here, as we'll be working with it extensively in the final three chapters of this book.

# Learning Django

Django (`http://djangoproject.com`) is a **rapid application development** (**RAD**) framework for building database-oriented web applications using Python. The Django framework is highly respected and is used to power thousands of web applications currently deployed across the internet. The major parts of Django include an object-relational mapper, an automatically generated admin interface, a flexible URL mapper, and a web templating system. Putting these elements together, Django allows you to quickly build sophisticated web applications to implement a wide variety of database-oriented systems.

In Django, you work with a **project** that is made up of a number of individual **apps**. Each app implements a specific set of functionality, for example, authenticating users, generating reports, or responding to API requests. When you create a project, you typically write one or more apps yourself and make use of a number of predefined apps that come built into Django.

One of the most useful built-in apps is the **admin interface**, which allows you to administer your web application, view and edit data, and so on. Other useful built-in apps implement persistent sessions, user authentication, site maps, user comments, sending emails, and viewing paginated data. A large number of user-contributed apps are also available.

Let's use Django to create a simple web application. We'll start by installing Django. The easiest way to do this is to use `pip`, the Python package manager. From the command line, type `pip install django`. If this doesn't work, for example, because you don't have `pip` installed, you can download a copy of Django from `https://www.djangoproject.com/download`.

Once it is installed, open up a terminal window and `cd` into the directory where you want to place your new web application's project. Then, type `django-admin startproject example`.

 Depending on how you installed Django, the `django-admin` program may not be directly accessible from the command line, because it is installed in a location that isn't on your path. If you get an error, you may need to find where `django-admin` was installed and add the path to your command. For example, on a Mac, the command is `/Library/Frameworks/Python.framework/Versions/current/bin/django-admin startproject example`. You may want to add the `django-admin` directory to your path to avoid having to type this out in full each time.

This will create a new Django project named `example`, which will be stored in a directory with the same name. This directory is just a container for your project; inside it, you will find the following:

**manage.py**

**example/**

    **__init__.py**

    **settings.py**

    **urls.py**

    **wsgi.py**

Let's take a closer look at these various files and folders:

- `manage.py` is a program generated automatically by Django. You'll be using this to run and update your project.
- The `example` subdirectory is a Python package that will hold various files related to your new project. As you can see, this is named after your project.
- `__init__.py` is an empty file that tells the Python interpreter to treat the `example` subdirectory as a Python package.
- The `settings.py` module holds various project-level settings.
- The `wsgi.py` script is used to run your project within a WSGI-compatible web server.

Now that we have a Django project, let's create a simple app that will run within it. Our app, which we will call `hello`, simply displays the following message to the user:

**Hello Number X.**

**X** is a number that increases each time the page is displayed. While this example app may seem trivial, it demonstrates a number of key features of Django:

- URL routing
- Views
- HTML templates
- The object-relational mapper

To create this app, `cd` into your outermost `example` directory and enter the following command:

```
python manage.py startapp hello
```

This will create a new sub-directory named `hello` within your outermost `example` directory. This directory is a Python package that holds the various parts of your new Django app. If you look in this directory, you will find the following items:

- `__init__.py` is another package initialization file, telling the Python interpreter to treat the `hello` directory as a Python package.
- `admin.py` is a module you can use to define the admin interface for your app. We won't be using this, so you can ignore it.
- The `migrations` directory holds the various **database migrations** for this app. The contents of this directory will be created automatically by the `manage.py` script when we define our database's structure.
- The `models.py` module holds the various **database models** used by this app. A database model is a Python class that defines the structure of a single database table. We'll look at this in more detail shortly.
- The `tests.py` module is the place to define various unit tests for your app.
- Finally, the `views.py` module will hold the various **view functions** that implement the behavior of your app. We'll be editing this module shortly.

Our next task is to tell the `example` project to use our newly created `hello` app. To do this, edit the `example/settings.py` file, and look for a variable named `INSTALLED_APPS`. This is a list of the apps that are used by the project. As you can see, a number of built-in apps are installed by default. Edit this list so that it looks like the following:

```
INSTALLED_APPS = (
    #'django.contrib.admin',
    'django.contrib.auth',
    'django.contrib.contenttypes',
```

```
    'django.contrib.sessions',
    'django.contrib.messages',
    'django.contrib.staticfiles',
    'hello'
)
```

Notice that we've commented out the `django.contrib.admin` app, as we won't want to use the admin interface for our simple example project. We've also added the `hello` app to our project.

Our next step is to set up the database model. Because our `hello` app needs to keep track of how often the *Hello* message has been displayed, we will create a model named `Counter` which keeps track of how often the message has been displayed. To do this, edit your `hello/models.py` module, and add the following to the end of it:

```
class Counter(models.Model):
    count = models.IntegerField()
```

A database model (that is, a subclass of the `django.db.models.Model` class) is a Python class that defines the structure of a database table. In our example, we've created a very simple database model—just one model, `Counter`, which has a single field named `count`. There's a lot more that can be done with database models, including defining relations between models, setting default behavior, adding custom methods to a model, and so on, but this is all we need for our example project.

Save the `models.py` file, then open up a terminal or command-line window, `cd` into your outermost `example` directory, and enter the following command:

**python manage.py makemigrations hello**

The `makemigrations` command looks at the database models you have defined for the `hello` app and figures out what changes have occurred to the database structure since the last time the command was run. Because this is the first time we've run this command, a new database table will be created that matches the structure of your `Counter` class.

If you look inside your `hello/migrations` directory, you'll see that a new file has been created: `0001_initial.py`. This file contains the detailed instructions needed by Django to create the database table corresponding to your database model.

Now that the migration file has been created, we need to apply it. To do this, enter the following command:

**python manage.py migrate**

The `migrate` command applies all unapplied database migrations. Because a number of standard apps are included in your project, they will have their own database migrations, which will be applied at the same time.

We now have a database that includes, among other things, our new `Counter` model. You might be wondering where this database is. By default, Django makes use of the SQLite database engine, creating a simple database on disk which it uses to store your project's data. You can change this if you want by editing the `DATABASES` setting in your `example/settings.py` module.

Now that we have a database, let's make use of it. Since our example project needs to display a message to the user, we next have to create two things: a **URL mapping** that tells Django which function to call when the user attempts to access the system and a **view function** which will respond when that URL is accessed.

In a real system, URL mappings can get quite sophisticated, but for our program, we're going to use a very basic mapping. Edit the `example/urls.py` module and add the following `import` statement to the top of it:

```
from hello import views
```

This makes the `hello` app's view functions (which we will create in the `hello/views.py` module) available for use in our URL mappings. Next, replace the existing definition for the `urlpatterns` variable with the following:

```
urlpatterns = [
    url('^$', views.say_hello)
]
```

Notice that we've removed the reference to the admin interface, since we aren't using it in our project. The `url()` function defines a single URL mapping that maps the rather cryptic-looking `'^$'` URL pattern to a function named `say_hello()` within our `hello/views.py` module. The `'^$'` string is a regular expression that will match against the top-level URL for our project. In other words, if the user accesses the project's top-level URL, the `views.say_hello()` function will be called to respond to the user's request.

Save the changes you have made to the `urls.py` module, and then edit the `hello/views.py` module. This is where you will define the view functions for the `hello` app. We're going to create a single function named `say_hello()` which will respond when the user accesses our project's top-level URL.

Before we write our `say_hello()` function, let's think for a moment what this function is supposed to do. We need to display a message that looks like the following:

**Hello Number X.**

The value for **X** is taken from our `Counter` database model and is incremented each time our view is called. So, our first step is to load a `Counter` record, creating it if it doesn't already exist, and then increment it. We can then display the **Hello Number X** message based on the counter's current value.

We start by importing the `Counter` class into our `views.py` module:

```
from hello.models import Counter
```

We then define our `say_hello()` function. In Django, a view function takes a **request** object, which provides information about the HTTP request that was received from the user's web browser, and returns a **response** object containing the information to be sent back to the user's web browser for display. This means that the basic structure of a Django view function looks like this:

```
def view_function(request):
    ...
    return response
```

In our case, we don't really care about the `request` object, as we don't need to use any of the information it may contain. We do, however, have to return a response.

Let's start by defining the first part of our view function. To do this, add the following to the end of your `views.py` module:

```
def say_hello(request):
```

Our view function needs to load the `Counter` record from the database, creating it if necessary. Using Django's object-relational mapper, we can do this using the `Counter` class directly:

```
counter = Counter.objects.first()
if counter == None:
    counter = Counter(count=0)
```

We then increment the counter and save it back into the database:

```
counter.count = counter.count + 1
counter.save()
```

We now have the value for **X** that we want to include in the **Hello Number X** message. Our final step is to create an HTTP response object that includes this message so that we can use it as the function's return value.

While there are many ways in which we can create an HTTP response object, we will use Django's built-in templating system to create the response. Doing this is easy:

```
return render(request, "say_hello.html",
              {'count' : counter.count})
```

The `render()` function takes the HTTP request object, the name of the template file to use, and a "context" dictionary that holds values to be included in the template. In this case, we will use the `say_hello.html` template and supply a value named `count`, which will be included in the template.

We have almost completed our example project. All that's left is to create the HTML template: inside the `hello` app's directory, create a new directory named `templates`, and then create a file named `say_hello.html` within it. Then, enter the following into this file:

```
<html>
  <head>
    <title>Hello Example</title>
  </head>
  <body>
    Hello Number {{ count }}.
  </body>
</html>
```

You can now run your project by typing the following into the command line:

```
python manage.py runserver
```

To test your program, open up a web browser and go to `http://127.0.0.1:8000`. All going well, you should see the following message appear in your web browser:

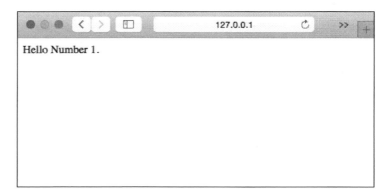

Reloading the page will cause the number to increment each time.

Of course, this example project is rather basic—there are lots of details we have skipped over, and the resulting program doesn't look particularly good yet—but we have covered most of the key features of Django that you need to know about:

- How to create projects and apps
- How to define and use database models
- How database migrations work
- How URL routing works to map from a URL to a view function
- How to write a simple view function
- How to create and use an HTML template

Now that we have seen how Django works, let's take a brief look at how GeoDjango extends the Django framework to allow you to create geospatial web applications.

# GeoDjango

The GeoDjango extension builds on Django's capabilities to add complete support for building geospatial web applications. In particular, it adds the following functionality to Django:

- **The model**:
    - The Django model is extended to allow you to store and retrieve geospatial data.
    - The Django ORM is extended to support spatial queries.
    - As geospatial features are read from the database, the object-relational mapper automatically converts them into GEOS objects, providing methods for querying and manipulating these features in a sophisticated way, similar to the interface provided by Shapely.
    - The model can import data from any OGR-supported vector-data source into the GeoDjango database.
    - GeoDjango can use *introspection* to see which attributes are available in a given OGR data source and automatically set up the model to store and import these attributes.

- **The template**:
    - Django's templating system is extended to allow the display of geospatial data using an embedded OpenLayers slippy map.

- **The admin interface**:
  - ° Django's admin interface is extended to allow the user to create and edit geospatial data using OpenLayers. The vector data is displayed on top of a base map provided by OpenStreetMap.

- **Distance and area calculators**:
  - ° The `django.contrib.gis.measure` package adds support for calculating and working with distances and areas.
  - ° Distances and areas can be converted between a range of standard units, for example, millimeters, yards, or miles.

- **IP-based geolocation**:
  - ° GeoDjango includes a wrapper around the MaxMind `GeoIP` API, making it possible to calculate locations based on a caller's IP address.
  - ° A location can be retrieved either as a lat/long coordinate or as a city and country name.

All told, the GeoDjango extension makes Django an excellent choice for developing geospatial web applications. In fact, ShapeEditor, the complete geospatial application we will be writing in the remainder of this book, will be built on top of the GeoDjango framework.

# Summary

In this chapter, we learned about the various tools and techniques involved in developing geospatial applications that can be accessed via a web interface. We saw how web applications can be structured, learned that web application frameworks can simplify the process of building a web application, and saw how user-interface libraries make the job of implementing web applications much easier. We then looked at the concept of web services and saw how to implement a great-circle distance calculator as a web service. We also looked at how map rendering can be implemented as a web service and saw how tile caching can speed up the process of displaying maps within a web browser.

We next looked at the concept of slippy maps and saw how these can be built using a stack of off-the-shelf components. We also examined a number of common protocols for sharing and manipulating geospatial data.

Finally, we took an in-depth look at three particular tools and techniques that we will make use of in the remainder of this book: the Tile Map Service (TMS) protocol, the OpenLayers user interface library, and the GeoDjango web application framework.

In the next chapter, we will start to build a complete mapping application using PostGIS, Mapnik, and GeoDjango.

# 11

# Putting It All Together – a Complete Mapping System

In these final three chapters of this book, we will bring together all the topics discussed in previous chapters to implement a sophisticated web-based mapping application called **ShapeEditor**.

In this chapter, we will:

- Look at the ShapeEditor system from the user's point of view in order to see how it will work

- Look at the various parts of the ShapeEditor in depth and see how they will be implemented in terms of data structures and functionality

- Set up a PostGIS database for the ShapeEditor to use

- Create the GeoDjango project and applications for the ShapeEditor system

- Define the ShapeEditor's database models

- Configure the GeoDjango admin interface for the ShapeEditor

- Use the admin interface to view and edit geospatial data within the ShapeEditor's database

## About the ShapeEditor

As we have seen, shapefiles are commonly used to store, make available, and transfer geospatial data. We have worked with shapefiles extensively in this book, obtaining freely available geospatial data in Shapefile format, writing programs to load data from a shapefile, and creating shapefiles programmatically.

While it is easy enough to edit the attributes associated with a shapefile's features, editing the features themselves is a lot more complicated. One approach is to install a GIS system and use it to import the data, make changes, and then export the data into another shapefile. While this works, it is hardly convenient if all you want to do is make a few changes to a shapefile's features. It would be much easier if we had a web application specifically designed for editing shapefiles.

This is precisely what we are going to implement: a web-based shapefile editor. Rather unimaginatively, we'll call this program **ShapeEditor**.

The following flowchart depicts the ShapeEditor's basic workflow:

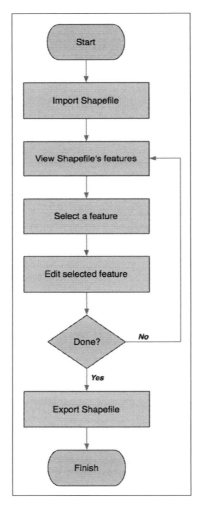

The user starts by importing a shapefile using the ShapeEditor's web interface, as shown in the following screen snapshot:

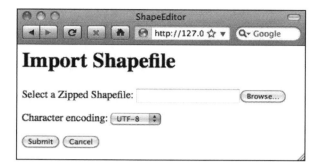

 Our ShapeEditor implementation wasn't chosen for its good looks; instead, it concentrates on getting the features working. It would be easy to add stylesheets and edit the HTML templates to improve the appearance of the application, but doing so would make the code harder to understand. This is why we've taken such a minimalist approach to the user interface. Making it pretty is an exercise left to the reader.

Once the shapefile has been imported, the user can view the shapefile's features on a map and can select a feature by clicking on it. In this case, we have imported the World Borders Dataset, used several times in this book:

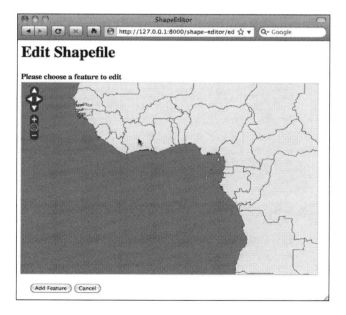

The user can then edit the selected feature's geometry as well as see a list of the attributes associated with that feature:

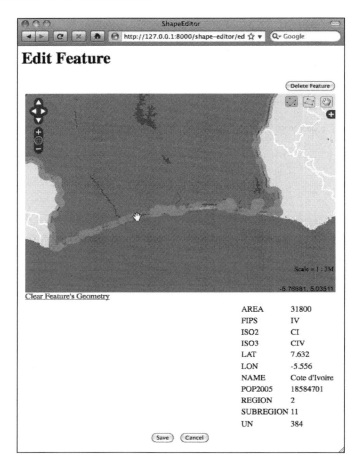

Once the user has finished making changes to the shapefile, he or she can export the shapefile again by clicking on the **Export** hyperlink on the main page:

That pretty much covers the ShapeEditor's functionality. It is a comparatively straightforward system, but it can be very useful if you need to work with geospatial data in shapefile format. And, of course, through the process of implementing the ShapeEditor, you will learn how to implement your own complex geospatial web applications using GeoDjango.

# Designing the ShapeEditor

Let's take a closer look at the various parts of the ShapeEditor in order to see what's involved in implementing it. The ShapeEditor is going to support the following activities:

- Importing geospatial features and attributes from a shapefile
- Allowing the user to select a feature to be edited
- Displaying the appropriate type of editor to allow the user to edit the feature's geometry
- Exporting geospatial features and attributes back to a shapefile

Let's take a closer look at each of these user activities in order to see how they will be implemented within the ShapeEditor system.

# Importing a shapefile

When the user imports a shapefile, we will store the contents of that shapefile in the database so that GeoDjango can work with it. Because we don't know in advance which types of geometries the shapefile will contain or what attributes might be associated with each feature, we need to have a generic representation of a shapefile's contents in the database rather than defining separate fields in the database for each of the shapefile's attributes.

To support this, we'll use the following collection of database objects:

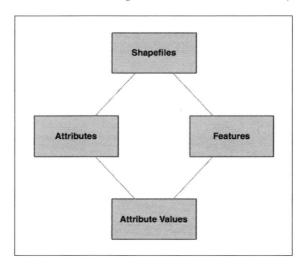

Each imported shapefile will be represented by a single Shapefile object in the database. Each Shapefile object will have a set of Attribute objects which define the name and data type for each of the shapefile's attributes. The Shapefile object will also have a set of Feature objects, one for each imported feature. The Feature objects will hold the geometry for each of the shapefile's features, and each feature will also have a set of AttributeValue objects, holding the value of each attribute of each feature.

To see how this works, let's imagine that we import the World Borders Dataset into the ShapeEditor. The contents of this shapefile would be stored in the database in the following way:

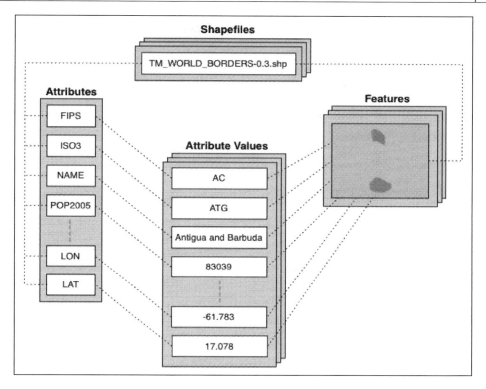

We will use a Shapefile object to represent the uploaded shapefile. This object will have a number of Attribute objects associated with it, one for each of the shapefile's attributes. There are also a number of Feature objects associated with the shapefile: the MultiPolygon geometry for each feature will be stored in the Feature object itself, while the attributes for each feature will be stored in a series of AttributeValue objects.

While this is a somewhat roundabout way of storing shapefile data in a database (it would be easier to use the ogrinspect management command to create a static GeoDjango model out of the shapefile's features and attributes), we have to do it this way because we don't know the shapefile's structure ahead of time, and it isn't practical to define a new database table whenever a shapefile is imported.

With this basic model in place to represent a shapefile's data in the database, we can continue designing the rest of the *Import Shapefile* logic.

Because shapefiles are represented on disk by a number of separate files, we expect the user to create a ZIP archive out of the shapefile and upload the zipped shapefile. This saves us having to handle multiple file uploads for a single shapefile and makes things more convenient for the user, as shapefiles often already come in ZIP format.

Once the ZIP archive has been uploaded, our code will need to decompress the archive and extract the individual files that make up the shapefile. We'll then have to read through the shapefile to find its attributes, create the appropriate `Attribute` objects, and then process the shapefile's features one at a time, creating `Feature` and `AttributeValue` objects as we go. All of this will be quite straightforward to implement.

# Selecting a feature

Before the user can edit a feature, we have to let the user select that feature. Unfortunately, GeoDjango's built-in slippy map interface won't allow us to select a feature by clicking on it. This is because GeoDjango can only display a single feature on a map at once, thanks to the way GeoDjango's geometry fields are implemented.

The usual way a GeoDjango application allows you to select a feature is by displaying a list of attributes (for example, city names) and then allowing you to choose a feature from that list. Unfortunately, this won't work for us either. Because the ShapeEditor allows the user to import *any* shapefile, there's no guarantee that the shapefile's attribute values can be used to select a feature. It may be that a shapefile has no attributes at all or has attributes that mean nothing to the end user—or, conversely, has dozens of attributes. There is no way of knowing which attribute to display or even whether there is a suitable attribute that can be used to select a feature. Because of this, we can't display a list of attributes when selecting the feature to edit.

Instead, we're going to take a completely different approach. We will bypass GeoDjango's built-in editor and instead use OpenLayers directly to display a map showing *all* the features in the imported shapefile. We'll then let the user click on a feature within the map to select it for editing.

Here is how we'll implement this particular feature:

OpenLayers needs to have a source of map tiles to display, so we'll create our own simple tile map server built on top of a Mapnik-based map renderer to display the shapefile's features stored in the database. We'll also write a simple **Click Handler** in JavaScript that intercepts clicks on the map and sends off an AJAX request to the server to see which feature the user clicked on. If the user does click on a feature (rather than just clicking on the map's background), the user's web browser will be redirected to the **Edit Feature** page so that they can edit the clicked-on feature.

There's a lot here, requiring a fair amount of custom coding, but the end result is a friendly interface to the ShapeEditor, allowing the user to simply point and click on a desired feature to edit it. In the process of building all this, we'll also learn how to use OpenLayers directly within a GeoDjango application and how to implement our own tile map server built on top of Mapnik.

# Editing a feature

To let the user edit a feature, we'll use GeoDjango's built-in geometry-editing widget. There is a slight amount of work required here, because we want to use this widget outside of GeoDjango's admin interface and will need to customize the interface slightly.

The only other issue that needs to be dealt with is the fact that we don't know in advance what type of feature we'll be editing. Shapefiles can hold any type of geometry, from Points and LineStrings through to MultiPolygons and GeometryCollections. Fortunately, all the features in a shapefile have to have the same geometry type, so we can store the geometry type in the `Shapefile` object and use it to select the appropriate type of editor when editing that shapefile's features.

# Exporting a shapefile

Exporting a shapefile involves the reverse of the importing process: we have to create a new shapefile on disk, define the various attributes that will be stored in the shapefile, and then process all the features and their attributes, writing them out to the shapefile. Once this has been done, we can create a ZIP archive from the contents of the shapefile and tell the user's web browser to download that ZIP archive to the user's hard disk.

# Prerequisites

Before we can start implementing the ShapeEditor, we need to make sure that the various libraries and tools it uses are installed on your computer. You probably already installed all of these when you worked through the previous chapters of this book, but just in case you haven't, please make sure you have installed the following software:

- GDAL/OGR version 1.10 or later
- PROJ.4 version 4.8 or later
- pyproj version 1.9 or later
- PostgreSQL version 9.4 or later
- PostGIS version 2.1 or later
- psycopg2 version 2.6 or later
- Mapnik version 2.2 or later
- Django version 1.8 or later

# Setting up the database

Because the ShapeEditor will make heavy use of PostGIS, we first need to set up a PostgreSQL user and database for the ShapeEditor to use and then enable the PostGIS extension for this database. Let's do that now:

1. Open a terminal or command-line window and type the following:

   ```
   createuser -P shapeeditor
   ```

    Don't forget to add the `-U postgres` command-line option or use `sudo` for this command if you need to run Postgres under a different user account.

2. You will be prompted to enter a password for the `shapeeditor` Postgres user. Make sure you remember the password you use, as you'll need to use it when setting up the ShapeEditor so that it can access the database. We next need to create the database itself:

   ```
   % createdb shapeeditor
   ```

    Once again, add the `-U` command-line option, or use `sudo` if you need to.

3. We then need to tell Postgres that the `shapeeditor` user can access the `shapeeditor` database:

   ```
   % psql -c "GRANT ALL PRIVILEGES ON DATABASE shapeeditor TO shapeeditor; "
   ```

4. Finally, we need to spatially-enable the `shapeeditor` database by turning on the PostGIS extension:

   ```
   % psql -d shapeeditor -c "CREATE EXTENSION postgis;"
   ```

    For all these commands, add the `-U` command-line option, or use `sudo` if you need to.

Congratulations! You have just set up a PostGIS database for the ShapeEditor application to use.

# Setting up the ShapeEditor project

We now have to create the Django project for our ShapeEditor system. To do this, `cd` into the directory where you want the project's directory to be placed, and type the following:

```
% django-admin.py startproject shapeEditor
```

> When you installed Django, it should have placed the `django-admin.py` program into your path, so you shouldn't need to tell the computer where this script resides.

All going well, Django will create a directory named `shapeEditor` with the following contents:

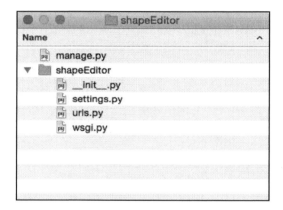

Now that the project has been created, we need to configure it. To do this, edit the `settings.py` file in the `shapeEditor` package directory. We need to tell our project how to access the database we set up, and we also want to enable the GeoDjango extension.

Start by searching for the `DATABASES` variable, and change it to look like the following:

```
DATABASES = {
    'default': {
        'ENGINE'   : 'django.contrib.gis.db.backends.postgis',
        'NAME'     : 'shapeeditor',
        'USER'     : 'shapeeditor',
        'PASSWORD' : '...'
    }
}
```

Make sure you enter the password you set up for the `shapeeditor` Postgres user.

Next, search for the `INSTALLED_APPS` variable, and add the following to the end of the list of installed applications:

```
'django.contrib.gis',
```

While we're editing the `settings.py` file, let's make one more change that will save us some trouble down the track. Go to the `MIDDLEWARE_CLASSES` setting, and comment out the `django.middleware.csrf.CsrfViewMiddleware` line. This entry causes the addition of extra error checking when processing forms to prevent **cross-site request forgery (CSRF)**. Implementing CSRF support requires adding extra code to our form templates, which we won't be doing here in order to keep things simple.

 If you deploy your own applications on the Internet, you should read the CSRF documentation on the Django web site and enable CSRF support. Otherwise, you may find your application subjected to cross-site request forgery attacks.

This completes the configuration of our ShapeEditor project.

# Defining the ShapeEditor's applications

We now have a Django project for our overall ShapeEditor system. We next need to break down our project into **applications**, following Django's design philosophy of having applications be small and relatively self-contained. Looking back at our design for the overall project, we can see several possible candidates for breaking the functionality into separate applications:

- Importing and exporting shapefiles
- Selecting features
- Editing features
- The tile map server

We're going to combine the first three into a single application called `shapefiles`, which will handle all the shapefile-related logic. We'll then have another application called `tms`, which implements our tile map server. Finally, we'll define one more application, which we'll called `shared`, to hold the database models and Python modules that are shared across these applications.

For example, we might have a module named `utils.py` that is needed by both the `shapefile` and `tms` applications. We'll place this into the `shared` application to make it clear that this code is designed to be shared by various parts of the system.

# Creating the shared application

The `shapeEditor.shared` application will hold the core database tables and Python modules we use throughout the system. Let's go ahead and create this application now. Use the `cd` command to change the current directory to the top-level `shapeEditor` directory and type the following:

```
python manage.py startapp shared
```

This will create a new Python package named `shared` that will hold the contents of the `shared` app. Note that, by default, a new application is placed in the topmost `shapeEditor` directory. This means you can import this application into your Python program like this:

```
import shared
```

Django's conventions say that applications in the topmost directory (or anywhere else in your Python path) are intended to be *reusable* — that is, you can take that application and use it in a different project. The applications we're defining here aren't like that; they can only work as part of the `shapeEditor` project, and we would like to be able to import them like this:

```
import shapeEditor.shared
```

To allow this, you have to move the newly-created `shared` package directory inside the `shapeEditor` project's subdirectory. Doing this from the command line is easy; simply `cd` into the outermost `shapeEditor` directory and type the following command:

```
mv shared shapeEditor
```

Alternatively, if you are running MS Windows, you should use the following command:

```
move shared shapeEditor
```

 Unfortunately, Django doesn't currently make it easy for you to create non-reusable applications. You have to create the application first and then move the directory into the project directory to make it non-reusable.

Inside the `shapeEditor.shared` package directory will be a number of files:

| File | Description |
|------|-------------|
| `__init__.py` | This is a standard Python package initialization file |
| `admin.py` | This module defines the admin interface for the `shapeEditor.shared` application |
| `migrations` | This directory will hold the various database migrations used by this application |
| `models.py` | This Python module holds the `shapeEditor.shared` application's database models |
| `tests.py` | This module can be used to hold the application's unit tests |
| `views.py` | This module is normally used to hold the application's view functions |

Go ahead and delete the `tests.py` and `views.py` modules, as we won't be using them for this application. You should end up with the following directory structure:

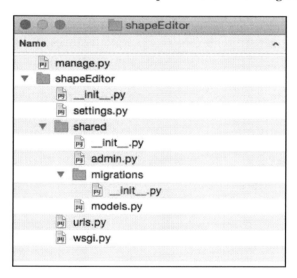

Since we have created the application itself, let's add it to our project. Edit the `settings.py` file again, and add the following entry to the `INSTALLED_APPS` list:

```
'shapeEditor.shared',
```

Now that we have our `shapeEditor.shared` application, let's start to put some useful things into it.

# Defining the data models

We already know which database objects we are going to need to store the uploaded shapefiles:

- The `Shapefile` object will represent a single uploaded shapefile

- Each shapefile will have a number of `Attribute` objects, giving the name, data type, and other information about each attribute within the shapefile

- Each shapefile will have a number of `Feature` objects which hold the geometry for each of the shapefile's features

- Each feature will have a set of `AttributeValue` objects which hold the value for each of the feature's attributes

Let's look at each of these in more detail and think about exactly what information will need to be stored in each object.

## The Shapefile object

When we import a shapefile, there are a few things we need to remember:

- The original name of the uploaded file. We will display this in the "list shapefiles" view so that the user can identify the shapefile within this list.

- The spatial reference system used by the shapefile. When we import the shapefile, we will convert it to use latitude and longitude coordinates using the WGS84 datum (EPSG 4326), but we need to remember the shapefile's original spatial reference system so that we can use it again when exporting the features. For simplicity, we're going to store the spatial reference system in WKT format.

- What type of geometry was stored in the shapefile. We'll need this to know which field in the `Feature` object holds the geometry.

## The Attribute object

When we export a shapefile, it has to have the same attributes as the original imported file. Because of this, we have to remember the shapefile's attributes. This is what the `Attribute` object does. We will need to remember the following information for each attribute:

- Which shapefile the attribute belongs to
- The name of the attribute

- The type of data stored in this attribute (string, floating-point number, and so on)
- The field width of the attribute, in characters
- The number of digits to display after the decimal point (for floating-point attributes)

All of this information comes directly from the shapefile's layer definition.

# The Feature object

Each feature in the imported shapefile will need to be stored in the database. Because PostGIS (and GeoDjango) uses different field types for different types of geometries, we need to define separate fields for each geometry type. Because of this, the Feature object will need to store the following information:

- The shapefile the feature belongs to
- The Point geometry, if the shapefile stores this type of geometry
- The MultiPoint geometry, if the shapefile stores this type of geometry
- The MultiLineString geometry, if the shapefile stores this type of geometry
- The MultiPolygon geometry, if the shapefile stores this type of geometry
- The GeometryCollection geometry, if the shapefile stores this type of geometry

**Isn't something missing?**

If you've been paying attention, you've probably noticed that some of the geometry types are missing. What about Polygons and LineStrings? Because of the way data is stored in a shapefile, it is impossible to know in advance whether a shapefile holds Polygons or MultiPolygons and, similarly, whether it holds LineStrings or MultiLineStrings (or Points or MultiPoints). The shapefile's internal structure makes no distinction between these geometry types. Because of this, a shapefile may claim to store Polygons when it really contains MultiPolygons and may make similar claims for LineString geometries. For more information, check out http://code.djangoproject.com/ticket/7218.

To work around this limitation, we store all Polygons as MultiPolygons, all LineStrings as MultiLineStrings, and all Points as MultiPoints. This is why we don't need Polygon, Point, or LineString fields in the Feature object.

# The AttributeValue object

The `AttributeValue` object holds the value for each of the feature's attributes. This object is quite straightforward, storing the following information:

- Which feature the attribute value is for
- Which attribute the value is for
- The attribute's value, as a Unicode string

For simplicity, we'll store all attribute values as strings.

# The models.py file

Now that we know what information we want to store in our database, it's easy to define our various model objects. To do this, edit the `models.py` file in the `shapeEditor.shared` directory, and make sure it looks like this:

```python
from django.contrib.gis.db import models


class Shapefile(models.Model):
    filename  = models.CharField(max_length=255)
    srs_wkt   = models.CharField(max_length=255)
    geom_type = models.CharField(max_length=50)


class Attribute(models.Model):
    shapefile = models.ForeignKey(Shapefile)
    name      = models.CharField(max_length=255)
    type      = models.IntegerField()
    width     = models.IntegerField()
    precision = models.IntegerField()


class Feature(models.Model):
    shapefile = models.ForeignKey(Shapefile)
    geom_point = models.PointField(srid=4326,
                                   blank=True, null=True)
    geom_multipoint = \
          models.MultiPointField(srid=4326,
                                 blank=True, null=True)
    geom_multilinestring = \
```

```
                models.MultiLineStringField(srid=4326,
                                        blank=True, null=True)
    geom_multipolygon = \
            models.MultiPolygonField(srid=4326,
                                    blank=True, null=True)
    geom_geometrycollection = \
            models.GeometryCollectionField(srid=4326,
                                        blank=True,
                                        null=True)


    objects = models.GeoManager()



class AttributeValue(models.Model):
    feature   = models.ForeignKey(Feature)
    attribute = models.ForeignKey(Attribute)
    value     = models.CharField(max_length=255,
                            blank=True, null=True)
```

There are a few things to be aware of here:

- The `from...import` statement at the top has changed. We're importing the GeoDjango models rather than the standard Django ones.

- We use `models.CharField` objects to represent character data and `models.IntegerField` objects to represent integer values. Django provides a whole raft of field types for you to use. GeoDjango also adds its own field types to store geometry fields, as you can see from the definition of the `Feature` object.

- To represent relations between two objects, we use a `models.ForeignKey` object.

- Because the `Feature` object will store geometry data, we want to allow GeoDjango to perform spatial queries using this data. To enable this, we define a `GeoManager()` instance for the `Feature` class.

- Several fields (in particular, the `geom_XXX` fields in the `Feature` object) have both `blank=True` and `null=True`. These are actually quite distinct: `blank=True` means that the admin interface allows the user to leave the field blank, while `null=True` tells the database that these fields can be set to `NULL` in the database. For the `Feature` object, we'll need both so that we don't get validation errors when entering geometries via the admin interface.

That's all we need to do (for now) to define our database models. After you've made these changes, save the file, `cd` into the topmost project directory, and type the following:

```
python manage.py makemigrations shared
```

As we saw in the previous chapter, the `makemigrations` command creates a database migration file for the given application. With this migration in place, we can now tell Django to create a database structure to match the contents of our database models:

```
python manage.py migrate
```

This command tells Django to check the models and create new database tables as required. You should now have a spatial database set up with the various database tables you have defined. Let's take a closer look at this database by typing the following:

```
psql shapeeditor
```

When you see the Postgres command prompt, type \d and press *Return*. You should see a list of all the database tables that have been created:

```
                       List of relations

 Schema |                 Name                  |   Type   |   Owner
--------+---------------------------------------+----------+------------
 public | auth_group                            | table    | shapeeditor
 public | auth_group_id_seq                     | sequence | shapeeditor
 public | auth_group_permissions                | table    | shapeeditor
 public | auth_group_permissions_id_seq         | sequence | shapeeditor
 public | auth_permission                       | table    | shapeeditor
 public | auth_permission_id_seq                | sequence | shapeeditor
 public | auth_user                             | table    | shapeeditor
 public | auth_user_groups                      | table    | shapeeditor
 public | auth_user_groups_id_seq               | sequence | shapeeditor
 public | auth_user_id_seq                      | sequence | shapeeditor
 public | auth_user_user_permissions            | table    | shapeeditor
 public | auth_user_user_permissions_id_seq     | sequence | shapeeditor
 public | django_admin_log                      | table    | shapeeditor
 public | django_admin_log_id_seq               | sequence | shapeeditor
 public | django_content_type                   | table    | shapeeditor
 public | django_content_type_id_seq            | sequence | shapeeditor
```

| public | django_migrations | | table | shapeeditor |
|--------|-------------------|---|----------|-------------|
| public | django_migrations_id_seq | | sequence | shapeeditor |
| public | django_session | | table | shapeeditor |
| public | geography_columns | | view | postgres |
| public | geometry_columns | | view | postgres |
| public | raster_columns | | view | postgres |
| public | raster_overviews | | view | postgres |
| public | shared_attribute | | table | shapeeditor |
| public | shared_attribute_id_seq | | sequence | shapeeditor |
| public | shared_attributevalue | | table | shapeeditor |
| public | shared_attributevalue_id_seq | | sequence | shapeeditor |
| public | shared_feature | | table | shapeeditor |
| public | shared_feature_id_seq | | sequence | shapeeditor |
| public | shared_shapefile | | table | shapeeditor |
| public | shared_shapefile_id_seq | | sequence | shapeeditor |
| public | spatial_ref_sys | | table | postgres |

`(32 rows)`

To make sure that each application's database tables are unique, Django adds the application name to the start of the table name. This means that the table names for the models we have created within the shared application are actually called `shared_shapefile`, `shared_feature`, and so on. We'll be working with these database tables directly later on, when we want to use Mapnik to generate maps using the imported Shapefile data.

When you have finished with the Postgres command-line client, type \q and press *Return* to quit `psql`.

Now that our database has been set up, let's create a "superuser" account so that we can access it. You can do this by entering the following command:

`python manage.py createsuperuser`

You'll be prompted to enter the username, e-mail address and password for a new superuser; we'll need this for the next section, where we explore GeoDjango's built-in admin interface.

# Playing with the admin system

The built-in **admin** application is enabled by default in new Django projects. Before we can use it, however, we need to register the various database models we want it to support. To do this, edit the `admin.py` module within the `shapeEditor/shared` directory, and enter the following into this file:

```
from django.contrib.gis import admin
from shapeEditor.shared.models import *

admin.site.register(Shapefile, admin.ModelAdmin)
admin.site.register(Feature, admin.GeoModelAdmin)
admin.site.register(Attribute, admin.ModelAdmin)
admin.site.register(AttributeValue, admin.ModelAdmin)
```

The `ModelAdmin` class tells Django how to display the model within the admin interface. Notice that we use the `GeoModelAdmin` class for the `Feature` class. Because the `Feature` object includes geometry fields, using the `GeoModelAdmin` class allows the admin interface to edit these geometry fields using a slippy map. We'll see how this works shortly.

Now that the `admin` module has been configured, let's try running it. Type the following into your terminal or command-line window:

```
python manage.py runserver
```

This will start up the Django server for your project. Open a web browser and navigate to the following URL:

```
http://127.0.0.1:8000/admin/shared
```

You should see the **Django administration** login page:

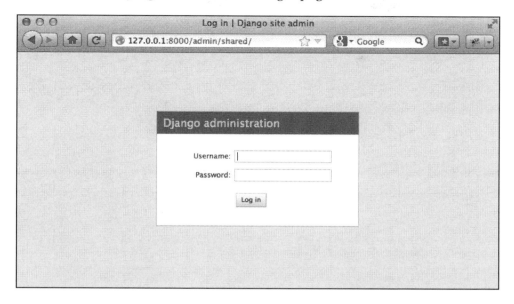

Enter the username and password for the superuser you created earlier, and you will see the main admin interface for the `shapeEditor.shared` application:

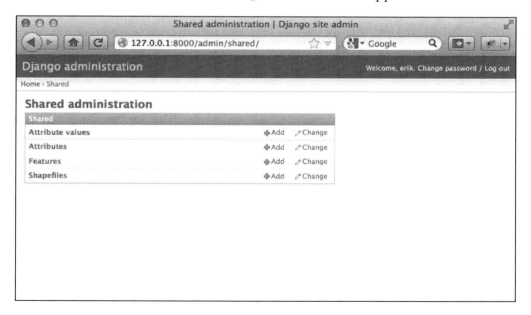

Let's use this admin interface to create a dummy shapefile. Click on the **Add** link in the **Shapefiles** row, and you will be presented with a basic input screen for entering a new shapefile:

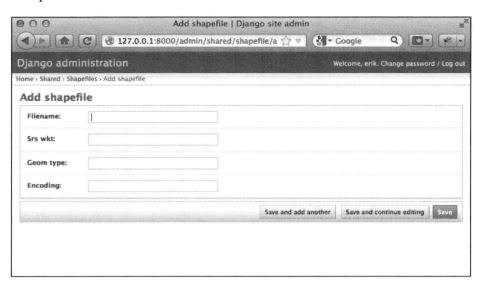

Enter some dummy values into the various fields (it doesn't matter what you enter), and click on the **Save** button to save the new `Shapefile` object into the database. A list of the shapefiles that are present in the database will be shown. At the moment, there is only the `Shapefile` record you just created:

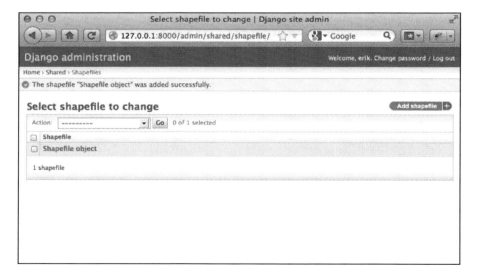

As you can see, the new shapefile object has been given a rather unhelpful label: **Shapefile object**. This is because we haven't yet told Django how to label the shapefile. To fix this, edit the `shared.models` file and add the following method to the end of the `Shapefile` class definition:

```
def __str__(self):
    return self.filename
```

The `__str__` method returns a human-readable summary of the `Shapefile` object's contents. In this case, we are showing the filename associated with the shapefile. If you then reload the web page, you can see that the shapefile now has a useful label:

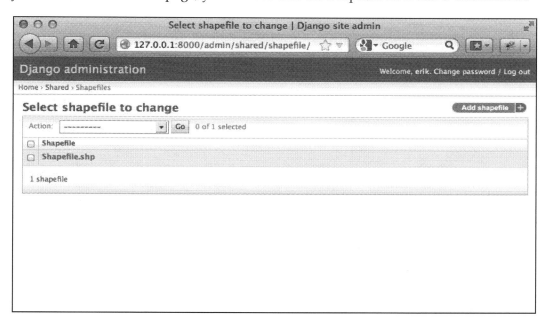

Go ahead and add the `__str__` method to the other model objects as well:

```
class Attribute(models.Model):
    ...
    def __str__(self):
        return self.name

class Feature(models.Model):
    ...
    def __str__(self):
```

```
        return str(self.id)

class AttributeValue(models.Model):
    ...
    def __str__(self):
        return self.value
```

While this may seem like busywork, it's actually quite useful for your database objects to be able to describe themselves. If you wanted to, you could further customize the admin interface, for example, by showing the attributes and features associated with the selected shapefile. For now, though, let's take a look at GeoDjango's built-in geometry editors.

Go back to the shared application's administration page (by clicking on the **Shared** hyperlink near the top of the window), and click on the **Add** button in the **Features** row. As with the shapefile, you will be asked to enter the details for a new feature. This time, however, the admin interface will use a slippy map to enter each of the different geometry types supported by the Feature object:

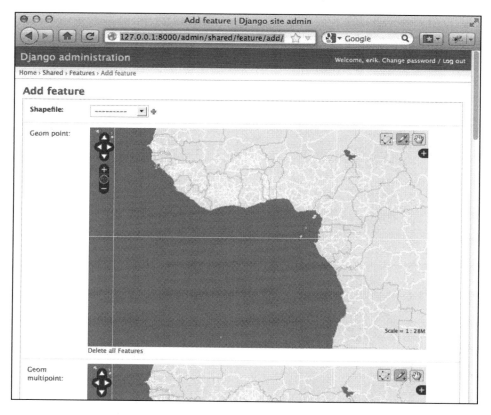

Obviously, having multiple slippy maps like this isn't quite what we want, and if we wanted to, we could set up a custom `GeoModelAdmin` subclass to avoid this, but that's not important right now. Instead, try selecting the shapefile to associate with this feature by choosing the shapefile you created from the **Shapefile** menu, and then scroll down to the **Geom multipolygon** field and try adding a polygon or two to the map. To do this, click on the map to start drawing a new polygon, click repeatedly to add points to the current polygon, or hold down the *Shift* key and click to finish creating a polygon. The interface can be a bit confusing at first, but it's certainly usable. We'll look at the various options for editing polygons later. For now, just click on the **Save** button at the very bottom of the page to save your new feature. If you edit it again, you'll see your saved geometry (or geometries) once again on the slippy maps.

This completes our tour of the admin interface. We won't be using this for end users, as we don't want to require users to log in before making changes to the shapefile data. We will, however, be borrowing some code from the admin application so that end users can edit their shapefile's features using a slippy map.

# Summary

You have now finished implementing the first part of the ShapeEditor application. Even at this early stage, you have made good progress, learning how GeoDjango works, designing the application, and laying the foundations for the functionality you will implement in the next two chapters.

In this chapter, you created your own GeoDjango project, designed the ShapeEditor system in detail, and broke it down into individual applications within the Django project. You defined the various database models that will be used by the ShapeEditor and set up a PostGIS database for storing the ShapeEditor's data. You then configured the built-in admin application so it could view and edit the database models you set up, and you used this application to view and edit your data. Finally, you saw how GeoDjango's `GeoModelAdmin` class allows the user to view and edit geospatial data using a slippy map.

In the next chapter, we will implement a view to display the list of available shapefiles as well as write the somewhat involved code for importing and exporting shapefiles via a web interface.

# 12
# ShapeEditor – Importing and Exporting Shapefiles

In this chapter, we will continue our implementation of the ShapeEditor application. We will start by implementing a list view to show the available shapefiles and then work through the details of importing and exporting shapefiles via a web interface.

In this chapter, we will learn:

- How to display a list of records using a Django template
- How to deal with the complexities of shapefile data, including issues with geometries and attribute data types
- How to import a shapefile's data using a web interface
- How to export a shapefile using a web interface

## Implementing the shapefile list view

When the user first opens the ShapeEditor, we want them to see a list of the previously uploaded shapefiles, with **Import**, **Edit**, **Export**, and **Delete** options. The Django application that implements this list view and its related functionality will be called shapefiles; let's go ahead and create this application now.

Open a terminal or command-line window, cd into the top-level shapeEditor directory, and enter the following command:

```
python manage.py startapp shapefiles
```

Once again, this creates the `shapefiles` application at the top level so that it is a reusable application. Move this inside the `shapeEditor` directory by typing this:

**mv shapefiles shapeEditor**

While we're at it, go into the `shapeEditor/shapefiles` directory and delete the `admin.py` and `tests.py` modules, as we won't need these. Then, edit the `shapeEditor/settings.py` module and add the following entry to the end of the `INSTALLED_APPS` list:

```
'shapeEditor.shapefiles',
```

Our `shapefiles` app won't define any database models of its own, but we need to keep the `models.py` file so that Django recognizes it as an application. The only other interesting part of the application is the `views.py` module, where we will define our "List Shapefiles" view. Let's go ahead and write a simple placeholder for this view; edit the `views.py` module and enter the following into it:

```
from django.http import HttpResponse

def list_shapefiles (request):
    return HttpResponse("in list_shapefiles")
```

 There is a lot of source code in this chapter, but you don't need to type it all in by hand if you don't want to. If you prefer, you can simply download the example code for this chapter, which includes all the changes made to the ShapeEditor system in this chapter.

We next need to tell our ShapeEditor project to call this view when the user accesses the topmost URL for the ShapeEditor system. To do this, edit the `urls.py` module and edit it so that it looks like the following:

```
from django.conf.urls import include, url
from django.contrib.gis import admin
import shapeEditor.shapefiles.views

urlpatterns = [
    url(r'^$', shapeEditor.shapefiles.views.list_shapefiles),
    url(r'^admin/', include(admin.site.urls)),
]
```

The first URL pattern maps from the topmost URL (which is identified by the regular expression `r'^$'`) to our `shapeEditor.shapefiles.views.list_shapefiles()` view function. This view acts as the user's starting point for the entire ShapeEditor system. The second URL pattern we define allows the user to access GeoDjango's admin interface via the `/admin` URL.

It's now time to test our new view function. Type the following command into your terminal window:

```
python manage.py runserver
```

Then, open your web browser and navigate to the following URL:

```
http://127.0.0.1:8000/
```

All going well, you should see **in list_shapefiles** appear in the browser window. This tells us that our `list_shapefile()` view function is being called in response to the top-level URL.

Now that we have a working view function, let's make it do something useful. Open the `views.py` module (in the `shapeEditor/shapefiles` directory), and edit its contents to look like the following:

```python
from django.http import HttpResponse
from django.shortcuts import render
from shapeEditor.shared.models import Shapefile


def list_shapefiles (request):
    shapefiles = Shapefile.objects.all().order_by('filename')
    return render(request, "list_shapefiles.html",
                  {'shapefiles' : shapefiles})
```

The `list_shapefiles()` view function now does two things:

- It loads the list of all Shapefile objects from the database into memory, sorted by filename

- It passes this list to a Django template (in a file named `list_shapefiles.html`), which is rendered into an HTML web page and returned back to the caller

Let's go ahead and create the `list_shapefiles.html` template. Create a directory called `templates` within the `shapeEditor/shapefiles` directory, and create a new file in this directory named `list_shapefiles.html`. This file should have the following contents:

```html
<html>
  <head>
    <title>ShapeEditor</title>
  </head>
  <body>
    <h1>ShapeEditor</h1>
{% if shapefiles %}
    <b>Available Shapefiles:</b>
    <table border="0" cellspacing="0" cellpadding="5"
           style="padding-left:20px">
{% for shapefile in shapefiles %}
      <tr>
        <td><font style="font-family:monospace">
          {{ shapefile.filename }}
        </font></td>
        <td> </td>
        <td>
          <a href="/edit/{{ shapefile.id }}">Edit</a>
        </td>
        <td> </td>
        <td>
          <a href="/export/{{ shapefile.id }}">Export</a>
        </td>
        <td> </td>
        <td>
          <a href="/delete/{{ shapefile.id }}">Delete</a>
        </td>
      </tr>
    {% endfor %}
    </table>
{% endif %}
    <button type="button"
            onClick='window.location="/import";'>
      Import New Shapefile
    </button>
  </body>
</html>
```

This template works as follows:

- If the `shapefiles` list is not empty, it creates an HTML table to display the list of shapefiles
- For each entry in the `shapefiles` list, a new row in the table is created
- Each table row consists of the shapefile's file name (in monospaced text), along with **Edit**, **Export**, and **Delete** hyperlinks
- Finally, an **Import New Shapefile** button is displayed at the bottom

We'll look at the hyperlinks used in this template shortly, but for now, just create the file, make sure the Django server is running, and reload your web browser. You should see the following page:

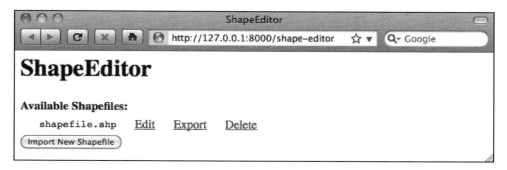

As you can see, the shapefile we created earlier in the admin interface is shown, along with the relevant hyperlinks and buttons to access the rest of the ShapeEditor's functionality:

- The **Edit** hyperlink will take the user to the `/edit/1` URL, which will let the user edit the shapefile with the given record ID
- The **Export** hyperlink will take the user to the `/export/1` URL, which will let the user download a copy of the shapefile with the given ID
- The **Delete** hyperlink will take the user to the `/delete/1` URL, which will let the user delete the given shapefile
- The **Import New Shapefile** button will take the user to the `/import` URL, which will let the user upload a new shapefile

You can explore these URLs by clicking on them if you want—they won't do anything other than displaying an error page, but you can see how these URLs link the various parts of the ShapeEditor's functionality together. You can also take a detailed look at the Django error page, which can be quite helpful in tracking down bugs.

Now that we have a working first page, let's start implementing the core functionality of the ShapeEditor system. We'll start with the logic required to import a shapefile.

# Importing shapefiles

The process of importing a shapefile involves the following steps:

1. Display a form prompting the user to upload the shapefile's ZIP archive.
2. Decompress the ZIP file to extract the uploaded shapefile.
3. Open the shapefile and read its data into the database.
4. Delete the temporary files we have created.

Let's work through each of these steps in turn.

## The Import Shapefile form

Let's start by creating a placeholder for the "Import Shapefile" view. Edit the `urls.py` module and add a new entry to the `urlpatterns` list:

```
url(r'^import$', shapeEditor.shapefiles.views.import_shapefile),
```

Then, edit the `shapeEditor/shapefiles/views.py` module and add a dummy `import_shapefile()` view function to respond to this URL:

```
def import_shapefile(request):
    return HttpResponse("More to come")
```

You can test this if you want: run the Django server, go to the main page, and click on the **Import New Shapefile** button. You should see the **More to come** message.

To let the user enter data, we're going to use a Django form. Forms are custom classes that define the various fields that will appear on the web page. In this case, our form will have just a single field that lets the user select the file to be uploaded. We're going to store this form in a file named `forms.py` in the `shapeEditor/shapefiles` directory. Go ahead and create this file, and then edit it to look like this:

```
from django import forms

class ImportShapefileForm(forms.Form):
    import_file = forms.FileField(label="Select a Zipped
    Shapefile")
```

The `FileField` class lets the user select a file to upload. As you can see, we give this field a custom label, which will be displayed in the web page.

Now that we have created the form, go back to `views.py` and change the definition of the `import_shapefile()` view function to look like this:

```
def import_shapefile(request):
    if request.method == "GET":
        form = ImportShapefileForm()
        return render(request, "import_shapefile.html",
                        {'form' : form})
    elif request.method == "POST":
        form = ImportShapefileForm(request.POST,
                                    request.FILES)
        if form.is_valid():
            shapefile = request.FILES['import_file']
            # More to come...
            return HttpResponseRedirect("/")

        return render(request, "import_shapefile.html",
                        {'form' : form})
```

Also, add these two `import` statements to the top of the module:

```
from django.http import HttpResponseRedirect
from shapeEditor.shapefiles.forms import ImportShapefileForm
```

Let's take a look at what is happening here: the `import_shapefile()` function will initially be called with an HTTP GET request; this will cause the function to create a new `ImportShapefileForm` object and then call `render()` to display that form to the user. When the form is submitted, the `import_shapefile()` function will be called with an HTTP POST request. In this case, an `ImportShapefileForm` will be created with the submitted data (`request.POST` and `request.FILES`), and the form will be checked to see that the entered data is valid. If so, we will extract the uploaded shapefile.

At this point, because we haven't implemented the actual importing code, we will simply redirect the user back to the top-level page. As the comment says, we'll add more code here shortly.

If the form was not valid, we will once again call `render()` to display the form to the user. In this case, Django will automatically display the error message(s) associated with the form so that the user can see why the validation failed.

To display the form, we'll use a Django template and pass the form object as a parameter. Let's create that template now—create a new file named `import_shapefile.html` in the `templates` directory, and enter the following text into this file:

```html
<html>
    <head>
        <title>ShapeEditor</title>
    </head>
    <body>
        <h1>Import Shapefile</h1>
        <form enctype="multipart/form-data" method="post"
            action="import">
            {{ form.as_p }}
            <input type="submit" value="Submit"/>
            <button type="button"
                onClick='window.location="/shape-editor";'>
                Cancel
            </button>
        </form>
    </body>
</html>
```

As you can see, this template defines an HTML `<form>` element and adds **Submit** and **Cancel** buttons to that form. The body of the form is not specified. Instead, we use `{{ form.as_p }}` to insert the form object into the template.

Let's test this out. Start up the Django web server if it is not already running, open a web browser, and enter the `http://127.0.0.1:8000` URL into the address bar. Then, click on the **Import New Shapefile** button. All going well, you should see the following page:

If you attempt to submit the form without uploading anything, an error message will appear saying that a shapefile is required. This is the default error-handling for any form: by default, all fields are required. If you do select a file for uploading, all that will happen is that the user will get redirected back to the main page; this is because we haven't implemented the import logic yet.

Now that we've created the form, let's work on the code required to process the uploaded shapefile.

# Extracting the uploaded shapefile

Because the process of importing data is going to be rather involved, we'll put this code into a separate module. Create a new file named shapefileIO.py within the shapeEditor/shapefiles directory, and add the following text into this file:

```
def import_data(shapefile):
    return "More to come..."
```

Since it's quite possible for the process of importing a shapefile to fail (for example, if the user uploads a file that isn't a ZIP archive), our import_data() function is going to return an error message if something goes wrong. Let's go back and change our view (and template) to call this import_data() function and display the returned error message, if any.

Edit the views.py module, and add the following highlighted lines to the import_shapefile() view function:

```
def import_shapefile(request):
    if request.method == "GET":
        form = ImportShapefileForm()
        return render_to_response("import_shapefile.html",
                                  {'form'   : form,
                                   'errMsg' : None})
    elif request.method == "POST":
        errMsg = None # initially.

        form = ImportShapefileForm(request.POST,
                                   request.FILES)
        if form.is_valid():
            shapefile = request.FILES['import_file']
            errMsg = shapefileIO.import_data(shapefile)
            if errMsg == None:
                return HttpResponseRedirect("/")
```

```
return render_to_response("import_shapefile.html",
                          {'form'   : form,
                           'errMsg' : errMsg})
```

You'll also need to add the following to the top of the file:

```
from django.shortcuts import render_to_response
from shapeEditor.shapefiles import shapefileIO
```

Now, edit the `import_shapefile.html` template and add the following lines to the file, immediately below the `<h1>Import Shapefile<h1>` line:

```
{% if errMsg %}
<b><i>{{ errMsg }}</i></b>
{% endif %}
```

This will display the error message to the user if it is not `None`.

Go ahead and try out your changes: click on the **Import New Shapefile** button, select a ZIP archive, and click on **Submit**. You should see the text **More to come...** appear at the top of the form, which is the error text returned by our dummy `import_data()` function.

We're now ready to start implementing the import logic. Edit the `shapefileIO.py` module again and get ready to write the body of the `import_data()` function. We'll take this one step at a time.

When we set up a form that includes a `FileField` object, Django returns to us an `UploadedFile` object representing the uploaded file. Our first task is to read the contents of the `UploadedFile` object and store it into a temporary file on disk so that we can work with it. Add the following to your `import_data()` function:

```
fd,fname = tempfile.mkstemp(suffix=".zip")
os.close(fd)

f = open(fname, "wb")
for chunk in shapefile.chunks():
    f.write(chunk)
f.close()
```

As you can see, we use the `tempfile` module from the Python standard library to create a temporary file, and we then copy the contents of the `shapefile` object into this file.

Because `tempfile.mkstemp()` returns both a file descriptor and a filename, we call `os.close(fd)` to close the file descriptor. This allows us to reopen the file using `open()` and write to it in the normal way.

We're now ready to open the temporary file and check whether it is indeed a ZIP archive containing the files that make up a shapefile. Here is how we can do this:

```
if not zipfile.is_zipfile(fname):
    os.remove(fname)
    return "Not a valid zip archive."

zip = zipfile.ZipFile(fname)

required_suffixes = [".shp", ".shx", ".dbf", ".prj"]
has_suffix = {}
for suffix in required_suffixes:
    has_suffix[suffix] = False

for info in zip.infolist():
    suffix = os.path.splitext(info.filename)[1].lower()
    if suffix in required_suffixes:
        has_suffix[suffix] = True

for suffix in required_suffixes:
    if not has_suffix[suffix]:
        zip.close()
        os.remove(fname)
        return "Archive missing required " + suffix + " file."
```

Notice that we use the Python standard library's `zipfile` module to check the contents of the uploaded ZIP archive, and we return a suitable error message if something is wrong. We also delete the temporary file before returning an error message so that we don't leave temporary files lying around.

Finally, now that we know that the uploaded file is a valid ZIP archive containing the files that make up a shapefile, we can extract these files and store them into a temporary directory:

```
shapefile_name = None
dir_name = tempfile.mkdtemp()
for info in zip.infolist():
```

```
        if info.filename.endswith(".shp"):
            shapefile_name = info.filename

        dst_file = os.path.join(dir_name, info.filename)
        f = open(dst_file, "wb")
        f.write(zip.read(info.filename))
        f.close()
    zip.close()
```

Notice that we create a temporary directory to hold the extracted files before copying the files into this directory. At the same time, we store the name of the main .shp file from the archive, as we'll need to use this name when we open the shapefile.

Because we've used some of the Python Standard Library modules in this code, you'll also need to add the following to the top of the module:

```
import os, os.path, tempfile, zipfile
```

# Importing the shapefile's contents

Now that we've extracted the shapefile's files out of the ZIP archive, we are ready to import the data from the uploaded shapefile. The process of importing the shapefile's contents involves the following steps:

1. Open the shapefile.
2. Add the Shapefile object to the database.
3. Define the shapefile's attributes.
4. Store the shapefile's features.
5. Store the shapefile's attributes.

Let's work through these steps one at a time.

## Opening the shapefile

We will use the OGR library to open the shapefile. Add the following to the end of your shapefileIO.py module:

```
    try:
        datasource   = ogr.Open(os.path.join(dir_name,
                                              shapefile_name))
        layer        = datasource.GetLayer(0)
        shapefile_ok = True
```

```
except:
    traceback.print_exc()
    shapefile_ok = False

if not shapefile_ok:
    os.remove(fname)
    shutil.rmtree(dirname)
    return "Not a valid shapefile."
```

Once again, if something goes wrong, we clean up our temporary files and return a suitable error message. We're also using the `traceback` library module to display debugging information in the web server's log, while returning a friendly error message that will be shown to the user.

 In this program, we will be using OGR directly to read and write shapefiles. GeoDjango provides its own Python interface to OGR in the `contrib.gis.gdal` package, but unfortunately GeoDjango's version doesn't implement writing to shapefiles. Because of this, we will use the OGR Python bindings directly, which requires you to install OGR separately.

Because this code uses a couple of Python standard library modules as well as the OGR library, we'll have to add the following `import` statements to the top of the `shapefileIO.py` module:

```
import shutil, traceback
from osgeo import ogr
```

# Adding the Shapefile object to the database

Now that we've successfully opened the shapefile, we are ready to read the data out of it. First off, we'll create the `Shapefile` object to represent this imported shapefile. To do this, add the following to the end of your `import_data()` function:

```
src_spatial_ref = layer.GetSpatialRef()
geom_type = layer.GetLayerDefn().GetGeomType()
geom_name = ogr.GeometryTypeToName(geom_type)
shapefile = Shapefile(filename=shapefile_name,
                      srs_wkt=src_spatial_ref.ExportToWkt(),
                      geom_type=geom_name)
shapefile.save()
```

As you can see, we get the spatial reference from the shapefile's layer as well as the name for the type of geometry stored in the layer. We then store the shapefile's name, the spatial reference, and the geometry type name into a `Shapefile` object, which we then save into the database.

To allow this code to work, we'll have to add the following `import` statement to the top of the `shapefileIO.py` module:

```
from shapeEditor.shared.models import Shapefile
```

## Defining the shapefile's attributes

Now that we've created a `Shapefile` object to represent the imported shapefile, our next task is to create `Attribute` objects describing the shapefile's attributes. We can do this by querying the OGR shapefile; add the following code to the end of the `import_data()` function:

```
attributes = []
layer_def = layer.GetLayerDefn()
for i in range(layer_def.GetFieldCount()):
    field_def = layer_def.GetFieldDefn(i)
    attr = Attribute(shapefile=shapefile,
                     name=field_def.GetName(),
                     type=field_def.GetType(),
                     width=field_def.GetWidth(),
                     precision=field_def.GetPrecision())
    attr.save()
    attributes.append(attr)
```

Notice that, as well as saving the `Attribute` objects into a database, we also create a separate list of these attributes in a variable named `attributes`. We'll use this later on, when we import the attribute values for each feature.

Don't forget to add the following `import` statement to the top of the module:

```
from shapeEditor.shared.models import Attribute
```

## Storing the shapefile's features

Our next task is to extract the shapefile's features and store them as `Feature` objects in the database. Because the shapefile's features can be in any spatial reference, we need to transform them into our internal spatial reference system (EPSG 4326, unprojected latitude and longitude values) before we can store them. To do this, we'll use an OGR `CoordinateTransformation` object.

Using OGR, it will be easy to scan through the shapefile's features, extract the geometry from each feature, transform them into the EPSG 4326 spatial reference, and convert them into a GeoDjango GEOS geometry object so that we can store it into the database. Unfortunately, this leaves us with two problems we have to solve:

- As we saw in the previous chapter, shapefiles are unable to distinguish between Polygons and MultiPolygons, between LineStrings and MultiLineStrings, and between Points and MultiPoints. If a Shapefile contains Polygons, some of the features may return a Polygon geometry, while others may return a MultiPolygon. Because all the features in the database must be of the same geometry type, we are going to have to *wrap* a Polygon geometry inside a MultiPolygon, a LineString geometry inside a MultiLineString, and a Point inside a MultiPoint to ensure that they are all of the same geometry type.

- Because the `Feature` object has separate fields for each type of geometry, we will have to decide which particular field within the `Feature` object will hold a given geometry. When we defined the `Feature` class, we had to create separate geometry fields for each of the geometry types; we now need to decide which of these fields will be used to store a given type of geometry.

Since these two tasks (wrapping a geometry and calculating the geometry field to use for a given geometry type) are general functions that we will need to use elsewhere, we'll store them in a separate module. Create a file named `utils.py` inside the `shapeEditor/shared` directory, and then add the following code to this module:

```python
from django.contrib.gis.geos.collections \
    import MultiPolygon, MultiLineString, MultiPoint

def wrap_geos_geometry(geometry):
    if geometry.geom_type == "Polygon":
        return MultiPolygon(geometry)
    elif geometry.geom_type == "LineString":
        return MultiLineString(geometry)
    elif geometry.geom_type == "Point":
        return MultiPoint(geometry)
    else:
        return geometry

def calc_geometry_field(geometry_type):
    if geometry_type == "Polygon":
        return "geom_multipolygon"
    elif geometry_type == "LineString":
```

```
        return "geom_multilinestring"
    elif geometry_type == "Point":
        return "geom_multipoint"
    else:
        return "geom_" + geometryType.lower()
```

> Every self-respecting Python program should have a `utils.py` module; it's about time we added one to the ShapeEditor.

With this module in place, we can now return to our `shapefileIO.py` module and complete the implementation of the `import_data()` function. To save the features to disk, we first have to set up a coordinate transformation object that will convert our features from the shapefile's spatial reference system into EPSG 4326. Add the following to the end of your `import_data()` function:

```
dst_spatial_ref = osr.SpatialReference()
dst_spatial_ref.ImportFromEPSG(4326)

coord_transform = osr.CoordinateTransformation(
                            src_spatial_ref,
                            dst_spatial_ref)
```

We can now iterate through the shapefile's features, creating a GeoDjango `GEOSGeometry` object for each feature:

```
for i in range(layer.GetFeatureCount()):
    src_feature = layer.GetFeature(i)
    src_geometry = src_feature.GetGeometryRef()
    src_geometry.Transform(coord_transform)
    geometry = GEOSGeometry(src_geometry.ExportToWkt())
    geometry = utils.wrap_geos_geometry(geometry)
```

Notice that we are using the `utils.wrap_geos_geometry()` function we wrote earlier to wrap Polygon, LineString, and Point geometries so that they can be saved into the database.

We now need to store the geometry inside a `Feature` object. To do this, we'll first calculate the name of the geometry field that will hold our geometry:

```
geom_field = utils.calc_geometry_field(geom_name)
```

Now that we know the name of the field, we can create a `Feature` object with the geometry stored in the correct field. Because the field name varies, we'll use a Python trick called *keyword argument unpacking* to do this. This involves creating a Python dictionary with the various fields we want to save into the `Feature` object:

```
fields = {}
fields['shapefile'] = shapefile
fields[geom_field] = geometry
```

We then use this dictionary as the set of keyword parameters passed to the `Feature` object's initializer. This has the effect of creating a new `Feature` object with the given fields, which we then save into the database:

```
feature = Feature(**fields)
feature.save()
```

Finally, add the following `import` statements to the top of the `shapefileIO.py` module:

```
from django.contrib.gis.geos.geometry import GEOSGeometry
from osgeo import osr
from shapeEditor.shared.models import Feature
from shapeEditor.shared import utils
```

# Storing the shapefile's attributes

Now that we've dealt with the feature's geometry, we can now look at importing the feature's attributes. The basic process involves iterating over the attributes, extracting each attribute value from the OGR feature, creating an `AttributeValue` object to store the value, and then saving it into the database. Our code will look something like the following:

```
for attr in attributes:
    value = ...
    attr_value = AttributeValue(feature=feature,
                                attribute=attr,
                                value=value)

    attr_value.save()
```

The challenge is to extract the attribute value from the feature. Because the OGR `Feature` object has different methods for different types of field values, we are going to have to check for the different field types, call the appropriate `GetFieldAsXXX()` method, convert the resulting value to a string, and then store this string into the `AttributeValue` object. Null values will also have to be handled appropriately. Because of all this complexity, we'll define a new `utils.py` function to do the hard work and simply call it from our `import_data()` function. We'll call this function `get_ogr_feature_attribute()`.

Note that because we have to extract and parse the attribute values from the file, the process of extracting the attribute value can actually fail, for example, if the shapefile included a type of attribute that we don't support. Because of this, we have to add error handling to our code. To support error handling, our `get_ogr_feature_attribute()` function will return a `(success, result)` tuple, where `success` will be `True` if and only if the attribute was successfully extracted, and `result` will either be the extracted attribute value (as a string) or an error message explaining why the operation failed.

Let's add the necessary code to our `import_data()` function to store the attribute values into the database and gracefully handle any conversion errors that might occur:

```
for attr in attributes:
    success,result = utils.get_ogr_feature_attribute(
                            attr, src_feature)
    if not success:
        os.remove(fname)
        shutil.rmtree(dir_name)
        shapefile.delete()
        return result

    attr_value = AttributeValue(feature=feature,
                                attribute=attr,
                                value=result)
    attr_value.save()
```

Notice that we pass the `Attribute` object and the OGR feature to the `get_ogr_feature_attribute()` function. If an error occurs, we clean up the temporary files, delete the shapefile we created earlier, and return the error message back to the caller. If the attribute was successfully extracted, we create a new `AttributeValue` object with the attribute's value and save it into the database.

Note that we use `shapefile.delete()` to remove the partially imported shapefile from the database. By default, Django will also automatically delete any records that are related to the record being deleted through a `ForeignKey` field. This means that the `Shapefile` object will be deleted along with all the related `Attribute`, `Feature`, and `AttributeValue` objects. With one line of code, we can completely remove all references to the shapefile's data.

Now, let's implement that `get_ogr_feature_attribute()` function. Add the following to `utils.py`:

```
def get_ogr_feature_attribute(attr, feature):
    attr_name = attr.name

    if not feature.IsFieldSet(attr_name):
        return (True, None)

    if attr.type == ogr.OFTInteger:
        value = str(feature.GetFieldAsInteger(attr_name))
    elif attr.type == ogr.OFTIntegerList:
        value = repr(feature.GetFieldAsIntegerList(attr_name))
    elif attr.type == ogr.OFTReal:
        value = feature.GetFieldAsDouble(attr_name)
        value = "%*.*f" % (attr.width, attr.precision, value)
    elif attr.type == ogr.OFTRealList:
        values = feature.GetFieldAsDoubleList(attr_name)
        str_values = []
        for value in values:
            str_values.append("%*.*f" % (attr.width,
                                         attr.precision, value))
        value = repr(str_values)
    elif attr.type == ogr.OFTString:
        value = feature.GetFieldAsString(attr_name)
    elif attr.type == ogr.OFTStringList:
        value = repr(feature.GetFieldAsStringList(attr_name))
    elif attr.type == ogr.OFTDate:
        parts = feature.GetFieldAsDateTime(attr_name)
        year,month,day,hour,minute,second,tzone = parts
        value = "%d,%d,%d,%d" % (year,month,day,tzone)
    elif attr.type == ogr.OFTTime:
        parts = feature.GetFieldAsDateTime(attr_name)
```

```
        year,month,day,hour,minute,second,tzone = parts
        value = "%d,%d,%d,%d" % (hour,minute,second,tzone)
elif attr.type == ogr.OFTDateTime:
    parts = feature.GetFieldAsDateTime(attr_name)
    year,month,day,hour,minute,second,tzone = parts
    value = "%d,%d,%d,%d,%d,%d,%d,%d" % (year,month,day,
                                          hour,minute,
                                          second,tzone)
else:
    return (False, "Unsupported attribute type: " +
                    str(attr.type))

return (True, value)
```

There's a lot of ugly code here relating to the extraction of different field types from the OGR feature. Don't worry too much about these details; the basic concept is that we extract the attribute's value in whatever format is needed for that type of attribute, convert the value(s) to a string if necessary, and then return the string back to the caller.

You'll also need to add the following to the top of utils.py so that your new function will work:

```
from osgeo import ogr
```

Finally, we'll have to add the following import statement to the top of the shapefileIO.py module:

```
from shapeEditor.shared.models import AttributeValue
```

# Cleaning up

Now that we've imported the shapefile's data, all that's left is to clean up our temporary files and tell the caller that the import succeeded. To do this, simply add the following lines to the end of your import_data() function:

```
os.remove(fname)
shutil.rmtree(dir_name)
return None
```

That's it!

To test all this out, grab a copy of the TM_WORLD_BORDERS-0.3 shapefile in ZIP file format. You can either use the original ZIP archive that you downloaded from the World Borders Dataset web site, or you can recompress the shapefile into a new ZIP archive. Then, run the ShapeEditor, click on the **Import New Shapefile** button, click on the button to choose a file to import, and select the ZIP archive containing the World Borders Dataset.

When you click on the **Submit** button, you'll have to wait a few seconds for the shapefile to be imported. All going well, the World Borders Dataset will appear in the list of imported shapefiles:

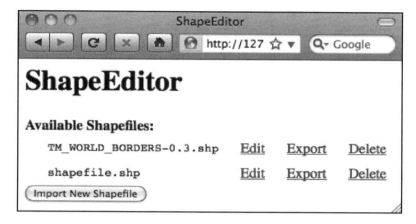

If a problem occurs, check the error message to see what might be wrong. Also, go back and make sure you have typed the code in exactly as described. If it works, congratulations! You have just implemented the most difficult part of the ShapeEditor system. It gets easier from here.

# Exporting shapefiles

We next need to implement the ability to export a shapefile. The process of exporting a shapefile is basically the reverse of the importing logic, and involves the following steps:

1. Create an OGR shapefile to receive the exported data.
2. Save the features and their attributes into the shapefile.
3. Compress the shapefile into a ZIP archive.
4. Delete our temporary files.
5. Send the ZIP file back to the user's web browser.

All this work will take place in the `shapefileIO.py` module, with help from some `utils.py` functions. Before we begin, let's define the `export_data()` function so that we have somewhere to place our code. Edit `shapefileIO.py`, and add the following new function:

```
def export_data(shapefile):
    return "More to come..."
```

While we're at it, let's create the "Export Shapefile" view function. This will call the `export_data()` function to do all the work. Edit the `shapefiles/views.py` file and add the following new function:

```
def export_shapefile(request, shapefile_id):
  try:
    shapefile = Shapefile.objects.get(id=shapefile_id)
  except Shapefile.DoesNotExist:
    raise Http404("No such shapefile")

  return shapefileIO.export_data(shapefile)
```

This is all pretty straightforward: we load the `Shapefile` object with the given ID from the database and pass it to our `export_data()` function. While you are editing this file, add the following `import` statement to the top:

```
from django.http import Http404
```

We next need to tell Django to call this view function in response to the `/export` URL. Edit the `urls.py` file (in the main `shapeEditor` directory), and add the following entry to the URL pattern list:

```
url(r'^export/(?P<shapefile_id>\d+)$',
        shapeEditor.shapefiles.views.export_shapefile),
```

The "List Shapefiles" view will call this URL when the user clicks on the **Export** hyperlink. This in turn will call our view function, which will call `shapefileIO.export_data()` to export the shapefile.

Let's now start implementing that `export_data()` function.

# Define the OGR shapefile

We'll use OGR to create a new shapefile to hold the exported features. Let's start by creating a temporary directory to hold the shapefile's contents; replace your placeholder version of export_data() with the following:

```
def export_data(shapefile):
    dst_dir = tempfile.mkdtemp()
    dst_file = os.path.join(dst_dir, shapefile.filename)
```

Now that we've got somewhere to store the shapefile (and a file name for it), we'll create a spatial reference for the shapefile to use, and set up the shapefile's data source and layer:

```
        dst_spatial_ref = osr.SpatialReference()
        dst_spatial_ref.ImportFromWkt(shapefile.srs_wkt)

        driver = ogr.GetDriverByName("ESRI Shapefile")
        datasource = driver.CreateDataSource(dst_file)
        layer = datasource.CreateLayer(shapefile.filename,
                                        dst_spatial_ref)
```

Now that we've created the shapefile itself, we next need to define the various fields that will hold the shapefile's attributes:

```
        for attr in shapefile.attribute_set.all():
            field = ogr.FieldDefn(attr.name, attr.type)
            field.SetWidth(attr.width)
            field.SetPrecision(attr.precision)
            layer.CreateField(field)
```

Notice how the information needed to define the field is taken directly from the Attribute object: Django makes iterating over the shapefile's attributes easy.

That completes the definition of the shapefile itself. We're now ready to start saving the shapefile's features.

# Saving the features into the shapefile

Because the shapefile can use any valid spatial reference, we'll need to transform its features from the spatial reference used internally (EPSG 4326) into the shapefile's own spatial reference. To do this, we'll need to create an `osr.CoordinateTransformation` object to do the transformation:

```
src_spatial_ref = osr.SpatialReference()
src_spatial_ref.ImportFromEPSG(4326)

coord_transform = osr.CoordinateTransformation(
                    src_spatial_ref, dst_spatial_ref)
```

We'll also need to know which geometry field in the `Feature` object holds the feature's geometry data:

```
geom_field = utils.calc_geometry_field(shapefile.geom_type)
```

With this information, we're ready to start exporting the shapefile's features:

```
for feature in shapefile.feature_set.all():
    geometry = getattr(feature, geom_field)
```

Right away, however, we encounter a problem. If you remember when we imported the shapefile, we had to *wrap* a Polygon, a LineString, or a Point geometry into a MultiPolygon, a MultiLineString, or a MultiPoint so that the geometry types would be consistent in the database. Now that we're exporting the shapefile, we need to *unwrap* the geometry so that features that had only one Polygon, LineString, or Point in their geometries are saved as Polygons, LineStrings, and Points rather than MultiPolygons, MultiLineStrings, and MultiPoints. We'll use a `utils.py` function to do this unwrapping:

```
geometry = utils.unwrap_geos_geometry(geometry)
```

We'll implement this `utils.py` function shortly.

Now that we've unwrapped the feature's geometry, we can go ahead and convert it back into an OGR geometry, transform it into the shapefile's own spatial reference system, and then create an OGR feature using that geometry:

```
dst_geometry = ogr.CreateGeometryFromWkt(geometry.wkt)
dst_geometry.Transform(coord_transform)

dst_feature = ogr.Feature(layer.GetLayerDefn())
dst_feature.SetGeometry(dst_geometry)
```

We next need to add the feature to the layer so that it gets saved into the shapefile:

```
layer.CreateFeature(dst_feature)
```

Finally, we need to close the shapefile to ensure that everything is saved to disk. OGR doesn't have an explicit "close" feature; instead, we need to remove our references to the layer and data source. This will have the effect of closing the shapefile, writing the shapefile's contents to disk:

```
layer      = None
datasource = None
```

Before we move on, let's add our new `unwrap_geos_geometry()` function to `utils.py`. This code is quite straightforward, pulling a single Polygon, LineString, or Point object out of a MultiPolygon, MultiLineString, or MultiPoint if they contain only one geometry:

```
def unwrap_geos_geometry(geometry):
    if geometry.geom_type in ["MultiPolygon",
                              "MultiLineString",
                              "MultiPoint"]:
        if len(geometry) == 1:
            geometry = geometry[0]
    return geometry
```

So far, so good: we've created the OGR feature, unwrapped the feature's geometry, and stored everything into the shapefile. Now we're ready to save the feature's attribute values.

# Saving the attributes into the shapefile

Our next task is to save the attribute values associated with each feature. When we imported the shapefile, we extracted the attribute values from the various OGR data types and converted them into strings so that they could be stored into the database. This was done using the `utils.get_ogr_feature_attribute()` function. We now have to do the opposite: store the string value back into an OGR attribute field. As before, we'll use a `utils.py` function to do the hard work. Add the following highlighted lines to the bottom of your `export_data()` function in the `shapefileIO.py` module:

```
        ...

        dst_feature = ogr.Feature(layer.GetLayerDefn())
        dst_feature.SetGeometry(dst_geometry)
```

```
            for attr_value in feature.attributevalue_set.all():
                utils.set_ogr_feature_attribute(
                        attr_value.attribute,
                        attr_value.value,
                        dst_feature)

            layer.CreateFeature(dst_feature)

    layer      = None
    datasource = None
```

Now, let's implement the set_ogr_feature_attribute() function within utils.py. As with the get_ogr_feature_attribute() function, set_ogr_feature_attribute() is rather tedious but straightforward: we have to deal with each OGR data type in turn, processing the string representation of the attribute value and calling the appropriate SetFieldXXX() method to set the field's value. Here is the relevant code:

```
    def set_ogr_feature_attribute(attr, value, feature):
        attr_name = attr.name

        if value == None:
            feature.UnsetField(attr_name)
            return

        if attr.type == ogr.OFTInteger:
            feature.SetField(attr_name, int(value))
        elif attr.type == ogr.OFTIntegerList:
            integers = eval(value)
            feature.SetFieldIntegerList(attr_name, integers)
        elif attr.type == ogr.OFTReal:
            feature.SetField(attr_name, float(value))
        elif attr.type == ogr.OFTRealList:
            floats = []
            for s in eval(value):
                floats.append(eval(s))
            feature.SetFieldDoubleList(attr_name, floats)
        elif attr.type == ogr.OFTString:
            feature.SetField(attr_name, value)
        elif attr.type == ogr.OFTStringList:
            strings = []
            for s in eval(value):
                strings.append(s.encode(encoding))
```

```
            feature.SetFieldStringList(attr_name, strings)
    elif attr.type == ogr.OFTDate:
        parts = value.split(",")
        year  = int(parts[0])
        month = int(parts[1])
        day   = int(parts[2])
        tzone = int(parts[3])
        feature.SetField(attr_name, year, month, day,
                          0, 0, 0, tzone)
    elif attr.type == ogr.OFTTime:
        parts  = value.split(",")
        hour   = int(parts[0])
        minute = int(parts[1])
        second = int(parts[2])
        tzone  = int(parts[3])
        feature.SetField(attr_name, 0, 0, 0,
                          hour, minute, second, tzone)
    elif attr.type == ogr.OFTDateTime:
        parts  = value.split(",")
        year   = int(parts[0])
        month  = int(parts[1])
        day    = int(parts[2])
        hour   = int(parts[3])
        minute = int(parts[4])
        second = int(parts[5])
        tzone  = int(parts[6])
        feature.SetField(attr_mame, year, month, day,
                          hour, minute, second, tzone)
```

# Compressing the shapefile

Now that we've exported the desired data into an OGR shapefile, we can compress it into a ZIP archive. Go back to the shapefileIO.py module and add the following to the end of your export_data() function:

```
temp = tempfile.TemporaryFile()
zip = zipfile.ZipFile(temp, 'w', zipfile.ZIP_DEFLATED)

shapefile_name = os.path.splitext(shapefile.filename)[0]

for fName in os.listdir(dst_dir):
    zip.write(os.path.join(dst_dir, fName), fName)

zip.close()
```

Notice that we use a temporary file, referred to by the `temp` variable, to store the ZIP archive's contents. We'll be returning the contents of the `temp` file to the user's web browser once the export process has finished.

# Deleting temporary files

We next have to clean up after ourselves by deleting the shapefile that we created earlier:

```
shutil.rmtree(dst_dir)
```

Notice that we don't have to remove the temporary ZIP archive, as that's done automatically for us by the `tempfile` module when the file is closed.

# Returning the ZIP archive to the user

The last step in exporting the shapefile is to send the ZIP archive to the user's web browser so that it can be downloaded onto the user's computer. To do this, we'll create a special type of `HttResponse` object called a `FileResponse`, which is used to download files. We first have to prepare the temporary file so that it can be used by the `FileResponse` object:

```
temp.flush()
temp.seek(0)
```

This ensures that the contents of the file have all been written to disk, and the current file position is set to the start of the file so the entire file's contents will be downloaded.

We can now prepare the `FileResponse` object so that the user's web browser will download it:

```
response = FileResponse(temp)
response['Content-type'] = "application/zip"
response['Content-Disposition'] = \
    "attachment; filename=" + shapefile_name + ".zip"
return response
```

As you can see, we set up the HTTP response header to indicate that we're returning a file attachment. This forces the user's browser to download the file rather than trying to display it. We also use the original shapefile's name as the name of the downloaded file.

This completes the definition of the `export_data()` function. There's only one more thing to do: add the following `import` statement to the top of the `shapefileIO.py` module:

```
from django.http import FileResponse
```

We've finally finished implementing the shapefile export feature. Test it out by running the server and clicking on the **Export** hyperlink beside one of your shapefiles. All going well, there'll be a slight pause and you'll be prompted to save your shapefile's ZIP archive to disk:

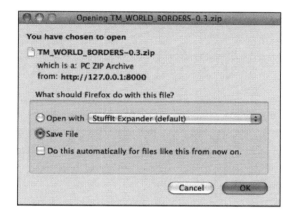

# Summary

In this chapter, we continued our implementation of the ShapeEditor by adding three important functions: the list view and the ability to import and export shapefiles. While these aren't very exciting features, they are a crucial part of the ShapeEditor.

In the process of implementing these features, we learned how to use Django's templating language to display a list of records within a web page. We saw how to use the `zipfile` standard library module to extract the contents of an uploaded shapefile before opening that shapefile using OGR, and we discussed the concept of wrapping and unwrapping geometries to deal with the quirky way these are handled by the shapefile format. Finally, we saw how to use OGR to create a new shapefile that can be compressed using the `zipfile` library before being returned to the caller using the Django web interface.

With this functionality out of the way, we can now turn our attention to the most interesting parts of the ShapeEditor: the code that displays and lets the user edit geometries using a slippy map interface. This will be the main focus of the final chapter of this book.

# 13
# ShapeEditor – Selecting and Editing Features

In this final chapter, we will implement the remaining features of the ShapeEditor system. A large part of this chapter will involve the use of OpenLayers and the creation of a Tile Map Server so that we can display a map with all the shapefile's features on it and allow the user to click on a feature to select it. We'll also implement the ability to add, edit, and delete features, and we'll conclude with an exploration of how the ShapeEditor can be used to work with geospatial data and serve as the springboard for your own geospatial development efforts.

In this chapter, we will learn how to:

- Implement a Tile Map Server using Mapnik and GeoDjango
- Use OpenLayers to display a slippy map on a web page
- Write a custom click handler for OpenLayers
- Use AJAX to send requests to the server
- Perform spatial queries using GeoDjango
- Use GeoDjango's built-in editing widgets in your own application
- Edit geospatial data using GeoDjango's built-in editing widgets
- Customize the interface for GeoDjango's editing widgets
- Add and delete records in a Django web application

Let's get started with the code that lets the user select the feature to be edited.

# Selecting the feature to edit

As we discussed in the *Designing ShapeEditor* section of *Chapter 11, Putting It All Together – a Complete Mapping System*, GeoDjango's built-in map widgets can only display a single feature at a time. In order to display a map with all the shapefile's features on it, we will have to use OpenLayers directly, along with a Tile Map Server and a custom AJAX-based click handler. The basic workflow will look like this:

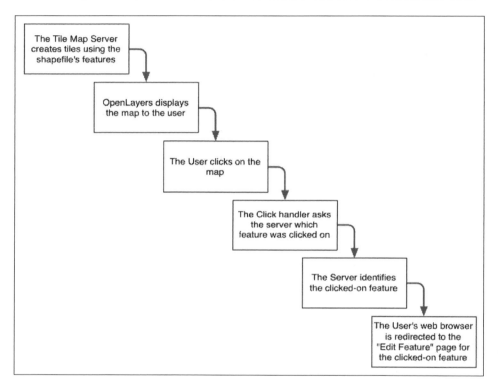

Let's start by implementing the Tile Map Server and then see what's involved in using OpenLayers, along with implementing a custom click handler and some server-side AJAX code to respond when the user clicks on the map.

# Implementing the Tile Map Server

As we discussed in *Chapter 10, Tools for Web-based Geospatial Development*, the **Tile Map Service (TMS)** protocol is a simple RESTful protocol for serving map Tiles. The TMS protocol includes calls to identify the various maps that can be displayed, along with information about the available map Tiles, as well as providing access to the map Tile images themselves.

Let's briefly review the terminology used by the TMS protocol:

- A **Tile Map Server** is the overall web server that is implementing the TMS protocol.

- A **Tile Map Service** provides access to a particular set of maps. There can be multiple Tile Map Services hosted by a single Tile Map Server.

- A **Tile Map** is a complete map of all or part of the Earth's surface, displaying a particular set of features or styled in a particular way. A Tile Map Service can provide access to more than one Tile Map.

- A **Tile Set** is a collection of Tiles displaying a given Tile Map at a given zoom level.

- A **Tile** is a single map image representing a small portion of the map being displayed by the Tile Set.

While this may sound confusing, it's actually not too complicated. We'll be implementing a Tile Map Server with just one Tile Map Service, which we'll call the ShapeEditor Tile Map Service. There will be one Tile Map for each shapefile that has been uploaded, and we'll support Tile Sets for a standard range of zoom levels. Finally, we'll use Mapnik to render the individual Tiles within the Tile Set.

Following the Django principle of breaking a large and complex system down into separate self-contained applications, we will implement the Tile Map Server as a separate application within the shapeEditor project. Start by using the cd command to set the current directory to your shapeEditor project directory, and then type the following:

```
python manage.py startapp tms
```

This creates our tms application in the top-level directory, making it a reusable application. Move the newly created directory into the shapeEditor sub-directory by typing the following command:

```
mv tms shapeEditor
```

This makes the tms application specific to our project. As usual, we won't need the admin.py and tests.py modules in the tms directory, so go ahead and delete them.

We next need to enable the application by editing our project's settings.py module and adding the following entry to the end of the INSTALLED_APPS list:

```
'shapeEditor.tms',
```

Next, we want to make our Tile Map Server's URLs available as part of the `shapeEditor` project. To do this, edit the top-level `urls.py` module (located inside the main `shapeEditor` directory), and add the following entry to the `urlpatterns` list:

```
url(r'^tms/', include(shapeEditor.tms.urls)),
```

You will also need to add the following `import` statement to the top of this module:

```
import shapeEditor.tms.urls
```

We now want to define the individual URLs provided by our Tile Map Server application. To do this, create a new module named `urls.py` inside the `tms` directory, and enter the following into this module:

```
# URLConf for the shapeEditor.tms application.

from django.conf.urls import url
from shapeEditor.tms.views import *

urlpatterns = [
    url(r'^$',
        root), # "/tms" calls root()
    url(r'^(?P<version>[0-9.]+)$',
        service), # eg, "/tms/1.0" calls service(version="1.0")
    url(r'^(?P<version>[0-9.]+)/(?P<shapefile_id>\d+)$',
        tileMap), # eg, "/tms/1.0/2" calls
                  # tileMap(version="1.0", shapefile_id=2)
    url(r'^(?P<version>[0-9.]+)/' +
        r'(?P<shapefile_id>\d+)/(?P<zoom>\d+)/' +
        r'(?P<x>\d+)/(?P<y>\d+)\.png$',
        tile), # eg, "/tms/1.0/2/3/4/5" calls
               # tile(version="1.0", shapefile_id=2, zoom=3, x=4, y=5)
]
```

These URL patterns are more complicated than the ones we've used in the past, because we're now extracting parameters from the URL. For example, consider the following URL:

```
http://127.0.0.1:8000/tms/1.0
```

Because of the way our URL modules are set up, the first part of this URL (`http://127.0.0.1:8000/tms/`) tells Django that this URL will be handled by the `tms.urls` module. The remainder of the URL, `1.0`, will be matched by the second regular expression in our `urls.py` module:

```
^(?P<version>[0-9.]+)$
```

This regular expression will extract the `1.0` portion of the URL and assign it to a parameter named `version`. This parameter is then passed on to the view function associated with this URL pattern, as follows:

```
service(version="1.0")
```

In this way, each of our URL patterns maps an incoming RESTful URL to the appropriate view function within our `tms` application. The included comments provide an example of how the regular expressions will map to the view functions.

Let's now set up these view functions. Edit the `views.py` module inside the `tms` directory, and add the following to this module:

```python
from django.http import HttpResponse

def root(request):
    return HttpResponse("Tile Map Server")

def service(request, version):
    return HttpResponse("Tile Map Service")

def tileMap(request, version, shapefile_id):
    return HttpResponse("Tile Map")

def tile(request, version, shapefile_id, zoom, x, y):
    return HttpResponse("Tile")
```

Obviously, these are only placeholder view functions, but they give us the basic structure for our Tile Map Server.

To check that this works, launch the ShapeEditor server by running the `python manage.py runserver` command, and point your web browser to `http://127.0.0.1:8000/tms`. You should see the text you entered into your placeholder `root()` view function.

Let's make that top-level view function do something useful. Go back to the `tms` application's `views.py` module, and change the `root()` function to look like the following:

```
def root(request):
    try:
        baseURL = request.build_absolute_uri()
        xml = []
        xml.append('<?xml version="1.0" encoding="utf-8" ?>')
        xml.append('<Services>')
        xml.append('  <TileMapService ' +
                   'title="ShapeEditor Tile Map Service" ' +
                   'version="1.0" href="' + baseURL + '/1.0"/>')
        xml.append('</Services>')
        response = "\n".join(xml)
        return HttpResponse(response, content_type="text/xml")
    except:
        traceback.print_exc()
        return HttpResponse("Error")
```

You'll also need to add the following `import` statement to the top of the module:

```
import traceback
```

This view function returns an XML-format response describing the one and only Tile Map Service supported by our TMS server. This Tile Map Service is identified by a version number, `1.0` (Tile Map Services are typically identified by version number). If you now go to `http://127.0.0.1:8000/tms`, you'll see the TMS response displayed in your web browser:

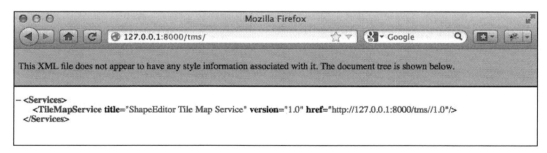

As you can see, this provides a list of the Tile Map Services that this TMS server provides. OpenLayers will use this to access our Tile Map Service.

**Error handling**

Notice that we've wrapped our TMS view function in a `try...except` statement and used the `traceback` standard library module to print out the exception if anything goes wrong. We're doing this because our code will be called directly by OpenLayers using AJAX; Django helpfully handles exceptions and returns an HTML error page to the caller, but in this case, OpenLayers won't display that page if there is an error in your code. Instead, all you'll see are broken image icons instead of a map, and the error itself will remain a mystery.

By wrapping our Python code in a `try...except` statement, we can catch any exceptions in our Python code and print them out. This will cause the error to appear in Django's web server log, so we can see what went wrong. This is a useful technique to use whenever you write AJAX request handlers in Python.

We're now ready to implement the Tile Map Service itself. Edit the `view.py` module again, and change the `service()` function to look like this:

```
def service(request, version):
    try:
        if version != "1.0":
            raise Http404

        baseURL = request.build_absolute_uri()
        xml = []
        xml.append('<?xml version="1.0" encoding="utf-8" ?>')
        xml.append('<TileMapService version="1.0" services="' +
                   baseURL + '">')
        xml.append('  <Title>ShapeEditor Tile Map Service' +
                   '</Title>')
        xml.append('  <Abstract></Abstract>')
        xml.append('  <TileMaps>')
        for shapefile in Shapefile.objects.all():
            id = str(shapefile.id)
            xml.append('    <TileMap title="' +
                       shapefile.filename + '"')
            xml.append('             srs="EPSG:4326"')
            xml.append('             href="'+baseURL+'/'+id+'"/>')
        xml.append('  </TileMaps>')
        xml.append('</TileMapService>')
        response = "\n".join(xml)
```

```
            return HttpResponse(response, content_type="text/xml")
        except:
            traceback.print_exc()
            return HttpResponse("Error")
```

You'll also need to add the following `import` statements to the top of the module:

```
from django.http import Http404
from shapeEditor.shared.models import Shapefile
```

Notice that this function raises an `Http404` exception if the version number is wrong. This exception tells Django to return an HTTP "not found" error, which is the standard error response when an incorrect URL has been used.

Assuming the version number is correct, we iterate over the various `Shapefile` objects in the database, listing each uploaded shapefile as a Tile Map.

If you save this file and enter `http://127.0.0.1:8000/tms/1.0` into your web browser, you should see a list of the available Tile Maps, in XML format:

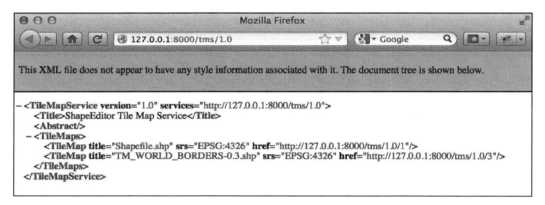

We next need to implement the `tileMap()` function to display the various Tile Sets available for a given Tile Map. Before we can do this, though, we're going to have to learn a bit about the notion of **zoom levels**.

As we have seen, a slippy map lets the user zoom in and out to view the map's contents. This zooming is done by controlling the map's zoom level. Typically, a zoom level is specified as a simple number: zoom level 0 is when the map is fully zoomed out, zoom level 1 is when the map is zoomed in once, and so on.

Let's start by considering the map when it is zoomed out completely (in other words, zoom level 0). In this case, we want the entire Earth's surface to be covered by just two map Tiles:

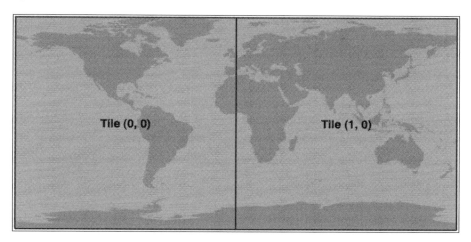

Each map Tile at this zoom level would cover 180 degrees of latitude and longitude. If each Tile were 256 pixels square, this would mean that each pixel would cover 180 / 256 = 0.703125 map units where, in this case, a map unit is a degree of latitude or longitude. This number is going to be very important when it comes to calculating the Tile Maps.

Now, whenever we zoom in (for example, by going from zoom level 0 to zoom level 1), the width and height of the visible area are halved. For example, at zoom level 1, the Earth's surface would be displayed as the following series of eight Tiles:

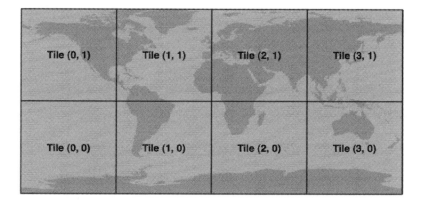

Following this pattern, we can calculate the number of map units covered by a single pixel on the map, for a given zoom level, using the following formula:

$$\text{Map units per pixel} = \frac{0.703125}{2^{\text{zoom level}}}$$

Since we'll be using this formula in our TMS server, let's go ahead and add the following code to the end of our `tms/views.py` module:

```python
def _unitsPerPixel(zoomLevel):
    return 0.703125 / math.pow(2, zoomLevel)
```

 Notice that we start the function name with an underscore; this is a standard Python convention for naming private functions within a module.

You'll also need to add an `import math` statement to the top of the file.

Next, we need to add some constants to the top of the module to define the size of each map Tile and how many zoom levels we support:

```python
MAX_ZOOM_LEVEL = 10
TILE_WIDTH     = 256
TILE_HEIGHT    = 256
```

With all this, we're finally ready to implement the `tileMap()` function to return information about the available Tile Sets for a given shapefile's Tile Map. Edit this function to look like the following:

```python
def tileMap(request, version, shapefile_id):
    if version != "1.0":
        raise Http404

    try:
        shapefile = Shapefile.objects.get(id=shapefile_id)
    except Shapefile.DoesNotExist:
        raise Http404

    try:
```

```
baseURL = request.build_absolute_uri()
xml = []
xml.append('<?xml version="1.0" encoding="utf-8" ?>')
xml.append('<TileMap version="1.0" ' +
           'tilemapservice="' + baseURL + '">')
xml.append('  <Title>' + shapefile.filename + '</Title>')
xml.append('  <Abstract></Abstract>')
xml.append('  <SRS>EPSG:4326</SRS>')
xml.append('  <BoundingBox minx="-180" miny="-90" ' +
           'maxx="180" maxy="90"/>')
xml.append('  <Origin x="-180" y="-90"/>')
xml.append('  <TileFormat width="' + str(TILE_WIDTH) +
           '" height="' + str(TILE_HEIGHT) + '" ' +
           'mime-type="image/png" extension="png"/>')
xml.append('  <TileSets profile="global-geodetic">')
for zoomLevel in range(0, MAX_ZOOM_LEVEL+1):
    href = baseURL + "/{}".format(zoomLevel)
    unitsPerPixel = "{}".format(_unitsPerPixel(zoomLevel))
    order = "{}".format(zoomLevel)

    xml.append('    <TileSet href="' + href + '" ' +
               'units-per-pixel="'+ unitsPerPixel + '"' +
               ' order="' + order + '"/>')
xml.append('  </TileSets>')
xml.append('</TileMap>')
response = "\n".join(xml)
return HttpResponse(response, content_type="text/xml")
except:
    traceback.print_exc()
    return HttpResponse("Error")
```

As you can see, we start with some basic error checking on the version and shapefile ID and then iterate through the available zoom levels to provide information about the available Tile Sets. If you save your changes and enter `http://127.0.0.1:8000/tms/1.0/2` into your web browser, you should see the following information about the Tile Map for the shapefile object with record ID 2:

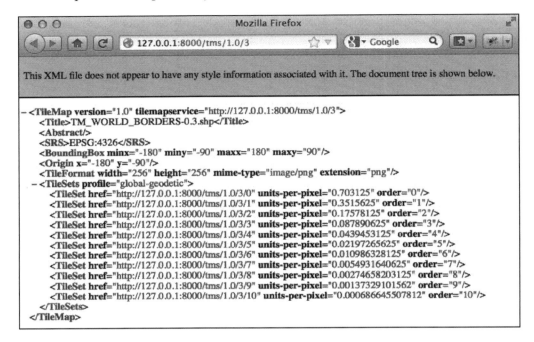

Notice that we provide a total of eleven zoom levels, from `0` to `10`, with an appropriately calculated `units-per-pixel` value for each zoom level.

We have now implemented three of the four view functions required to implement our own Tile Map Server. For the final function, `tile()`, we are going to write our own Tile renderer. The `tile()` function accepts a Tile Map Service version, a shapefile ID, a zoom level, and the X and Y coordinates of the desired Tile:

```
def tile(request, version, shapefile_id, zoom, x, y):
    ...
```

This function needs to generate the appropriate map Tile and return the rendered image to the caller. Before we implement this function, let's take a step back and think about what the map rendering should look like.

We want the map to include the outline of the various features within the given shapefile. However, by themselves, these features won't look very meaningful:

It isn't until these features are shown in context, by displaying a **base map** behind the features, that we can see what they are supposed to represent:

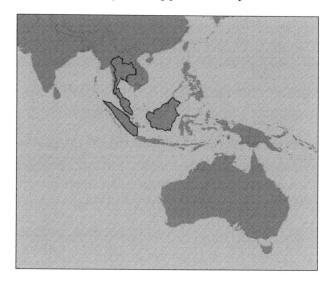

Because of this, we're going to have to display a base map on which the features themselves are drawn. Let's build that base map, and then we can use this, along with the shapefile's features, to render the map Tiles.

# Setting up the base map

For our base map, we're going to use the World Borders Dataset we've used several times throughout this book. While this dataset doesn't look great when zoomed right in, it works well as a base map on which we can draw the shapefile's features.

We'll start by creating a database model to hold the base map's data. Because the base map will be specific to our Tile Map Server application, we want to add a database table specific to this application. To do this, edit the `models.py` module inside the `tms` application directory, and change this file to look like the following:

```python
from django.contrib.gis.db import models

class BaseMap(models.Model):
    name     = models.CharField(max_length=50)
    geometry = models.MultiPolygonField(srid=4326)

    objects = models.GeoManager()

    def __str__(self):
        return self.name
```

 Don't forget to change the `import` statement at the top of the file.

As you can see, we're storing the country names as well as their geometries, which happen to be MultiPolygons. Now, from the command line, `cd` into your project directory and type the following commands:

```
% python manage.py makemigrations tms
% python manage.py migrate tms
```

This will create the database table used by the `BaseMap` object.

Now that we have somewhere to store the base map, let's import the data. Place a copy of the World Borders Dataset shapefile somewhere convenient, and type the following into the command-line window you had open previously:

```
% python manage.py shell
```

This runs a Python interactive shell with your project's settings and paths installed. Now create the following variable, replacing the text with the absolute path to the World Borders Dataset's shapefile:

```
>>> shapefile = "/path/to/TM_WORLD_BORDERS-0.3.shp"
```

Then, type the following:

```
>>> from django.contrib.gis.utils import LayerMapping
>>> from shapeEditor.tms.models import BaseMap
>>> mapping = LayerMapping(BaseMap, shapefile, {'name' : "NAME",
'geometry' : "MULTIPOLYGON"}, transform=False, encoding="iso-8859-1")
>>> mapping.save(strict=True, verbose=True)
```

We're using GeoDjango's `LayerMapping` module to import the data from this shapefile into our database. The various countries will be displayed as they are imported, which will take a few seconds.

Once this has been done, you can check the imported data by typing commands into the interactive shell, for example:

```
>>> print(BaseMap.objects.count())
246
>>> print(BaseMap.objects.all())
[<BaseMap: Antigua and Barbuda>, <BaseMap: Algeria>, <BaseMap:
Azerbaijan>, <BaseMap: Albania>, <BaseMap: Armenia>, <BaseMap: Angola>,
<BaseMap: American Samoa>, <BaseMap: Argentina>, <BaseMap: Australia>,
<BaseMap: Bahrain>, <BaseMap: Barbados>, <BaseMap: Bermuda>, <BaseMap:
Bahamas>, <BaseMap: Bangladesh>, <BaseMap: Belize>, <BaseMap: Bosnia and
Herzegovina>, <BaseMap: Bolivia>, <BaseMap: Burma>, <BaseMap: Benin>,
<BaseMap: Solomon Islands>, '...(remaining elements truncated)...']
```

Feel free to play some more if you want; the Django tutorial includes several examples of exploring your data objects using the interactive shell. When you are done, press *Ctrl + D* to exit.

Because this base map is going to be part of the ShapeEditor project itself (the application won't run without it), it would be good if Django could treat that data as part of the project's source code. That way, if we ever had to rebuild the database from scratch, the base map would be reinstalled automatically.

Django allows you to do this by creating what is known as a **fixture**. A fixture is a set of data that can be loaded into the database on demand, either manually, or automatically when the database is initialized. We'll save our base map data into a fixture so that Django can reload that data as required.

Create a directory named `fixtures` within the `tms` application directory. Then, in a terminal window, `cd` into the `shapeEditor` project directory and type the following:

```
% python manage.py dumpdata tms > shapeEditor/tms/fixtures/initial_data.
json
```

This will create a fixture named `initial_data.json` for the `tms` application. As the name suggests, the contents of this fixture will be loaded automatically if Django ever has to reinitialize the database.

Now that we have a base map, let's use it to implement our Tile-rendering code.

# Tile rendering

Using our knowledge of Mapnik, we're going to implement the TMS server's `tile()` function. Our generated map will consist of two layers: a **base layer** showing the base map and a **feature layer** showing the features in the imported shapefile. Since all our data is stored in a PostGIS database, we'll be using a `mapnik.PostGIS` data source for both layers.

Our `tile()` function will involve five steps:

1. Parsing the query parameters.
2. Setting up the map.
3. Defining the base layer.
4. Defining the feature layer.
5. Rendering the map.

Let's work through each of these in turn.

## Parsing the query parameters

Edit the `tms` application's `views.py` module, and delete the dummy code we had in the `tile()` function. We'll add our parsing code one step at a time, starting with some basic error-checking code to ensure that the version number is correct and that the shapefile exists, and once again wrapping our code in a `try...except` statement to catch typos and other errors:

```
try:
    if version != "1.0":
```

```
    raise Http404

try:
    shapefile = Shapefile.objects.get(id=shapefile_id)
except Shapefile.DoesNotExist:
    raise Http404
```

We now need to convert the query parameters (which Django passes to us as strings) into integers so that we can work with them:

```
zoom = int(zoom)
x    = int(x)
y    = int(y)
```

We can now check that the zoom level is correct:

```
if zoom < 0 or zoom > MAX_ZOOM_LEVEL:
    raise Http404
```

Our next step is to convert the supplied x and y parameters into the minimum and maximum latitude and longitude values covered by the Tile. This requires us to use the _unitsPerPixel() function we defined earlier to calculate the amount of the Earth's surface covered by the Tile for the current zoom level:

```
xExtent = _unitsPerPixel(zoom) * TILE_WIDTH
yExtent = _unitsPerPixel(zoom) * TILE_HEIGHT

minLong = x * xExtent - 180.0
minLat  = y * yExtent - 90.0
maxLong = minLong + xExtent
maxLat  = minLat  + yExtent
```

Finally, we can add some rudimentary error checking to ensure that the Tile's coordinates are valid:

```
if (minLong < -180 or maxLong > 180 or
    minLat < -90 or maxLat > 90):
    raise Http404
```

## Setting up the map

We're now ready to create the mapnik.Map object to represent the map. This is straightforward:

```
map = mapnik.Map(TILE_WIDTH, TILE_HEIGHT,
                 "+proj=longlat +datum=WGS84")
map.background = mapnik.Color("#7391ad")
```

## Defining the base layer

We now want to define the layer that draws our base map. To do this, we have to set up a `mapnik.PostGIS` data source for the layer:

```
dbSettings = settings.DATABASES['default']
datasource = \
    mapnik.PostGIS(user=dbSettings['USER'],
                   password=dbSettings['PASSWORD'],
                   dbname=dbSettings['NAME'],
                   table='tms_basemap',
                   srid=4326,
                   geometry_field="geometry",
                   geometry_table='tms_basemap')
```

As you can see, we get the name of the database, the username, and the password from our project's `settings` module. We then create a PostGIS data source using these settings. With this data source, we can now create the base layer itself:

```
baseLayer = mapnik.Layer("baseLayer")
baseLayer.datasource = datasource
baseLayer.styles.append("baseLayerStyle")
```

We now need to set up the layer's style. In this case, we'll use a single rule with two symbolizers: a `PolygonSymbolizer`, which draws the interior of the base map's polygons, and a `LineSymbolizer` to draw the polygon outlines:

```
rule = mapnik.Rule()

rule.symbols.append(
    mapnik.PolygonSymbolizer(mapnik.Color("#b5d19c")))
rule.symbols.append(
    mapnik.LineSymbolizer(mapnik.Color("#404040"), 0.2))

style = mapnik.Style()
style.rules.append(rule)
```

Finally, we can add the base layer and its style to the map:

```
map.append_style("baseLayerStyle", style)
map.layers.append(baseLayer)
```

# Defining the feature layer

Our next task is to add another layer to draw the shapefile's features onto the map. Once again, we'll set up a `mapnik.PostGIS` data source for the new layer:

```
geometry_field = \
    utils.calc_geometry_field(shapefile.geom_type)

query = '(select ' + geometry_field \
        + ' from "shared_feature" where' \
        + ' shapefile_id=' + str(shapefile.id) + ') as geom'

datasource = \
    mapnik.PostGIS(user=dbSettings['USER'],
                   password=dbSettings['PASSWORD'],
                   dbname=dbSettings['NAME'],
                   table=query,
                   srid=4326,
                   geometry_field=geometry_field,
                   geometry_table='shared_feature')
```

In this case, we are calling `utils.calc_geometry_field()` to see which field in the `shared_feature` table contains the geometry we're going to display.

We're now ready to create the new layer itself:

```
featureLayer = mapnik.Layer("featureLayer")
featureLayer.datasource = datasource
featureLayer.styles.append("featureLayerStyle")
```

Next, we want to define the styles used by the feature layer. As before, we'll have just a single rule, but in this case, we'll use different symbolizers depending on the type of feature we are displaying:

```
rule = mapnik.Rule()

if shapefile.geom_type in ["Point", "MultiPoint"]:
    rule.symbols.append(mapnik.PointSymbolizer())
elif shapefile.geom_type in ["LineString", "MultiLineString"]:
    rule.symbols.append(
        mapnik.LineSymbolizer(mapnik.Color("#000000"), 0.5))
elif shapefile.geom_type in ["Polygon", "MultiPolygon"]:
    rule.symbols.append(
```

```
            mapnik.PolygonSymbolizer(mapnik.Color("#f7edee")))
        rule.symbols.append(
            mapnik.LineSymbolizer(mapnik.Color("#000000"), 0.5))

    style = mapnik.Style()
    style.rules.append(rule)
```

Finally, we can add our new feature layer to the map:

```
    map.append_style("featureLayerStyle", style)
    map.layers.append(featureLayer)
```

## Rendering the map Tile

We looked at using Mapnik to render map images in *Chapter 7, Using Python and Mapnik to Generate Maps*. The basic process of rendering a map Tile is the same, except that we won't be storing the results into an image file on disk. Instead, we'll create a `mapnik.Image` object, convert it into raw image data in PNG format, and return that data back to the caller using an `HttpResponse` object:

```
    map.zoom_to_box(mapnik.Box2d(minLong, minLat,
                                  maxLong, maxLat))
    image = mapnik.Image(TILE_WIDTH, TILE_HEIGHT)
    mapnik.render(map, image)
    imageData = image.tostring('png')

    return HttpResponse(imageData, content_type="image/png")
```

All that's left now is to add our error-catching code to the end of the function:

```
except:
    traceback.print_exc()
    return HttpResponse("Error")
```

That completes the implementation of our Tile Map Server's `tile()` function. Let's tidy up and do some testing.

# Completing the Tile Map Server

Because we've referred to some new modules in our `views.py` module, we'll have to add some extra import statements to the top of the file:

```
import mapnik
from django.conf import settings
from shapeEditor.shared import utils
```

In theory, our Tile Map Server should now be ready to go. Let's test it out. If you don't currently have the Django web server running, `cd` into the `shapeEditor` project directory and type the following:

**% python manage.py runserver**

Start up your web browser and enter the following URL into the address bar:

`http://127.0.0.1:8000/tms/1.0/2/0/0/0.png`

All going well, you should see a 256 x 256 pixel map Tile appear in your web browser:

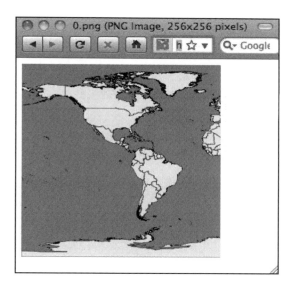

**Problems?**

If an error occurs, there are two likely causes: you might have made a mistake typing in the code, or you might have gotten the record ID of the shapefile wrong. Check the web server log in the terminal window you used to run the `python manage.py runserver` command: when a Python exception occurs, the traceback will be printed out in this window. This will tell you if you have a syntax or other error, or if an `Http404` exception was raised.

If you do get an `Http404` exception, it's most likely because you're using the wrong record ID for the shapefile. The URL is structured like this:

```
http://path/to/tms/<version>/<shapefile_
id>/<zoom>/<x>/<y>.png
```

If you've been working through these chapters in order, the record ID of the World Borders Dataset shapefile you imported earlier should be 2, but if you've imported other shapefiles in the meantime or created more shapefile records while playing with the admin interface, you may need to use a different record ID. To see what record ID a given shapefile has, go to `http://127.0.0.1:8000` and click on the **Edit** hyperlink for the desired shapefile. You'll see a **Page Not Found** error, but the final part of the URL will be the record ID of the shapefile. Replace the record ID in the previous URL with the correct ID, and the map Tile should appear.

Once you've reached the point of seeing the previous image in your web browser, you deserve a pat on the back—congratulations, you have just implemented your own working Tile Map Server!

# Using OpenLayers to display the map

Now that we have our TMS server up and running, we can use the OpenLayers library to display the rendered map Tiles within a slippy map. This slippy map will be used within our "Edit Shapefile" view function to display all the shapefile's features, allowing the user to select a feature within the shapefile to edit.

Let's implement this "Edit Shapefile" view, which we'll call `edit_shapefile()`. Edit the `urls.py` module within the main `shapeEditor` directory, and add the following entry to the end of the `urlpatterns` list:

```
url(r'^edit/(?P<shapefile_id>\d+)$',
    shapeEditor.shapefiles.views.edit_shapefile)
```

This will pass any incoming URLs of the form `/edit/N` to the `edit_shapefile()` view function within our `shapeEditor.shapefiles` application.

Let's implement this function. Edit the `shapeEditor.shapefiles` application's `views.py` module and add the following code to the end of this file:

```
def edit_shapefile(request, shapefile_id):
    try:
        shapefile = Shapefile.objects.get(id=shapefile_id)
    except Shapefile.DoesNotExist:
        return HttpResponseNotFound()

    tms_url = "http://" + request.get_host() + "/tms/"

    return render(request, "select_feature.html",
                  {'shapefile' : shapefile,
                   'tms_url'    : tms_url})
```

As you can see, we obtain the desired `Shapefile` object, calculate the URL used to access our TMS server, and pass both of these values to a template called `select_feature.html`. This template is where all the hard work will take place.

Now, we need to write the template. Start by creating a new file named `select_feature.html` in the `shapeEditor.shapefiles` application's `templates` directory, and enter the following into this file:

```
<html>
  <head>
    <title>ShapeEditor</title>
    <style type="text/css">
      div#map {
        width:  600px;
        height: 400px;
        border: 1px solid #ccc;
      }
    </style>
  </head>
  <body>
    <h1>Edit Shapefile</h1>
    <b>Please choose a feature to edit</b>
    <br/>
    <div id="map" class="map"></div>
    <br/>
```

```
    <div style="margin-left:20px">
      <button type="button"
              onClick='window.location="/";'>
        Cancel
      </button>
    </div>
  </body>
</html>
```

This is only the basic outline for this template, but it gives us something to work with. With the Django development server running (`python manage.py runserver` in a terminal window), go to `http://127.0.0.1:8000` and click on the **Edit** hyperlink for a shapefile. You should see the basic outline for the `select feature` page:

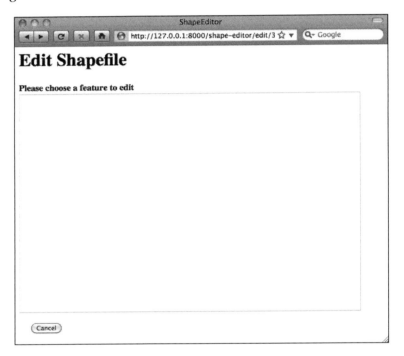

Notice that we've created a `<div>` element to hold the OpenLayers map, and we use a CSS stylesheet to give the map a fixed size and border. The map itself isn't being displayed yet because we haven't written the JavaScript code needed to launch OpenLayers. Let's do that now.

Add the following to the `<head>` section of your template:

```
<link rel="stylesheet"
      href="http://openlayers.org/en/v3.10.1/css/ol.css"
      type="text/css">
<script src="http://openlayers.org/en/v3.10.1/build/ol.js"
        type="text/javascript">
</script>
<script src="http://code.jquery.com/jquery-2.1.4.min.js"
        type="text/javascript">
</script>
<script type="text/javascript">
  function init() {
  }
</script>
```

Also, change the `<body>` tag definition to look like this:

```
<body onload="init()">
```

Notice that there are three `<script>` tags: the first loads the `OpenLayers.js` library from the `http://openlayers.org` web site, the second one loads the JQuery library from `http://code.jquery.com` (we'll need this later), and the final `<script>` tag is used to hold the JavaScript code that we'll write to create the map. We've also defined a JavaScript function called `init()`, which will be called when the page is loaded.

Let's implement that initialization function. The following code should all be inserted between the `function init() {` line and its corresponding `}`, which marks the end of the function.

We'll start by defining a variable named `url_template` containing the URL to use to access our map Tiles:

```
    var url_template = '{{ tms_url }}/1.0/{{ shapefile.id }}/{z}/{x}/
{y}.png';
```

Notice that we use Django's special `{{ ... }}` syntax to embed the URL of our Tile Map Server and the ID of the shapefile into our template. The strings `{z}`, `{x}`, and `{y}` at the end of our template will act as placeholders that we will replace with the zoom level and coordinate for the desired map Tile.

We next need to define the map projection OpenLayers should use for this map:

```
var projection = ol.proj.get('EPSG:4326');
```

Remember that EPSG code 4326 represents unprojected latitude and longitude coordinates on the WGS84 datum; this is the projection used by our underlying map data.

Our next step is to define an OpenLayers **Source** object, which represents the source of the map data to be displayed. Unfortunately, OpenLayers version 3 does not include a built-in source for Tile Map Servers, so we have to do a bit more work to obtain the map data from our TMS server:

```
var source = new ol.source.XYZ({
    crossOrigin: 'null',
    wrapX: false,
    projection: projection,
    tileUrlFunction: function(tileCoord) {
      var z = tileCoord[0] - 1;
      var x = tileCoord[1];
      var y = Math.pow(2, z) + tileCoord[2];
      return url_template.replace('{z}', z.toString())
                         .replace('{x}', x.toString())
                         .replace('{y}', y.toString());
    },
});
```

As you can see, we define a `tileUrlFunction` to calculate the URL to use to obtain a given map Tile. We convert the zoom level and the X and Y coordinates supplied by OpenLayers into the values required by our TMS server, and we then use JavaScript's `replace()` function to replace the placeholders within our URL template with these calculated values.

Now that we have the source defined, we can create an OpenLayers **Tile Layer** object to retrieve map Tiles from this source:

```
var layer = new ol.layer.Tile({source: source,
                               projection: projection,
                               });
```

We then set up an OpenLayers **View** object to set the initial zoom and display point for our map:

```
var view = new ol.View({center: [0, 0],
                        zoom: 1,
                        projection: projection,
                        });
```

Finally, we define an OpenLayers **Map** object, which will display our one and only map layer:

```
var map = new ol.Map({target: "map",
                      layers: [layer],
                      view: view});
}
```

Notice that we pass in the ID of our `<div>` element as the `target` parameter. This tells OpenLayers to display the map within the `<div>` element with that ID.

This completes the implementation of our `init()` function. Let's test what we've written. Save your changes, start up the Django web server if it isn't already running, and point your web browser to `http://127.0.0.1:8000`. Click on the **Edit** hyperlink for the shapefile you imported, and you should see a working slippy map:

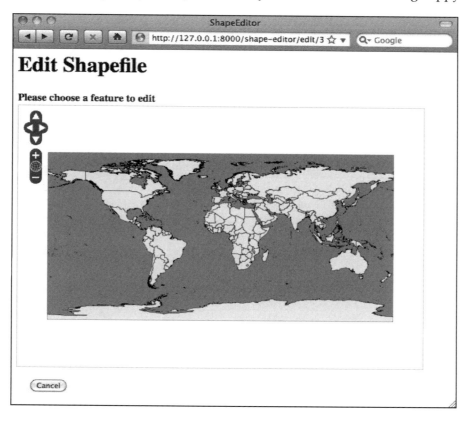

You can zoom in and out, pan around, and click to your heart's content. Of course, nothing actually works yet (apart from the **Cancel** button), but we have got a slippy map working with our Tile Map Server and the OpenLayers JavaScript widget. That's quite an achievement!

**What if it doesn't work?**

If the map isn't being shown for some reason, there are several possible causes. First, check the Django web server log, as we are printing any Python exceptions there. If that doesn't reveal the problem, look at your web browser's error console window to see whether there are any errors at the JavaScript level. Because we are now writing JavaScript code, error messages will appear within the web browser rather than in Django's server log. In Firefox, you can view JavaScript errors by selecting the **Error Console** item from the **Tools** menu. Other browsers have similar windows for showing JavaScript errors.

JavaScript debugging can be quite tricky, even for people experienced with developing web-based applications. If you do get stuck, you may find the following article helpful: `http://www.webmonkey.com/2010/02/javascript_debugging_for_beginners`

# Intercepting mouse clicks

When the user clicks on the map, we want to intercept that mouse click, identify the map coordinate that the user clicked on, and then ask the server to identify the clicked-on feature (if any). To intercept mouse clicks, we will add an **event listener** function to the map. Doing this in OpenLayers is easy: simply edit your `select_feature.html` template and add the following Javascript code to the end of your `init()` function:

```
map.on("singleclick", function(e) {
  Alert("Click");
});
```

This will cause the **Click** message to be displayed whenever the user clicks on the map. To test it out, reload the **Edit Shapefile** web page and try clicking on the map. You should see the following message:

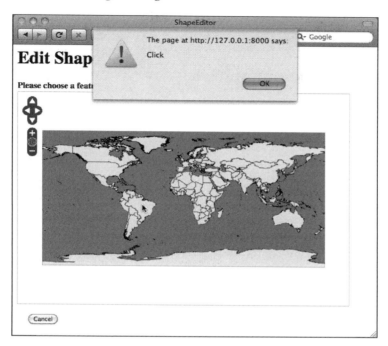

So far, so good. Notice that our click handler only intercepts single clicks; if you double-click on the map, it will still zoom in.

If your map isn't working, you may have made a mistake typing in the JavaScript code. Open your browser's JavaScript console or log window, and reload the page. An error message will appear in this window if there is a problem with your JavaScript code.

Let's now implement the real code to respond to the user's mouse click. When the user clicks on the map, we're going to send the clicked-on latitude and longitude value to the server using an AJAX request. The server will return the URL of the "Edit Shapefile" page for the clicked-on feature or an empty string if no feature was clicked on. If a URL is returned, we'll then redirect the user's web browser to that URL.

To make the AJAX call, we're going to use the JQuery library's `jQuery.ajax()` function. Replace the `alert("Click");` line with the following:

```
var request = jQuery.ajax({
        url      : "/find_feature",
        data     : {shapefile_id : {{ shapefile.id }},
                   latitude      : e.coordinate[1],
                   longitude     : e.coordinate[0] },
        success : function(response) {
                    if (response != "") {
                       window.location.href = response;
                    }
                  }
});
```

As you can see, the `jQuery.ajax()` function accepts the URL to send the request to (in the `url` entry), a set of parameters to send to the server (in the `data` entry), and a function to call when the response is received (in the `success` entry). When we make the request, the query parameters sent to the server will consist of the record ID of the shapefile and the clicked-on latitude and longitude values; when the response is received, our `success` function will be called with the data returned by the server.

 JQuery actually passes more information than just the returned data to the `success` function, but because of the way Javascript works, we can safely ignore these additional parameters.

Now that we've finished implementing our HTML template and the JavaScript code to make it work, let's now write the Python code to actually find a feature based on where the user clicked.

# Implementing the "Find Feature" view

We now need to write the view function that receives the AJAX request, checks to see which feature was clicked on (if any), and returns a suitable URL to use to redirect the user's web browser to the "edit" page for that clicked-on feature. To implement this, we're going to make use of GeoDjango's spatial query functions.

Let's start by adding the "Find Feature" view itself. To do this, edit the `shapefiles.views` module again, and add the following placeholder code:

```
def find_feature(request):
    return HttpResponse("")
```

Returning an empty string tells our AJAX callback function that no feature was clicked on. We'll replace this with some proper spatial queries shortly. First, though, we need to add a URL pattern so that incoming requests will get forwarded to the `find_feature()` view function. Open the top-level `urls.py` module and add the following entry to the URL pattern list:

```
url(r'^find_feature$',
    shapeEditor.shapefiles.views.find_feature),
```

You should now be able to run the ShapeEditor, click on the **Edit** hyperlink for an uploaded shapefile, see a map showing the various features within the shapefile, and click somewhere on the map. In response, the system should do—absolutely nothing! This is because our `find_feature()` function is returning an empty string, so the system thinks that the user didn't click on a feature and so ignores the mouse click.

> In this case, "absolutely nothing" is good news. As long as no error messages are being displayed either at the Python or JavaScript level, the AJAX code is running correctly. So go ahead and try this, even though nothing happens, just to make sure that you haven't got any bugs in your code. You should see the AJAX calls in the list of incoming HTTP requests being received by the server.

Before we implement the `find_feature()` function, let's take a step back and think what it means for the user to click on a feature's geometry. The ShapeEditor supports a complete range of possible geometry types: Point, LineString, Polygon, MultiPoint, MultiLineString, MultiPolygon, and GeometryCollection. Seeing if the user clicked on a Polygon or MultiPolygon feature is straightforward enough: we simply check whether the clicked-on point is inside the polygon's bounds. But because lines and points have no interior (their area will always be zero), a given coordinate could never be inside a Point or a LineString geometry. It might get infinitely close, but the user can never actually click inside a Point or a LineString.

Consider the following spatial query:

```
SELECT * FROM features WHERE ST_Contains(feature.geometry, clickPt)
```

This is not going to work, because the click point can never be inside a Point or a LineString geometry. Instead, we have to allow for the situation where the user clicks *close to* the feature rather than within it. To do this, we'll calculate a search radius, in map units, and then use the `DWithin` spatial query function to find all features within the given search radius of the clicked-on point.

Unfortunately, we have a problem here. When we used the ST_DWithin spatial query in *Chapter 8, Working with Spatial Data*, we used it to calculate all features within a given number of meters of a given point. We could do this because the features we were working with were stored in a PostGIS **Geography** column. In this case, however, our spatial data is not stored in a Geography column. Instead, it is stored in a **Geometry** column. This means that the search radius we supply to Django's DWithin spatial query function needs to be measured in degrees of latitude and longitude rather than in meters.

 Unfortunately, we can't use Geography columns for the ShapeEditor because of constraints in the way Geography columns work. Instead, we are going to have to calculate the search radius as a number of degrees.

Because the user can click anywhere on the Earth's surface, we will have to calculate the search radius based on the user's click location. This is because the relationship between map coordinates (latitude/longitude values) and actual distances on the Earth's surface can vary widely depending on whereabouts on the Earth the user clicked: a degree at the equator equals a distance of 111 kilometers, while a degree in Sweden is only half that much.

To ensure that we have a consistent search radius everywhere in the world, we will use the PROJ.4 library to calculate the search radius in map units given the clicked-on location and a desired linear distance. Let's add this function to our `shared.utils` module:

```
def calc_search_radius(latitude, longitude, distance):
    geod = pyproj.Geod(ellps="WGS84")

    x,y,angle = geod.fwd(longitude, latitude, 0, distance)
    radius = y-latitude

    x,y,angle = geod.fwd(longitude, latitude, 90, distance)
    radius = max(radius, x-longitude)

    x,y,angle = geod.fwd(longitude, latitude, 180, distance)
    radius = max(radius, latitude-y)

    x,y,angle = geod.fwd(longitude, latitude, 270, distance)
    radius = max(radius, longitude-x)

    return radius
```

This function calculates the distance, in map units, of a given linear distance measured in meters. It calculates the lat/long coordinates for four points directly north, south, east, and west of the starting location and the given number of meters away from that point. It then calculates the difference in latitude or longitude between the starting location and the end point:

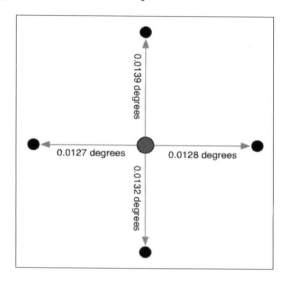

Finally, it takes the largest of these differences and returns it as the search radius, which is measured in degrees of latitude or longitude.

Because our `utils.py` module is now using `pyproj`, add the following `import` statement to the top of this module:

```
import pyproj
```

With the `calc_search_radius()` function written, we can now use Django's `DWithin` spatial query to identify all features close to the clicked-on location. The general process of doing this in GeoDjango is to use the `filter()` function to create a spatial query, as shown in the following example:

```
query = Feature.objects.filter(geometry__dwithin=(pt, radius))
```

This creates a query set that returns only those `Feature` objects that match the given criteria. GeoDjango cleverly adds support for spatial queries to Django's built-in filtering capabilities; in this case, the `geometry__dwithin=(pt, radius)` parameter tells GeoDjango to perform the `DWithin` spatial query using the two supplied parameters on the field named `geometry` within the `Feature` object.

Thus, this statement will be translated by GeoDjango into a spatial database query that looks something like this:

```
SELECT * from feature WHERE ST_DWithin(geometry, pt, radius)
```

 Notice that the `geometry__dwithin` keyword parameter includes two underscore characters; Django uses a double underscore to separate the field name from the filter function's name.

Knowing this, and having the `utils.calc_search_radius()` function implemented, we can finally implement our `find_feature()` view function. Edit the `shapefile.views` module and replace the body of the `find_feature()` function with the following:

```python
def find_feature(request):
    try:
        shapefile_id = int(request.GET['shapefile_id'])
        latitude     = float(request.GET['latitude'])
        longitude    = float(request.GET['longitude'])

        shapefile = Shapefile.objects.get(id=shapefile_id)
        pt = Point(longitude, latitude)
        radius = utils.calc_search_radius(latitude, longitude, 100)

        if shapefile.geom_type == "Point":
            query = Feature.objects.filter(
                geom_point__dwithin=(pt, radius))
        elif shapefile.geom_type in ["LineString", "MultiLineString"]:
            query = Feature.objects.filter(
                geom_multilinestring__dwithin=(pt, radius))
        elif shapefile.geom_type in ["Polygon", "MultiPolygon"]:
            query = Feature.objects.filter(
                geom_multipolygon__dwithin=(pt, radius))
        elif shapefile.geom_type == "MultiPoint":
            query = Feature.objects.filter(
                geom_multipoint__dwithin=(pt, radius))
        elif shapefile.geom_type == "GeometryCollection":
            query = feature.objects.filter(
                geom_geometrycollection__dwithin=(pt, radius))
        else:
```

```
        print "Unsupported geometry: " + shapefile.geom_type
        return HttpResponse("")

    if query.count() != 1:
        return HttpResponse("")

    feature = query[0]
    return HttpResponse("/edit_feature/" +
                        str(shapefile_id)+"/"+str(feature.id))
except:
    traceback.print_exc()
    return HttpResponse("")
```

There's a lot here, so let's take this one step at a time. First off, we've wrapped all our code inside a try...except statement:

```
def find_feature(request):
    try:
        ...
    except:
        traceback.print_exc()
        return HttpResponse("")
```

This is the same technique we used when implementing the Tile Map Server; it means that any Python errors in your code will be displayed in the web server's log, and the AJAX function will return gracefully rather than crashing.

We then extract the supplied query parameters, converting them from strings to numbers, load the desired Shapefile object, create a GeoDjango Point object out of the clicked-on coordinates, and calculate the search radius in degrees:

```
shapefile_id = int(request.GET['shapefile_id'])
latitude     = float(request.GET['latitude'])
longitude    = float(request.GET['longitude'])

shapefile = Shapefile.objects.get(id=shapefile_id)
pt = Point(longitude, latitude)
radius = utils.calc_search_radius(latitude, longitude, 100)
```

Notice that we use a hardwired search radius of 100 meters: this is enough to let the user select a point or line feature by clicking close to it, without being so large that the user might accidentally click on the wrong feature.

With this done, we're now ready to perform the spatial query. Because our `Feature` object has separate fields to hold each different type of geometry, we have to build the query based on the geometry's type:

```
if shapefile.geom_type == "Point":
  query = Feature.objects.filter(
            geom_point__dwithin=(pt, radius))
elif shapefile.geom_type in ["LineString", "MultiLineString"]:
  query = Feature.objects.filter(
            geom_multilinestring__dwithin=(pt, radius))
elif shapefile.geom_type in ["Polygon", "MultiPolygon"]:
  query = Feature.objects.filter(
            geom_multipolygon__dwithin=(pt, radius))
elif shapefile.geom_type == "MultiPoint":
  query = Feature.objects.filter(
            geom_multipoint__dwithin=(pt, radius))
elif shapefile.geom_type == "GeometryCollection":
  query = feature.objects.filter(
            geom_geometrycollection__dwithin=(pt, radius))
else:
  print("Unsupported geometry: " + shapefile.geom_type)
  return HttpResponse("")
```

In each case, we choose the appropriate geometry field and use `__dwithin` to perform a spatial query on the appropriate field in the `Feature` object.

Once we've created the appropriate spatial query, we simply check to see whether the query returned exactly one `Feature` object. If not, we return an empty string back to the AJAX handler's callback function to tell it that the user did not click on a feature:

```
if query.count() != 1:
  return HttpResponse("")
```

If there is exactly one matching feature, we get the clicked-on feature and use it to build a URL redirecting the user's web browser to the "Edit Feature" URL for the clicked-on feature:

```
feature = query[0]
return HttpResponse("/edit_feature/" +
                    str(shapefile_id)+"/"+str(feature.id))
```

After typing in all this code, add the following `import` statements to the top of the `views.py` module:

```
import traceback
from django.contrib.gis.geos import Point
from shapeEditor.shared.models import Feature
from shapeEditor.shared import utils
```

This completes our `find_feature()` view function. Save your changes, run the Django web server if it is not already running, and try clicking on a shapefile's features. If you click on the ocean, nothing should happen—but if you click on a feature, you should see your web browser redirected to a URL of this form:

```
http://127.0.0.1:8000/edit_feature/X/Y
```

Here, `X` is the record ID of the shapefile, and `Y` is the record ID of the clicked-on feature. Of course, at this stage, you'll get a **Page Not Found** error, because you haven't written that page yet. But at least you can click on a feature to select it, which is a major milestone in the development of the ShapeEditor application. Congratulations!

# Editing features

Now that we know which feature the user wants to edit, our next task is to implement the "Edit Feature" page itself. To do this, we are going to have to create a custom form with a single input field, named `geometry`, that uses a suitable map-editing widget for editing the feature's geometry.

The process of building this form is a bit involved, thanks to the fact that we have to create a new `django.contrib.gis.forms.Form` subclass on the fly to handle the different types of geometries that can be edited. Let's put this complexity into a new function within the `shared.utils` module, which we'll call `get_map_form()`.

Edit the `utils.py` module and type in the following code:

```
def get_map_form(shapefile):
    geometry_field = calc_geometry_field(shapefile.geom_type)

    if geometry_field == "geom_multipoint":
        field = forms.MultiPointField
    elif geometry_field == "geom_multilinestring":
        field = forms.MultiLineStringField
```

```
    elif geometry_field == "geom_multipolygon":
        field = forms.MultiPolygonField
    elif geometry_field == "geom_geometrycollection":
        field = forms.GeometryCollectionField
    else:
        raise RuntimeError("Unsupported field: " + geometry_field)

    widget = forms.OpenLayersWidget()

    class MapForm(forms.Form):
        geometry = field(widget=widget)

    return MapForm
```

You'll also need to add the following `import` statement to the top of the file:

```
from django.contrib.gis import forms
```

The `get_map_form()` function selects the type of field to edit based on the shapefile's `geom_type` attribute. For example, if the shapefile contains Point or MultiPoint geometries, we select the `MultiPointField` class for editing the shapefile's data. Once the field type has been selected, we dynamically create a new `django.contrib.gis.forms.Form` subclass that uses an instance of that form, with an `OpenLayersWidget` for editing the geometry's data.

Notice that the `get_map_form()` function returns the `MapForm` *class* rather than an instance of that class; we'll use the returned class to create the appropriate `MapForm` instances as we need them.

With this function behind us, we can now implement the rest of the "Edit Feature" view. Let's start by setting up the view's URL: open the `urls.py` module and add the following to the list of URL patterns:

```
url(r'^edit_feature/(?P<shapefile_id>\d+)/(?P<feature_id>\d+)$',
    shapeEditor.shapefiles.views.edit_feature),
```

We're now ready to implement the view function itself. Edit the `shapefiles.views` module and start defining the `edit_feature()` function:

```
def edit_feature(request, shapefile_id, feature_id):
    try:
        shapefile = Shapefile.objects.get(id=shapefile_id)
    except ShapeFile.DoesNotExist:
```

```
      return HttpResponseNotFound()

   try:
      feature = Feature.objects.get(id=feature_id)
   except Feature.DoesNotExist:
      return HttpResponseNotFound()
```

So far, this is quite straightforward: we load the `Shapefile` object for the current shapefile and the `Feature` object for the feature we are editing. We next want to load into memory a list of that feature's attributes so that they can be displayed to the user:

```
   attributes = []
   for attr_value in feature.attributevalue_set.all():
      attributes.append([attr_value.attribute.name,
                         attr_value.value])
   attributes.sort()
```

This is where things get interesting. We need to create a Django `Form` object (actually, an instance of the `MapForm` class created dynamically by the `get_map_form()` function we wrote earlier), and use this form instance to display the feature to be edited. When the form is submitted, we'll extract the updated geometry and save it back into the `Feature` object again before redirecting the user back to the "Edit Shapefile"page to select another feature.

As we saw when we created the "Import Shapefile" form, the basic Django idiom for processing a form is as follows:

```
   if request.method == "GET":
       form = MyForm()
       return render(request, "template.html",
                     {'form' : form})
   elif request.method == "POST":
       form = MyForm(request.POST)
       if form.is_valid():
           # Extract and save the form's contents here...
           return HttpResponseRedirect("/somewhere/else")
       return render(request, "template.html",
                     {'form' : form})
```

When the form is to be displayed for the first time, `request.method` will have a value of GET. In this case, we create a new form object and display the form as part of an HTML template. When the form is submitted by the user, `request.method` will have the value POST. In this case, a new form object is created that is bound to the submitted POST arguments. The form's contents are then checked, and if they are valid, they are saved and the user is redirected to some other page. If the form is not valid, it will be displayed again along with a suitable error message.

Let's see how this idiom is used by the "Edit Feature" view. Add the following to the end of your new view function:

```
geometry_field = \
    utils.calc_geometry_field(shapefile.geom_type)
form_class = utils.get_map_form(shapefile)

if request.method == "GET":
  wkt = getattr(feature, geometry_field)
  form = form_class({'geometry' : wkt})

  return render(request, "edit_feature.html",
                {'shapefile'  : shapefile,
                 'form'       : form,
                 'attributes' : attributes})
elif request.method == "POST":
  form = form_class(request.POST)
  try:
    if form.is_valid():
      wkt = form.cleaned_data['geometry']
      setattr(feature, geometry_field, wkt)
      feature.save()
      return HttpResponseRedirect("/edit/" +
                                       shapefile_id)
  except ValueError:
    pass

  return render(request, "edit_feature.html",
                {'shapefile'  : shapefile,
                 'form'       : form,
                 'attributes' : attributes})
```

As you can see, we call `utils.get_map_form()` to create a new `django.forms.Form` subclass, which will be used to edit the feature's geometry. We also call `utils.calc_geometry_field()` to see which field in the `Feature` object should be edited.

The rest of this function pretty much follows the Django idiom for form processing. The only interesting thing to note is that we get and set the geometry field (using the `getattr()` and `setattr()` functions, respectively) in WKT format. GeoDjango treats geometry fields as if they were character fields that hold the geometry in WKT format. The GeoDjango JavaScript code then takes that WKT data (which is stored in a hidden form field named `geometry`) and passes it to OpenLayers for display as a vector geometry. OpenLayers allows the user to edit that vector geometry, and the updated geometry is stored back into the hidden `geometry` field as WKT data. We then extract that updated geometry's WKT text and store it back into the `Feature` object.

That's all you need to know about the `edit_feature()` view function. Let's now create the template used by this view. Create a new file named `edit_feature.html` within the `shapefiles` application's `templates` directory, and enter the following text into it:

```
<html>
  <head>
    <title>ShapeEditor</title>
    {{ form.media }}
  </head>
  <body>
    <h1>Edit Feature</h1>
    <form method="POST" action="">
      <table>
        {{ form.as_table }}
        <tr>
          <td></td>
          <td align="right">
            <table>
{% for attr in attributes %}
              <tr>
                <td>{{ attr.0 }}</td>
                <td>{{ attr.1 }}</td>
              </tr>
{% endfor %}
            </table>
          </td>
        </tr>
        <tr>
          <td></td>
          <td align="center">
```

```
                    <input type="submit" value="Save"/>
                     
                    <button type="button" onClick='window.location="/edit/{{
shapefile.id }}";'>
                        Cancel
                    </button>
                </td>
            </tr>
        </table>
    </form>
  </body>
</html>
```

This template uses an HTML table to display the form and calls the `form.as_table` template function to render the form as HTML table rows. We then display a list of the feature's attributes as additional rows within this table and, finally, add **Save** and **Cancel** buttons to the bottom of the form.

With all this code written, we are finally able to edit features within the ShapeEditor:

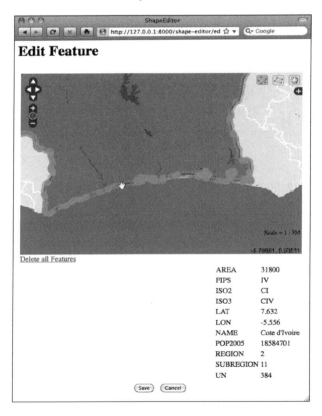

Within this editor, you can make use of a number of GeoDjango's built-in features to edit a geometry:

- You can click on the **Edit Geometry** tool () to select a feature for editing.
- You can click on the **Add Geometry** tool () to start drawing a new geometry.
- When a geometry is selected, you can click on a dark circle and drag it to move the endpoints of a line segment.
- When a geometry is selected, you can click on a light circle to split an existing line segment in two, creating a new point which can then be dragged.
- If you hold the mouse down over a dark circle, you can press the *Delete* key (or type *D*) to delete that point. Note that this only works if the geometry has more than three points.
- You can click on the **Delete all Features** hyperlink to delete the current feature's geometries. We'll look at this hyperlink in more detail shortly.

Once you have finished editing the feature, you can click on the **Save** button to save the edited features or the **Cancel** button to abandon the changes.

While this is all working well, there is one rather annoying quirk: GeoDjango lets the user remove the geometries from a map using a hyperlink named **Delete all Features**. Since we're currently editing a single feature within the shapefile, this hyperlink is rather confusingly named: what it actually does is delete the *geometries* for this feature, not the feature itself. Let's change the text of this hyperlink to something more meaningful.

Go to the copy of Django that you downloaded, and navigate to the `contrib/gis/templates/gis` directory. In this directory is a file named `openlayers.html`. Take a copy of this file, and move it into your `shapefiles` application's `templates` directory, renaming it to `openlayers-custom.html`.

Open your copy of this file, and look near the bottom for the text `Delete all Features`. Change this to `Clear Feature's Geometry`, and save your changes.

So far, so good. Now, we need to tell the GeoDjango editing widget to use our custom version of the `openlayers.html` file. To do this, edit your `utils.py` module and find your definition of the `get_map_form()` function. Add the following code immediately after the line that reads `widget = forms.OpenLayersWidget()`:

```
widget.template_name = "openlayers-custom.html"
```

If you then try editing a feature, you'll see that your customized version of the `openlayers.html` file is being used:

By replacing the template, passing parameters to the widget when it is created, and creating your own custom subclass of the `BaseGeometryWidget` class, you can make various changes to the appearance and functionality of the geometry-editing widget. If you want to see what is possible, take a look at the modules in the `django.contrib.gis` directory.

# Adding features

We'll next implement the ability to add a new feature. To do this, we'll put an **Add Feature** button onto the "Edit Shapefile" view. Clicking on this button will call the "Edit Feature" URL, but without a feature ID. We'll then modify the "Edit Feature" view so that if no feature ID is given, a new `Feature` object is created.

Open the `shapefiles` application's `views.py` module, find the `edit_shapefile()` function, and add the following highlighted lines to this function:

```
def edit_shapefile(request, shapefile_id):
    try:
        shapefile = Shapefile.objects.get(id=shapefile_id)
    except Shapefile.DoesNotExist:
        raise Http404

    tms_url = "http://"+request.get_host()+"/tms/"
    find_feature_url = "http://" + request.get_host() \
                     + "/editor/find_feature"
    add_feature_url = "http://" + request.get_host() \
                    + "/edit_feature/" + str(shapefile_id)

    return render(request, "select_feature.html",
                  {'shapefile'        : shapefile,
                   'find_feature_url' : find_feature_url,
                   'add_feature_url'  : add_feature_url,
                   'tms_url'          : tms_url})
```

Then, edit the `select_feature.html` template and add the following highlighted lines to the body of this template:

```
<body onload="init()">
  <h1>Edit Shapefile</h1>
  <b>Please choose a feature to edit</b>
  <br/>
  <div id="map" class="map"></div>
  <br/>
  <div style="margin-left:20px">
    <button type="button"
    onClick='window.location="{{ add_feature_url }}";'>
      Add Feature
    </button>
    <button type="button"
      onClick='window.location="/";'>
      Cancel
    </button>
  </div>
</body>
```

This will place an **Add Feature** button onto the "Select Feature" page. Clicking on that button will call the `http://127.0.0.1:8000/edit_feature/N` URL (where N is the record ID of the current shapefile). As you can see, this URL supplies the ID of the desired shapefile but not the ID of the feature to edit. This is because we're adding a new feature rather than editing an existing one.

We next need to add a URL pattern to support this URL. Open the `urls.py` module and add the following entry to the URL pattern list:

```
url(r'^edit_feature/(?P<shapefile_id>\d+)$',
    shapeEditor.shapefiles.views.edit_feature),
```

Then, go back to `views.py` and change the function definition for the `edit_feature()` function to look like this:

```
def edit_feature(request, shapefile_id, feature_id=None):
```

Notice that the `feature_id` parameter is now optional. Now, find the following block of code:

```
try:
    feature = Feature.objects.get(id=feature_id)
except Feature.DoesNotExist:
    return HttpResponseNotFound()
```

You need to replace this block with the following:

```
if feature_id == None:
  feature = Feature(shapefile=shapefile)
else:
  try:
    feature = Feature.objects.get(id=feature_id)
  except Feature.DoesNotExist:
    return HttpResponseNotFound()
```

This will create a new `Feature` object if the `feature_id` value is not specified, but it will still fail if an invalid feature ID is specified.

With these changes, you should be able to add a new feature to the shapefile. Go ahead and try it out: run the Django web server if it's not already running, and click on the **Edit** hyperlink for your imported shapefile. Then, click on the **Add New Feature** hyperlink, and try creating a new feature. The new feature should appear within the "Select Feature" view:

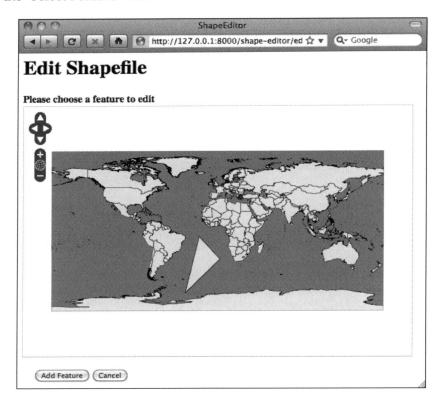

# Deleting features

We next want to let the user delete an existing feature. To do this, we'll add a **Delete Feature** button to the "Edit Feature" view. Clicking on this button will redirect the user to the "Delete Feature" view for that feature.

Edit the `edit_feature.html` template, and add the following highlighted lines to the `<form>` section of the template:

```
<form method="POST" action="">
  <table>
    <tr>
      <td></td>
      <td align="right">
        <input type="submit" name="delete"
               value="Delete Feature"/>
      </td>
    </tr>
    {{ form.as_table }}
    ...
```

Notice that we've used `<input type="submit">` for this button. This will submit the form with an extra POST parameter named `delete`. Now, go back to the `shapefiles.views` module and add the following to the top of the `edit_feature()` function:

```
if request.method == "POST" and "delete" in request.POST:
    return HttpResponseRedirect("/delete_feature/" +
                                shapefile_id+"/"+feature_id)
```

We next want to implement the "Delete Feature" view. Open the top-level `urls.py` module and add the following to the list of URL patterns:

```
url(r'^delete_feature/(?P<shapefile_id>\d+)/(?P<feature_id>\d+)$',
    shapeEditor.shapefiles.views.delete_feature),
```

Next, create a new file named `delete_feature.html` in the `shapeEditor/shapefiles/templates` directory, and enter the following text into this file:

```
<html>
  <head>
    <title>ShapeEditor</title>
  </head>
  <body>
    <h1>Delete Feature</h1>
    <form method="POST">
```

```
        Are you sure you want to delete this feature?
        <p/>
        <button type="submit" name="confirm"
                value="1">Delete</button>
         
        <button type="submit" name="confirm"
                value="0">Cancel</button>
     </form>
  </body>
</html>
```

This is a simple HTML form that confirms the deletion. When the form is submitted, the POST parameter named `confirm` will be set to `1` if the user wishes to delete the feature. Let's now implement the view that uses this template. Open the `shapefiles.views` module and add the following new view function:

```
def delete_feature(request, shapefile_id, feature_id):
  try:
    feature = Feature.objects.get(id=feature_id)
  except Feature.DoesNotExist:
    return HttpResponseNotFound()

  if request.method == "POST":
    if request.POST['confirm'] == "1":
      feature.delete()
    return HttpResponseRedirect("/edit/" +
                                  shapefile_id)

  return render(request, "delete_feature.html")
```

As you can see, deleting features is quite straightforward.

# Deleting shapefiles

The final piece of functionality we'll need to implement is the "Delete Shapefile" view. This will let the user delete an entire uploaded shapefile. The process is basically the same as for deleting features: we've already got a **Delete** hyperlink on the main page, so all we have to do is implement the underlying view.

Go to the top-level `urls.py` module and add the following entry to the URL pattern list:

```
url(r'^delete/(?P<shapefile_id>\d+)$',
    shapeEditor.shapefiles.views.delete_shapefile),
```

Then, edit the `shapefiles.views` module and add the following new view function:

```
def delete_shapefile(request, shapefile_id):
  try:
    shapefile = Shapefile.objects.get(id=shapefile_id)
  except Shapefile.DoesNotExist:
    return HttpResponseNotFound()

  if request.method == "GET":
    return render(request, "delete_shapefile.html",
                  {'shapefile' : shapefile})
  elif request.method == "POST":
    if request.POST['confirm'] == "1":
      shapefile.delete()
    return HttpResponseRedirect("/")
```

Notice that we're passing the `Shapefile` object to the template. This is because we want to display some information about the shapefile on the confirmation page.

 Remember that `shapefile.delete()` doesn't just delete the `Shapefile` object itself; it also deletes all the objects associated with the `Shapefile` through `ForeignKey` fields. This means that the one call to `shapefile.delete()` will also delete all the `Attribute`, `Feature`, and `AttributeValue` objects associated with that shapefile.

Finally, create a new template named `delete_shapefile.html`, and enter the following text into this file:

```
<html>
  <head>
    <title>ShapeEditor</title>
  </head>
  <body>
    <h1>Delete Shapefile</h1>
    <form method="POST">
      Are you sure you want to delete the
      "{{ shapefile.filename }}" shapefile?
      <p/>
```

```
        <button type="submit" name="confirm"
              value="1">Delete</button>
         
        <button type="submit" name="confirm"
              value="0">Cancel</button>
     </form>
   </body>
</html>
```

You should now be able to click on the **Delete** hyperlink to delete a shapefile. Go ahead and try it; you can always re-import your shapefile if you need it.

# Using the ShapeEditor

Congratulations! You have now finished implementing the last of the ShapeEditor's features, and you have a complete working geospatial application built using GeoDjango. Using the ShapeEditor, you can import shapefiles, view their features and attributes, make changes to the features' geometries, add and delete features, and then export the shapefile again.

This is certainly a useful application. Even if you don't have a full-blown GIS system installed, you can now make quick and easy changes to a shapefile's contents using the ShapeEditor. And, of course, the ShapeEditor is a great starting point for the development of your own geospatial applications.

# Further improvements and enhancements

As with any new application, there are a number of ways in which the ShapeEditor could be improved. Here are a few examples:

- Adding user signup and login so that each user has his or her own private set of shapefiles, rather than every user seeing the entire list of all the uploaded shapefiles.
- Adding the ability to edit a feature's attribute values.
- Using CSS stylesheets, and possibly a user-interface library such as Bootstrap, to improve the look of the system's web pages.
- Using a higher-resolution base map. An obvious candidate for this would be the GSHHS high-resolution shoreline database.

- Adding a Tile cache for our TMS server.

- Using JavaScript to add a **please wait** pop-up message while a shapefile is being imported or exported.

- Improving the reusability of the ShapeEditor's codebase. We've concentrated on learning how to use GeoDjango to build a working system, but with a suitable redesign, the code could be made much more generic so that it can be used in other applications as well.

Feel free to make these improvements; you will learn a lot more about GeoDjango and about geospatial development in general. As you work with the ShapeEditor, you'll probably come up with your own list of things you'd like to improve.

# Summary

In this chapter, we finished implementing a sophisticated geospatial web application using GeoDjango, Mapnik, PostGIS, OGR, and pyproj. This application is useful in its own right as well as being a springboard to developing your own geospatial web applications.

We learned that we can easily create our own Tile Map Server using Mapnik and GeoDjango. We saw how to use OpenLayers in our own web pages and how OpenLayers can be made to work with our Tile Map Server. We learned how to intercept mouse clicks using OpenLayers and how to use JQuery's AJAX functionality to send requests to the server for processing.

We then saw how to use Proj.4 to calculate a search radius measured in degrees of latitude and longitude and how to use GeoDjango's query functions to identify features close to the point where the user clicked. We also looked at how to use GeoDjango's editing forms to let the user view and edit the contents of a geometry.

Finally, we saw how to handle the addition of new features to the system and how we can use a template to confirm the deletion of a feature or a shapefile. We also learned how to customize the look and feel of the built-in GeoDjango editing widgets.

This completes our exploration of GeoDjango and completes this book. Hopefully, you have learned a lot about geospatial development and how to create geospatial applications using Python. With these tools at your disposal, you are now ready to start developing your own complex geospatial systems. Have fun!

# Index

projection 23
shapes 32, 33
units 22, 23
**cross-site request forgery (CSRF) 317**
**cylindrical projections**
about 24, 25
equal-area cylindrical projection 25
Mercator projection 25
universal transverse Mercator projection 25

# D

**dash length 197**
**data access layer 274**
**database**
creating 159
enabling, spatially 160
Postgres user account, creating 159
setting up 159
user access, enabling 160
**database migrations 296**
**database models 296**
**data models, ShapeEditor**
attribute 320
AttributeValue object 322
defining 320
feature 321
models.py file 322-325
shapefile 320
**data source 54, 180**
**data sources, Mapnik**
about 188
Gdal 189, 190
MemoryDatasource 190, 191
PostGIS 189
shapefile 188
**Data Tier 274**
**datums**
about 31, 123
changing 123
changing, to combine older and newer
TIGER data 127-129
NAD 27 31
NAD 83 31
WGS 84 31
**Digital Elevation Model (DEM) 34**
**Digital Raster Graphic (DRG) 34**

**DISTAL**
about 209
application workflow 209-212
using 242
**DISTAL application**
database, building 212-215
database, designing 212-215
data, downloading 216
data, importing 216
implementing 224, 225
select area script 228-233
select country script 226, 227
show results script 236, 237
**distance**
about 19
angular distance 19
linear distance 20
traveling distance 20, 21
**Distance-based Identification of Shorelines,
Towns, and Lakes.** *See* **DISTAL**
**Django**
about 294-301
URL 294
**DSG (feature designation code) field 222**

# E

**Editing API**
URL 80
**equal-area cylindrical projection 25**
**equidistant projection 26**
**European Petroleum Survey
Group (EPSG) 166**
**event listener function 390**
**EveryBlock**
URL 69
**exterior ring 33**

# F

**FC (feature classification) field 222**
**feature layer 378**
**features**
adding 406-408
deleting 409, 410
editing 399-406

# M

**Mapnik**
about 69-73, 178
documentation 75
example code 73, 74
example map, creating 183-187
exploring 178-182
installing 69-71
symbolizers 72
URL 69
**Mapnik concepts**
about 188
data sources 188
filters 191-193
map rendering 205, 206
maps and layers 203, 204
rules 191-193
styles 193
symbolizers 194
**map overlays 281**
**MapProxy**
URL 290
**MapServer 11**
**Mercator projection 25**
**meridians 19**
**micro-formats**
about 35
Geography Markup Language (GML) 35
GeoJSON 35
Well-known Binary (WKB) 35
Well-known Text (WKT) 35
**migrations directory 296**
**models.py module 296**

# N

**National Elevation Dataset (NED)**
about 100
data format 101
data, obtaining 101
data, using 102-104
**National Map Viewer**
reference 101
**Natural Earth**
about 85, 96, 97
cultural map data 85

data format 86, 97
physical map data 86
raster data, obtaining 98
raster data, using 98
URL 85
vector data, obtaining 86
vector data, using 86
**nodata value, GDAL 50**
**nodes 79**
**non-US place names**
about 221-224
download link 221
**NT (name type) field 222**

# O

**OGR**
about 54, 55
example code 55-57
**OGR coordinate transformation 124**
**Open Geospatial Consortium**
about 13
URL 13
**OpenLayers**
about 290-293
URL 290
**OpenLayers source object 388**
**OpenLayers Tile layer object 388**
**OpenStreetMap**
about 78
APIs 80
data format 79
data, obtaining 80
data, using 80
data, working with 81
mirrors and extracts 81
Planet.osm database 80, 81
URL 69, 78
**OpenStreetMap data**
reference link 279
**OpenStreetMap geocoder 12**
**orthographic projection 27**
**orthorectification 93**
**osm2pgsql tool**
reference 81
**Overpass API**
URL 80

# S